Nuclear Disarmament in International Law

Nuclear Disarmament in International Law

by Haralambos Athanasopulos

McFarland & Company, Inc., Publishers
Jefferson, North Carolina, and London

Library of Congress Cataloguing-in-Publication Data

Athanasopulos, Haralambos, 1957–
Nuclear disarmament in international law / by Haralambos Athanasopulos.
p. cm.
Includes bibliographical references and index.
ISBN 0-7864-0587-2 (library binding : 50# alkaline paper) ∞
1. Nuclear disarmament. 2. Nuclear weapons (International law)
I. Title.
KZ5675.A89 2000
341.7'33—dc21 99-53082
CIP

British Library Cataloguing-in-Publication data are available

Manufactured in the United States of America

McFarland & Company, Inc., Publishers
Box 611, Jefferson, North Carolina 28640
www.mcfarlandpub.com

In memory of my father

Table of Contents

List of Abbreviations

ABM Anti-Ballistic Missile
ALBM Air-Launched Ballistic Missile
ALCM Air-Launched Cruise Missile
BMD Ballistic Missile Defense
CAS Committee on Assurances of Supply
CTBT Comprehensive Test Ban Treaty
GLBM Ground-Launched Ballistic Missile
GLCM Ground-Launched Cruise Missile
IAEA International Atomic Energy Agency
ICBM Intercontinental Ballistic Missile
ICJ International Court of Justice
IMA International Monitoring Agency
INF Intermediate Nuclear Forces
INFCE International Nuclear Fuel Cycle Evaluation
IRBM Intermediate Range Ballistic Missile
LRINF Long-Range Intermediate Nuclear Forces
LTBT Limited Test Ban Treaty
MIRV Multiple Independently-Targetable Reentry Vehicle
NFPZ Nuclear-Free Peace Zone
NPT Nonproliferation Treaty
NST Nuclear and Space Talks
NTM National Technical Means
NWFZ Nuclear Weapon-Free Zone
PNET Peaceful Nuclear Explosions Treaty
SALT Strategic Arms Limitation Talks
SCC Standing Consultative Commission
SDI Strategic Defense Initiative
SLBM Sea-Launched Ballistic Missile
SLCM Sea-Launched Cruise Missile
SNDV Strategic Nuclear Delivery Vehicle
SRAM Short-Range Attack Missile
START Strategic Arms Reduction Talks
TTBT Threshold Test Ban Treaty
UN United Nations
ZOPFAN Zone of Peace, Freedom and Neutrality

Introduction

In December 1938, two German physicists, Otto Hahn and Fritz Strassmann, working at the Kaiser Wilhelm Institute in Berlin, performed a revolutionary experiment which resulted in the splitting of the uranium atom. As a result of this experiment, it was soon realized that if proper conditions were created, the fission of uranium could provide Germany with a weapon of unprecedented explosive power and destructive capability. In 1939, Albert Einstein wrote a letter to President Franklin Roosevelt warning him about the alarming possibility that the Hahn-Strassmann scientific breakthrough could lead to the development of a German atomic bomb. This warning compelled President Roosevelt that year to take the initial step in the American effort to build an atomic bomb.

After intensive scientific research during World War II, American nuclear scientists managed to develop the first atomic bomb. In July 1945, the United States War Department announced the development of a weapon that was potentially destructive beyond the wildest stretches of the imagination. Subsequently, in a remote corner of the Alamogordo Air Force Base, in the state of New Mexico, at 5:30 in the morning of July 16, 1945, the first atomic bomb was successfully tested. The successful detonation at Alamogordo was a scientific victory of the most startling and conclusive sort in the nuclear field. The Alamogordo test showed that science had delved into the inert structure of matter and revealed the secret power of the atom hidden since the creation of time and the universe. Above all, the successful testing of the first atomic bomb brought the world into the nuclear age.

It was recognized that the release of the power of the atom would be a great source of energy, but attention focused largely on its destructive force. The splitting of the uranium atom created the most devastating weapon ever known to the human race. In fact, the devastation of Hiroshima and Nagasaki in 1945 proved to the entire world that the atomic bomb was not just one more weapon; it was the ultimate weapon of mass destruction.

Unlike their conventional counterparts, nuclear weapons, because of their immediate blast effects and because of the long-term effects of nuclear radiation and fallout, are capable of annihilating the entire human race and its planet. Since it is estimated that approximately 500 heavy strategic nuclear weapons would be more than enough to destroy Eurasia and North America, there should be no doubt that the present existence of about 40,000 strategic and tactical nuclear weapons is more than enough to destroy humanity and the planet many times over.

Since the beginning of the nuclear age, the technological advances made in nuclear weapons and their delivery systems have resulted in the development and production of ever more destructive and sophisticated weapons. The existence of both strategic nuclear weapons with intercontinental ranges, and various types of tactical and battlefield nuclear weapons, enables the nuclear superpowers and other nuclear weapon states to target and destroy any part of the planet. Contributing to this lethal reach are nuclear weapons deliverable by land-based intercontinental ballistic missiles, by strategic bombers and fighters, by submarines and surface warships, and by other tactical missile systems.

As a result of the failure to achieve global nuclear disarmament through the instrumental value and power of international law, civilization lives in fear of its annihilation in a global thermonuclear war. In particular, the Cold War between East and West, and especially the nuclear arms race and confrontation between the Soviet Union and the United States, brought the entire world to the brink of a nuclear holocaust which could have been completed within 30 minutes from the time Soviet and American strategic nuclear missiles were launched.

There can be no doubt that a global thermonuclear war would destroy civilization. It might not bring about the immediate extinction of the entire human race; people might, for a time, continue to exist on Earth. However, the long-term effects of nuclear radiation and fallout would cause fatal diseases and deformities among those who survived such a holocaust, and the ecological disasters would destroy the processes of food production and, generally, the means of supporting life. Thus the survivors would be living in a stone age, surrounded by a radioactive environment that would condemn them to slow death.

By any account, nuclear weapons are inherently evil and capable of destroying civilization. For the first time in human history, a manmade doomsday machine has been created. It poses enormous challenges and dilemmas connected with the very survival of humanity.

Despite their destructive consequences, the First and Second World Wars (waged by conventional weapons) were not capable of annihilating civilization. But nuclear weapons can achieve a global human holocaust. The existence of these weapons and the potential danger of their use challenge the very survival of humanity and the legal values and principles of humanity created by the United Nations Charter adopted in 1945.

The UN Charter was designed to serve the legal objective of saving succeeding generations from the scourge of war, which has brought untold sorrow to mankind, and to maintain peace and security, including the protection of fundamental human rights and the dignity and worth of each person. Nuclear weapons pose an ultimate challenge to these fundamental legal principles and values. Additionally, they defeat the traditional concept of just war, including the waging of war on the basis of self-defense. In short, the very existence of nuclear weapons and the potential for their use threatens the rule of law.

The New International Law of Nuclear Disarmament

The failure to achieve nuclear disarmament at the beginning of the nuclear age, particularly before the Cold War, led to the arms race between the Soviet Union and the United States. In addition to the superpowers' nuclearization and that of the other so-called great powers, namely Britain, France and China, in the postwar years, a new nuclear age began in the 1970s as a result of the proliferation of nuclear weapons among a number of other states. Despite the abundant existence of strategic and tactical weapons in the nuclear arsenals of the superpowers and other members of the so-called Nuclear Club, the horizontal proliferation of nuclear weapons has presented new threats to regional and global peace and security.

The Cold War produced strategic, political, and legal obstacles to the quest for global and comprehensive nuclear disarmament through an effective international legal process. Nevertheless, even during the Cold War a new international law of nuclear arms control and disarmament began to develop and to evolve on a step-by-step basis. The development of this new law played a significant role in the international legal effort to place limitations on nuclear arms and nuclear behavior, and also to prevent the eruption of a global thermonuclear war. Moreover, this new international law of arms control and disarmament formulated new legal norms, principles, and methods for approaching and resolving the problem of nuclear disarmament.

With the end of the Cold War in the 1980s and the emergence of a new era of global détente, the major causes of the nuclear arms race and major obstacles that resulted in the failure of nuclear disarmament during the Cold War have been significantly reduced. In particular, the nuclear disarmament process between the two nuclear superpowers, as represented by their INF, START I and START II treaties, among other bilateral legal instruments, shows that a new era of superpower denuclearization has begun in the post–Cold War era. The superpowers' lawmaking processes have not only expanded the norms and principles of the new international law of nuclear disarmament but have also created an innovative and dynamic international verification system.

With the end of the Cold War, the constant threat of a direct and intentional global nuclear war between the two nuclear superpowers has been substantially reduced, at least as a political issue. As a strict military issue, however, the threat of a global thermonuclear war due to an unauthorized or accidental use of nuclear weapons by the superpowers or due to their involvement in certain future conflicts still remains. The threat of a nuclear war will be entirely eliminated only when the last nuclear weapons are effectively eliminated. Until then, the quest for global nuclear disarmament must continue to be the highest priority of the entire world.

In the new political and legal environment, the world has a unique opportunity to create a nuclear weapons–free world through the instrumental value and the power of international law. The study that follows will attempt to establish that comprehensive nuclear disarmament is not only required by the new international law but is also feasible and effective.

Scope and Methodological Approach of This Study

The study comprehensively analyzes the applicable rules of the new international law of peace and nuclear disarmament as they relate to the problem of nuclear disarmament. It will also discuss methodological approaches and institutional changes whose adoption will assist in the creation of a nuclear weapons–free, post–Cold War world. Since the world community has witnessed both the nuclear arms race and the international legal race for nuclear disarmament, this study will examine the implications of these two opposing tendencies, including their mutual interaction.

The study comprises nine chapters. Chapter 1 will discuss the advent of the nuclear age and nuclear weapons and their legal impact on global peace and security in the postwar era. It will focus on the organizational role and institutional capabilities of the United Nations to legally resolve the question of nuclear disarmament through the instrumental power of international law at the beginning of the nuclear age.

Chapter 2 will concentrate on the advent of the Cold War, the beginning of the superpowers' nuclear arms race, and the initiatives of the United Nations in nuclear disarmament during the period 1945–1950. This chapter will discuss the negative impact of the Cold War on the effort to create an international legal regime of nuclear disarmament. It will address the rejection of the Baruch and Gromyko Plans for global nuclear disarmament. Additionally, this chapter will discuss the role of the United Nations and its Atomic Energy Commission in nuclear disarmament and the failure to achieve such disarmament on the basis of international law at the very beginning of the nuclear age.

Chapter 3 will discuss the globalization of the Cold War, the expansion of the superpowers' nuclear arms race, and the UN nuclear disarmament efforts from 1951 through 1962. It will consider the dimensions of the superpowers' relentless nuclear arms race and the Cuban Missile Crisis of 1962, which brought the superpowers to the brink of a thermonuclear war. It will analyze the UN multilateral approaches to nuclear disarmament, and it will also examine the legal issues involved in the search for effective nuclear disarmament.

Chapter 4 will concentrate on the further escalation of the superpowers' nuclear arms race and their efforts at détente, 1963–1975. It will analyze the legal regimes and the impact of the Limited Test Ban Treaty and the SALT I Agreement on the superpowers' bilateral nuclear arms control efforts. It will point out that superpower détente during 1963–1975 proved capable of creating a new international law of nuclear arms control and disarmament, which exercised a positive impact on the management and control of the nuclear arms race.

Chapter 5 will discuss the UN nuclear disarmament initiatives and approaches in the period 1963–1975. In particular, it will discuss the Outer Space Treaty, the Nonproliferation Treaty, and the Seabed Treaty (all of which were concluded during this period), including their legal impact on global nuclear arms control and disarmament. This chapter will also analyze the Treaty of Tlatelolco of 1967, which established the Latin American Nuclear Weapon-Free Zone, and its legal impact on regional nuclear disarmament. The analysis in this chapter will show that, during 1963–1975, the UN developed a new body of regional and global international law on nuclear weapons.

Chapter 6 will analyze the continuation of the superpowers' nuclear arms race and their relevant legal relations in the years 1976–1985. This chapter will discuss the conclusion of the Threshold Test Ban Treaty, the Peaceful Nuclear Explosions Treaty, and the SALT II agreements during this period, and their impact on the superpowers' nuclear arms control and disarmament processes. It will also discuss the START and INF negotiations and proposals. Chapter 6 will analyze the legality of the U.S. Strategic Defense Initiative program in view of the Anti-Ballistic Missile Treaty and other applicable rules of international law.

Chapter 7 focuses on UN nuclear disarmament efforts and the expansion of the international law of nuclear arms control and regional nuclear weapons nonproliferation, 1975–1985. It will concentrate on the UN agenda on nuclear disarmament and its impact through the rule of international law. It will analyze the Moon Treaty, the Convention on the Physical Protection of Nuclear Materials, and the contribution of these treaties to the quest for nuclear disarmament.

Chapter 8 is devoted to a discussion of the forces that resulted in the end of the Cold War and the end of the East-West ideological conflict, rivalry, and threat of nuclear confrontation during the period from 1986 to 1997. In the context of this analysis, the disintegration of the Soviet Union and the emergence of Russia as a new nuclear superpower will be addressed. This chapter will examine the conclusion of the INF, the START I and START II treaties during 1986–1993, and these treaties' legal impact on the superpowers' nuclear disarmament. The chapter will argue that, regarding the new international law of nuclear disarmament, a total superpower denuclearization is both feasible and effective in the post–Cold War era.

Chapter 9 discusses global nuclear disarmament and the role of the United Nations in the post–Cold War era. It examines relevant developments since 1986 and explores the feasibility and effectiveness of disarmament. It questions the legality of the use, development, possession, and deployment of nuclear weapons.

After concluding that such activities are illegal under the new international law of peace and nuclear disarmament, Chapter 9 points out that global nuclear disarmament is both feasible and effective and is required by the new international law of nuclear disarmament.

The study ends with a conclusion and a comment on future prospects. It will be argued that global nuclear disarmament can be achieved through international law by 2010.

Chapter 1

The Advent of the Nuclear Age and Its Impact on the Postwar World Peace and Legal Order

The Development of the Atomic Bomb

Alfred Nobel, the inventor of dynamite, said that he wished he could produce a substance or a machine of such frightful efficacy for wholesale devastation that wars would thereafter become altogether impossible.[1] In that direction, in December 1938, two German physicists, Otto Hahn and Fritz Strassmann, working at the Kaiser Wilhelm Institute in Berlin, performed a revolutionary experiment: They bombarded uranium with neutrons and split the uranium atom into two substances nearly equal in atomic weight, one of which they originally believed was radium. The two scientists could not at first explain what had happened to a small fraction of the original mass of uranium which, in the experiment, had completely vanished, since it was inconceivable to them that an atom could be divided.[2]

It was soon realized that Hahn and Strassmann had split the uranium atom. They had proved the validity of Einstein's equation, $E=MC^2$. It was further realized that if proper conditions were created, the fission of uranium could provide Germany with a weapon of unprecedented explosive power and destructive capability.[3]

The alarming possibility that the Hahn-Strassmann scientific breakthrough could lead to the development of a German atomic bomb persuaded President Roosevelt to take the initial step in October 1939 to build an atomic bomb in the United States.[4] By the end of 1942 the construction of such a weapon was beginning to look inevitable.[5]

Between 1943 and 1945 the United States concerned itself with the production of fissionable material, especially uranium-235 and plutonium, the question of calculating the critical size of a chain-reacting unit, and the technical issue of the assembly and detonation of a bomb. The determination of the size of an atomic bomb, its assembly, and detonation represented enormous scientific problems.[6] Those difficulties were successfully overcome and on July 1, 1945, the U.S. War Department reported that

> A weapon has been developed that is potentially destructive beyond the wildest nightmares of the imagination; a weapon so ideally suited to a sudden unannounced attack that a country's major cities might be destroyed overnight by an ostensibly friendly power.[7]

In a remote corner of the Alamogordo Air Force Base, at 5:30 in the morning of July 16, 1945, the first atomic bomb was successfully tested. Its explosion caused an enormous fireball as bright as several midday suns, a mushroom cloud that extended 41,000 feet into the stratosphere, a tremendous crash, a crater 1,200 feet in diameter, and a crumpled forty-ton tower one-half mile away from the explosion.[8]

The successful explosion of the first atomic bomb at Alamogordo was a startling scientific victory for research in the nuclear field.[9] It was a revolutionary breakthrough that split the nuclei of the atoms of the uranium-235 by a process of nuclear fission and thus generated a huge amount of energy.[10] In retrospect, the costly[11] but successful American efforts to build an atomic bomb introduced the nuclear age to civilization.[12]

Beyond the recognition that the release of the power of the atom would be a tremendous source of energy,[13] the splitting of the atom also created the most devastating weapon ever known. The absolute weapon of destruction, which essentially consisted of four separate weapons combined in one,[14] had been built. The wish of Alfred Nobel to build such a destructive weapon to make war impossible was fulfilled.[15]

The Legal Impact of the Atomic Bomb on International Law and Postwar World Peace and Order

Even though the atomic bomb had not been developed when the United Nations Charter was adopted in June of 1945,[16] the charter nevertheless provides the constitutional and structural foundation of the postwar order. It fundamentally changed the concept of war as an instrument of international conflict resolution. War as an act of force was outlawed by Article 2 paragraph 4, which imposes a legal obligation on member states to refrain in their international relations from the threat or use of force.[17] The charter's initial but loose legal objective was primarily the regulation of armaments rather than global and comprehensive disarmament.[18]

The UN Charter provided the legal regime for the establishment of a warless world. However, it is arguable that in view of the failure of the disarmament regime of the League of Nations, the United Nations should have been more interested in providing a new legal regime and machinery for disarmament.

Although Article 11 paragraph 1 of the charter provides the General Assembly with discretionary power to consider the principles governing disarmament and the regulation of armaments, and although Article 26 imposes an obligation on the Security Council to formulate plans and to establish a system to regulate armaments, the charter failed to lay down the legal framework of a mandatory disarmament system for the postwar era. Furthermore, Article 43 paragraph 1, at least in legal-technical terms, seems to require member states to maintain their own armed forces, since the Security Council has the legal power to ask any member state to make available its armed forces to maintain and restore international peace and order through UN peacekeeping operations.[19] The legal objective of the charter to regulate armaments aims to create a military balance among member states, which would further prevent aggressive and expansionist wars.

We need to remember that the physical realities of the atomic bomb, as a revolutionary means of warfare and as an immediate threat to humankind's survival, had been the concern of nuclear scientists even before the use of the bomb against Japan. Nuclear scientists Niels Bohr, Leo Szilard and James Franck had maintained that the only way to effectively prevent an atomic arms race, and thus a nuclear Armageddon, was through the international legal control of atomic energy and the legal safeguards of inspection by international bodies, which would ensure that no nation possessed atomic bombs.[20]

Understandably, however, the advent of the bomb immediately influenced professional thinking about the management of war itself as practiced in the prenuclear age. The release of the destructive power of the atom profoundly changed traditional legal thinking about the value of war as an instrument of international conflict resolution and, in particular, about the use of the atomic bomb.[21]

The possibility of atomic war between belligerent parties began to persuade the world community that such a war would assure mutual destruction. Atomic war would defy the objectives of war, if it ever had any, as traditionally conceived. Similarly, even the idea of waging atomic war led to a reconsideration of the doctrines of just war and of military necessity: A war fought with atomic bombs would cause unprecedented devastation; this, in turn, would put in question the conceptual and juridical justification of these doctrines. The waging of a nuclear war according to the doctrine of self-defense, as traditionally conceived and juridically justified, would clearly exceed the legal bounds.

Chapter 2

Cold War, Superpower Nuclear Armaments and United Nations Nuclear Disarmament Initiatives (1945–1950)

The Atomic Bomb and the Eruption of the Cold War (1945–1950)

As a consequence of the Cold War, the Truman administration formulated its strategy of containing the Soviet communist threat by military bloc building.[22] Relying on its atomic monopoly, the United States added new military and strategic dimensions to its Cold War relations with the Soviets.[23] Even though President Truman had stated in 1945 that the American atomic bomb was no threat to any nation, but a sacred trust which the United States would retain indefinitely, he nevertheless viewed the American atomic bomb and nuclear monopoly as the most effective means of dictating his own terms to the Soviets in the postwar years.[24]

America's reliance on its atomic arsenal and the contemplation of its use to confront Soviet military aggression against the Western bloc led the United States to engage in a unilateral nuclear arms buildup, which increased American atomic power to 50 nuclear bombs by the end of 1948[25]; the Soviet Union at the time lacked any nuclear weapon capabilities. Such an atomic buildup clearly demonstrated American military superiority over the Soviets in the early years of the Cold War. This superiority must have been perceived by the Soviets not only as a threat to their security and as a form of military-political blackmail, but also as a provocation to their desire to develop their own atomic bomb to respond to the American atomic monopoly and military superiority with nuclear weapons.

UN Nuclear Disarmament Proposals and the UN Atomic Energy Commission (1945–1950)

President Truman was determined to maintain America's atomic monopoly in the postwar years. In 1945, he rejected proposals by some members of his administration for an international legal regime to control the peaceful application of atomic energy and to prevent a nuclear arms race with the Soviets.[26] In the same year, the Truman administration refused to share atomic secrets with the Soviets as a way to prevent the development of a Soviet atomic bomb to counterweight the American atomic monopoly. Instead, President Truman stated that the Soviets had to build an atomic bomb on their own and, if they were successful, the United States would stay ahead.[27]

These statements of President Truman at the very beginning of the nuclear age, at a time of growing conflict in American-Soviet relations, not only provoked the Soviets to develop their own bomb, but also clearly revealed American policy to maintain qualitative and quantitative nuclear superiority over the Soviets in the event the Soviet Union succeeded in developing its own bomb.

President Truman relied on the mistaken prediction that the Soviets would need at least 20 years to develop their own bomb.[28] He viewed the atomic monopoly of the United States as a powerful political and military instrument for safeguarding the global interests of his country and to further neutralize any potential Soviet obstacle to America's expanding world hegemony in the postwar era.[29]

Despite the growing stand-off between the United States and the Soviet Union, the legal process of nuclear disarmament got underway at the United Nations in 1946. Based on the Agreed Declaration of November 15, 1945,[30] the General Assembly established the United Nations Atomic Energy Commission, which was entrusted with the task of formulating plans to ensure the atomic energy would only be used for peaceful purposes.[31] The UN General Assembly adopted on January 24, 1946, Resolution 1(I), which called for the total elimination of atomic weapons.

At the first meeting of the Atomic Energy Commission, in November 1946, the United States submitted a plan for the elimination of all nuclear weapons, which became known as the Baruch Plan, after Bernard Baruch, the American representative to the United Nations and author of the American legal proposal for nuclear disarmament.

The Baruch Plan called for the creation of an international atomic energy development authority to be entrusted with all phases of the use and development of nuclear energy. This authority would enjoy a monopoly over all activities involving nuclear energy; it would have power to inspect, manage, and license all such activities. Use of the atomic bomb as a military weapon was to be legally banned; manufacturing of nuclear bombs was to stop; and existing stockpiles were to be destroyed. The Baruch Plan also included a system of sanctions that could be brought into play by majority vote of the Security Council. The plan emphasized the strengthening and effectiveness of international law as the most fundamental instrument in achieving effective nuclear disarmament and control of the peaceful applications of atomic energy.[32]

Although the General Assembly adopted the Baruch Plan on December 31, 1946, it was rejected by the Soviet Union and its allies. The Soviets objected to the approach of "control before disarmament."[33] The American initiative was also unacceptable to the Soviet leadership on the ground that Soviet research into nuclear weapons would be checked at a time when United States nuclear scientists had already acquired the knowledge to construct such weapons. In the final analysis, the Soviets felt that the Baruch Plan would require them to give up development of nuclear weapons at once whereas the United States would retain its atomic arsenal at least until after the proposed UN authority was functioning.[34]

At the second meeting of the UN Atomic Energy Commission, the Soviet Union introduced its own proposal for nuclear disarmament and control of atomic energy, the Gromyko Plan, named after Andrei Gromyko, Soviet Representative to the United Nations. The Gromyko Plan comprised two stages. The first called for an international convention to prohibit the production and use of atomic weapons. This would be followed within six months by an international agreement providing penalties for violations. The second stage called for the creation of two United Nations committees; one would plan for the exchange of scientific information in the nuclear field; the other would work on a system of safeguards against violations of the treaty. In addition, the Gromyko Plan called for the destruction of all atomic weapons within three months of the treaty's ratification.[35]

The Gromyko Plan was not acceptable to the United States, which thought that it would require the United States to destroy its stocks of nuclear bombs before the international authority began to function. The United States was simply not willing to give up its atomic monopoly before a functioning and effective system of international atomic control and surveillance was in place.[36]

In retrospect, neither the Baruch nor the Gromyko Plan was a realistic legal approach to the problem of nuclear disarmament and atomic control at the beginning of the nuclear age. Although the Baruch Plan had great appeal, since the United States, possessing the monopoly of nuclear weapons, offered to dismantle them and to make its civil nuclear knowledge available to other states,[37] its adoption would have required the Soviets to renounce the development of nuclear weapons. Thus it would have preserved the American atomic monopoly, at least for some time. For its part, the Gromyko Plan was also flawed. The United States could hardly be expected to destroy its nuclear stockpiles without being able to verify through effective means of inspection what the Soviet side was doing.[38]

Although it is accurate to say that both American and Soviet proposals for an international legal regime on nuclear disarmament were inadequate, it must be remembered that lack of good faith, mutual trust and confidence between the two superpowers became a major negative factor in the disarmament process. In essence, this prevented the superpowers from achieving, through further negotiations and compromises, the adoption of an effective legal regime requiring nuclear disarmament and promoting the peaceful uses of atomic energy. As a result of distrust and rivalry, the future arms race became largely unmanageable: The United States was seeking to extend its lead in the development of nuclear technology and weapons and the Soviets were working hard to catch up.[39]

Further negotiations conducted in 1946 under the auspices of the United Nations proved fruitless. The Soviets used their veto in the Security Council to prevent the adoption of any specific legal plan for the regulation of nuclear energy and the elimination of nuclear weapons. Even though, at the urging of the General Assembly, the Atomic Energy Commission continued its nuclear disarmament negotiating, no progress occurred. Shortly thereafter, the Soviet Union refused even to participate, because the representative of the Nationalist government of China continued to represent Communist China. As a consequence, the Security Council dissolved the Atomic Energy Commission in 1952.

The first postwar attempts to achieve nuclear disarmament and prevent a superpower nuclear arms race thus proved a failure.[40] However, despite the failure of the United Nations to legally control and regulate both atomic energy and nuclear arms, from the perspective of bilateral treaty arrangements, the peace treaties signed by the Allies with Bulgaria, Finland, Hungary, Italy and Romania on February 19, 1947, prohibited the possession, construction or testing of nuclear weapons by the latter states.[41]

The Soviet Atomic Bomb (1949): A Response to the American Atomic Monopoly

The inability of the United Nations to adopt a legal regime on nuclear disarmament, the continuation of the Cold War, and, most significantly, the atomic monopoly of the United States and its nuclear strategic planning against the Soviets, led the Soviet Union to develop its own atomic bomb, which it successfully tested in 1949.[42] Although Stalin had publicly denigrated the strategic significance of atomic weapons as early as 1946, when he said that the atomic bomb was intended to intimidate the weak-nerved,[43] the atomic diplomacy and secrecy[44] of the West and the growing American nuclear arsenal in the early years of the Cold War had a direct negative impact on Soviet national security.

Soviet leadership was also persuaded that, in the nuclear age, the most effective response to Western atomic monopoly and military bloc building was the development of a Soviet atomic bomb, which would restore the military balance between East and West. The Soviets viewed the development of their own nuclear bomb in the belief that not only the Soviet Union, but also the world as a whole, would be safer if there were a socialist nuclear bomb to balance the capitalist one.[45]

There were plausible Soviet arguments to justify the development of their own atomic bomb and thus end the American atomic monopoly, which admittedly posed a threat to their national security. The Soviet acquisition of atomic weapon capabilities in 1949 marked the beginning of the atomic arms race between the two superpowers. President Truman and his advisers were shocked when they were informed that the Soviets had successfully detonated their own atomic bomb. President Truman's response to the Soviet bomb was his assurance to the American public on September 23, 1949, that the United States had sufficient countermeasures to the Soviet atomic bomb capability. This, of course, meant that Truman was determined to expand America's atomic weapon programs and to proceed with the development of a far more destructive weapon, the hydrogen bomb.[46]

Chapter 3

Globalization of the Cold War, Expansion of the Superpower Nuclear Arms Race and United Nations Nuclear Disarmament Efforts (1951–1962)

Cold War in Asia and the Korean War (1950)

The globalization of the Cold War in the 1950s and, in particular, the eruption of a "hot war" in Korea clearly showed that the East-West ideological conflict had become a determinative factor in superpower confrontation and rivalry. The United States and the Soviet Union viewed each other as motivated mainly by aggressive and offensive designs.[47] Especially in 1954, when the Federal Republic of Germany was granted membership in NATO and Germany's military rearmament began,[48] the Soviets felt compelled, perhaps justifiably, to establish the Warsaw Pact in May of 1955.[49] The Soviets were deeply troubled by two related developments in American security policy during the culmination of the Cold War in the 1950s. The first was what the Soviets called American "pactomania" and "capitalist encirclement"; the second was the apparent U.S. willingness to develop nuclear weapons and strategies capable of launching a nuclear first strike against the Soviet Union.[50]

The H-bomb and the Growing Club of Nuclear Powers

The successful development of the Soviet atomic bomb in 1949 ended the atomic monopoly of the United States and, above all, restored a kind of military balance between the superpowers; both nations now possessed nuclear weapons. This nuclear balance must have convinced both superpowers, particularly the United States, that any further American strategy to maintain nuclear superiority over the Soviet Union would result in a nuclear arms race. It also persuaded both superpowers to seriously reenter the international legal process of nuclear disarmament, either on a bilateral level or under the auspices of the United Nations.

However, President Truman failed to exploit the prospects for disarmament created by the end of the American atomic monopoly and the reality of Soviet scientific potential to compete with the United States in nuclear armaments. He chose not to initiate a new negotiation on the elimination of nuclear weapons or at least on their control. On the contrary, shocked by the Soviet Union's unexpected development of an atomic bomb, President Truman decided to further expand America's nuclear arms program by ordering the construction of the hydrogen bomb (H-bomb).[51] On November 1, 1952, the hydrogen bomb was successfully tested by the United States.[52] Its detonation yielded an unexpected energy equivalent to ten megatons (ten million tons of TNT), an amount about 1,000 times greater than the energy released by the atomic bomb dropped on Hiroshima (some 13 kilotons).[53] Once more, the continued insistence of the United States on maintaining nuclear superiority over the Soviets proved to have an unfortunate side effect: The Soviet Union almost immediately responded by successfully developing and testing its own hydrogen bomb on August 12, 1953.[54]

Beyond the direct rivalry of the superpowers, the successful detonation of the British atomic and H-bombs in 1952 and 1957, and the explosion of the French nuclear bomb in 1960, evidenced the proliferation of nuclear weapons that began to take place.[55] It can thus be seen that during the 1950s, in addition to the rapid expansion of the superpower arms race, the nuclear powers club was already expanding. This situation can be attributed to the inability of the United Nations to adopt a legal regime regulating nuclear disarmament and nuclear proliferation.

The Expansion of the Superpower Nuclear Arms Race in the 1950s

President Eisenhower's policy of massive retaliation required for its implementation a huge American nuclear weapons buildup. Although such a buildup would lead to the escalation of the nuclear arms race and competition with the Soviets, the Eisenhower administration proceeded in 1954 with the development and successful testing of lightweight nuclear warheads. In the following year it decided to approve the development of the Atlas missile, America's first intercontinental ballistic missile (ICBM), which was designed to carry a one-megaton nuclear warhead 5,500 nautical miles. In the same year, the administration approved the development of America's first intermediate range ballistic missile (IRBM), the Thor, which could carry a nuclear warhead 1,500 miles. In 1957, administration approval was given to yet another Air Force ICBM, a solid-fueled missile called the Minuteman. When the Minuteman became operational in 1962, it replaced the manned bomber as the primary component of America's strategic forces.[56]

On the other side, the Soviet Union, under the leadership of Nikita Khrushchev, who after Stalin's death in 1953 became head of the Soviet Communist

Party, was understandably concerned with the American nuclear buildup. The doctrine of massive retaliation as promulgated by the Eisenhower administration, the anti-communism and anti-Sovietism in the United States, and the agitation in East Germany, Poland and Hungary became substantial factors in shaping Soviet nuclear strategy and expanding the Soviet nuclear arsenal, thus escalating the nuclear arms race during the 1950s.[57]

Khrushchev viewed the American doctrine of massive retaliation as atomic blackmail, and was conscious of his country's nuclear inferiority. As a result, the Soviets expanded their own nuclear weapons program; by 1955 they had amassed a nuclear arsenal of approximately 400 atomic and thermonuclear weapons.[58] Khrushchev's military strategy was thus the opposite of Stalin's: The latter had relied on enormous conventional forces; nuclear weapons now received primary strategic significance from the Soviet leadership.[59]

The Cuban Missile Crisis (October 1962) and Its Aftermath

Beyond the continuation of America's massive nuclear buildup and the nuclearization of NATO's forces in Europe, the Kennedy administration also formulated its own nuclear strategic doctrine of flexible response. In June 1962, President Kennedy's Secretary of Defense, Robert McNamara, explained that a more flexible nuclear strategy was needed to implement a damage limitation strategy. As explained by McNamara, in a Soviet nuclear attack on America's allies, or one limited to American military installations, the new nuclear strategy would enable the United States to attempt to avoid damage to its own cities by retaliating initially only against Soviet military installations (a counterforce attack), rather than Soviet cities (a countervalue attack). McNamara believed that superior American nuclear forces and weapons systems were required to implement his damage limitation strategy and give the United States an assured destruction capability — that is, sufficient nuclear forces, even after a Soviet first-strike — to retaliate against Soviet military installations and, if necessary, Soviet cities as well.[60]

Furthermore, during the Kennedy years, the Cold War rhetoric was intensified and concretized in the form of the Berlin Crisis of 1961, which led to the erection of the Berlin Wall in the same year,[61] and which, in turn, became the symbol of the East-West conflict and division in the years which followed. As is well known, however, the Cuban Missile Crisis of 1962 became the most pivotal episode of the nuclear age, bringing the superpowers to the brink of nuclear war. The Cuban Missile Crisis, or the Caribbean Crisis as it was called by the Soviets, which lasted 13 days in October of 1962, was, in fact, the culmination of the superpowers' Cold War rivalry and the ultimate result of their unrestrained nuclear arms race.[62]

Fortunately, rational thinking prevailed. An accord was reached between

Kennedy and Khrushchev through which the Soviets agreed to withdraw their nuclear missiles from Cuba and the United States pledged not to invade Cuba and to remove its Jupiter nuclear missiles deployed in Turkey.[63]

Nonetheless, the Cuban Missile Crisis persuaded the superpowers that their confrontations could lead to nuclear war and that dispute management was necessary. In short, the Cuban Missile Crisis and its final deflation was a classic case study of a near-nuclear war. It played an important role in convincing both superpowers of the need to avoid direct confrontation and of the need to expedite negotiations to conclude nuclear disarmament and arms control agreements through the international legal process.

UN Legal Initiatives on Nuclear Disarmament (1951–1962)

The Establishment of UN Disarmament Organs and Nuclear Disarmament Proposals (1951–1955)

Early in 1952 the General Assembly created the UN Disarmament Commission, which replaced the already dissolved UN Atomic Energy Commission and the UN Commission for Conventional Armaments and consolidated them into a single UN Disarmament Commission. This new commission, composed of the permanent members of the Security Council and Canada, assumed responsibility to work toward both nuclear and conventional disarmament; it remained the primary institutional organ until 1957.[64] Its main task was to prepare legal proposals for the regulation, limitation and balanced reduction of all armed forces and all armaments, conventional and nuclear, in a coordinated, comprehensive program. Such proposals were to include legal measures for the elimination of all major weapons adaptable to mass destruction as well as measures for effective international control of atomic energy to ensure the prohibition of atomic weapons and the use of atomic energy for peaceful purposes only.[65]

Despite the intensity of the Cold War and the escalation of the nuclear arms race between the superpowers in the 1950s, nuclear disarmament proposals were made by the Soviet Union and the Western powers in the United Nations. On April 5, 1952, the United States submitted to the General Assembly a plan for disclosure and verification of all armed forces and all armaments, including atomic, as a first legal step toward disarmament. The process of disclosure and verification was to take place in five stages, proceeding from the less secret to the more secret weapons, and was to be completed within two years. The Soviet Union, however, objected to the idea of stages and rejected the U.S. plan on the ground that it was aimed at "getting information from other people while concealing data on atomic weapons and secret weapons at home."[66]

On December 8, 1953, President Eisenhower, speaking in the General

Assembly, put forward his "Atoms for Peace" proposal. He suggested the creation of an international atomic energy agency to which nations would make joint contributions of fissionable materials to promote the peaceful uses of atomic energy.[67] Although the initial and early contributions to the plan would be small, President Eisenhower maintained that his proposal had the virtue of avoiding the complicated issues and problems that would be involved in setting up a world-wide system of international inspection and control. The agency, he continued, would be responsible for the impounding, storage and protection of the contributed materials and would devise methods for their allocation and peaceful uses.[68] The Soviets agreed to participate in the talks and negotiations proposed by Eisenhower's "Atoms for Peace" plan, and on December 21, 1953, they put forward an additional proposal calling on all states to assume a solemn and unconditional obligation not to employ atomic, hydrogen or other weapons of mass destruction.[69]

At the summit conference in Geneva on July 21, 1955, held by the United States, the Soviet Union, France and the United Kingdom, President Eisenhower stated that complete nuclear disarmament was no longer technically feasible. The number of nuclear weapons stockpiled had been greatly increased and thus there was no longer any way to verify whether a country that had agreed to destroy its nuclear weapons had in fact hidden enough of them away to be able to launch a surprise nuclear attack. Eisenhower proposed an alternative plan for "Open Skies," which would allow reciprocal aerial inspection by the United States and the Soviet Union and an exchange of blueprints of their military bases.[70]

During its further negotiation and elaboration by the UN Disarmament Subcommittee, which convened on August 29, 1955, the Open Skies proposal was not accepted by the Soviet Union. The Soviets continued to adhere to their traditional legal position to oppose on-site verification measures of nuclear disarmament agreements.[71] Moreover, on September 19, 1955, more concrete objections by the Soviet Union came directly from Soviet Premier Nikolai Bulganin in a letter to President Eisenhower. He maintained that the U.S. Open Skies plan did not include overseas installations and that it would not lead to successful disarmament since it omitted mention of the necessity for reduction of armaments and prohibition of nuclear weapons.[72]

The UN Agenda on Nuclear Disarmament and the Expansion of Its Disarmament Machinery (1956–1958)

Nuclear disarmament negotiations resumed in 1956 despite the tension caused by the Soviet Union's suppression of the Hungarian uprising and Soviet threats of war during the Anglo-French Attack on the Suez Canal the previous year. Nuclear testing, in particular, had become a major problem in nuclear disarmament and in the superpower nuclear arms race.[73] The 1957 session of the UN Disarmament Subcommittee, which proved to be its last, witnessed the most intensive effort by its members to find common ground on partial measures of nuclear disarmament through serious and extensive negotiations.[74]

The Soviets later submitted several proposals which, among other points, included an obligation not to test nuclear weapons for five years, the prohibition of atomic military units beyond national frontiers, and a prohibition on placing nuclear weapons at the disposal of states that did not currently have them.[75] Additionally, Soviet Premier Bulganin accepted the Rapacki Plan submitted to the United Nations on October 2, 1957, by Polish Foreign Minister Adam Rapacki. This plan proposed the creation of a Nuclear Weapon-Free Zone (NWFZ) in Central Europe that would have included both Germanys, Poland and Czechoslovakia. The plan provided that no nuclear weapons be stationed or produced within the denuclearized zone. The Rapacki Plan was rejected by the Western powers.[76]

In July 1957 the International Atomic Energy Agency (IAEA) officially came into existence. The principal aim of the IAEA is to accelerate and enlarge the contribution of atomic energy to peace, health and prosperity throughout the world. Above all, the agency is to ensure that special fissionable and other nuclear materials provided by it to its member states will not be used for any military purposes by those states. It also has the legal task to make sure that assistance provided by it, or at its request, or under its supervision or control will not be used to further any military purpose by the recipient member state.[77]

The IAEA has been empowered with legal safeguards and verification techniques, which among others, include: the examination of the design of specialized equipment and facilities, including nuclear reactors and their approval only if they will not further any military purpose; the right to call for and receive reports from its recipient member states; the right to approve the scientific means to be used for the chemical processing of irradiated materials solely on the basis that they will not be used for military applications; and the right to conduct on-site inspections by inspectors designated by the agency after consultation with the recipient state concerned. Its inspectors have the right of access to nuclear facilities and data and to anyone whose occupation involves fissionable materials.[78]

In conclusion, the legal power of the agency's inspectors to make on-site inspections on the territory of the recipient state concerned constituted a legal breakthrough in the effort to verify that such a state does not use nuclear material received from the IAEA for military applications. This legal technique of on-site inspection could be of the utmost practicality in ensuring effective implementation of nuclear disarmament agreement, as well as the prevention of the proliferation of nuclear weapons.[79]

In 1958 the Disarmament Commission was enlarged to 25 members. The Soviets boycotted further work of the commission because of a dispute over its membership: The Soviets wished to enlarge it to include seven additional members, including Austria, Bulgaria, Ceylon, Finland, Indonesia, Romania and the Sudan. Nonetheless, negotiations on nuclear disarmament continued in several other fora. The United States and the Soviet Union also convened a group of experts who met at the Geneva Conference on the discontinuance of nuclear weapons tests in 1958. They concluded that the development of satellite technology made it technically feasible to set up a workable and effective control system to detect violations of an agreement on worldwide cessation of nuclear weapon tests. A second conference of experts convened at Geneva in November 1958 to study methods to help prevent a surprise nuclear attack. However, no joint report was agreed upon.[80]

The UN Agenda on General and Complete Disarmament (1959–1962)

At the beginning of 1959 the United Nations established the Ten-Nation Disarmament Committee. Among other nuclear disarmament proposals and initiatives at the start of that year, the joint communiqué issued by Nikita Khrushchev and Harold MacMillan revealed that the two leaders had agreed to further study the issue of nuclear disengagement in Europe, coupled with a system of inspection and the intensification of the test ban negotiations. But by the end of 1959 the UN agenda was mainly concerned with general and complete disarmament. Substantial legal efforts were then undertaken to meet the goals and objectives posed by the UN concept of such disarmament. Indeed, the General Assembly, at its 14th session, declared this disarmament the fundamental legal strategy and goal of the United Nations in its further negotiations on disarmament.[81]

The new item "General and Complete Disarmament" was placed on the agenda of the General Assembly's 14th session at the request of the Soviet Union, on whose behalf Premier Khrushchev, addressing the assembly on September 18, 1959, proposed a new program of general and complete disarmament, which included the following proposals: complete prohibition of atomic and hydrogen weapons — discontinuance of the production of all types of these weapons, their elimination from the armaments of the states, and destruction of stockpiles of same; complete discontinuance of the production of rocket weapons of all types and ranges, including spare rockets for military purposes and their production; and the dismantling of all rocket-launching installations.[82]

While the 1959 Soviet plan on general and complete disarmament (nuclear and conventional) constituted a comprehensive proposal which, if accepted, would have led to a new order under the rule of law, the United States rejected it. On the goal of complete disarmament, the United States inappropriately raised questions about the type of international police force to be established, what principles of international law should govern the use of force, and what internal security forces would be required by the nations of the world if existing armaments were abolished.[83]

Despite the failure of negotiations conducted under the aegis of the United Nations in 1959, it is worth noting that the Antarctic Treaty was signed at Washington, on December 1, 1959, and entered into force on June 23, 1961. This treaty, initially signed by a dozen states, including the United States and the Soviet Union, is of particular significance to nuclear disarmament. It adopted the principle of the peaceful uses of the entire Antarctic region. It not only prohibits the militarization of the region but specifically prohibits the installation of military bases of any type; it bans the deployment of nuclear weapons and any other kind of military weapons; and it prohibits the explosion or testing of nuclear weapons in the region.

Article I of the treaty provides that: "1. Antarctica shall be used for peaceful purposes only. There should be prohibited, *inter alia,* any measures of a military nature, such as the establishment of military bases and fortifications, the carrying out of military maneuvers, as well as the testing of any type of weapons. 2. The present Treaty shall not prevent the use of military personnel or equipment for scientific research or for any other peaceful purpose."

Article V of the treaty states that: "1. Any nuclear explosions in Antarctica and the disposal there of radioactive waste material shall be prohibited. 2. In the event of the conclusion of international agreements concerning the use of nuclear energy, including nuclear explosions and the disposal of radioactive waste material, to which all of the contracting parties whose representatives are entitled to participate in the meetings provided for under Article IX are parties, the rules established under such agreements shall apply in Antarctica."

The Antarctic Treaty can certainly be regarded as one of the most fundamental legal instruments concluded since the end of World War II insofar as the creation of a demilitarized and denuclearized region is concerned. It made the Antarctic a demilitarized and denuclearized zone, and provided a system of verification and inspection techniques to safeguard effective implementation. It was also the first postwar multilateral treaty to shift the interest of the United Nations from the goal of general and complete disarmament to the more specific goal of regional nuclear disarmament and the prevention of regional nuclearization. It constitutes the starting point in the UN drive for the development of an international legal regime against regional nuclear proliferation.[84]

In 1961 the superpowers announced that they had reached an understanding to continue an exchange of views on questions relating to disarmament and the resumption of negotiations in an appropriate body whose composition was to be agreed upon. They jointly submitted a statement of agreed principles on the multilateral negotiating process of disarmament to the General Assembly. As a result, the assembly, on April 21, 1961, unanimously adopted by Resolution 1617 (XV) the joint Soviet-American statement on agreed principles of disarmament. This resolution provided that further disarmament negotiations would focus on the elimination of all stockpiles of nuclear weapons and the cessation of their production, and the elimination of all means of delivery of nuclear weapons and weapons of mass destruction in general.[85]

During 1962 the nuclear disarmament negotiations continued under the aegis of the United Nations. The Conference of the Eighteen-Nation Committee on Disarmament opened in Geneva on March 15, 1962, at the Foreign Ministers' level.[86] Although France decided not to participate, because it believed that it might be possible for the disarmament problem to be discussed later by powers that could effectively contribute to its solution, the Foreign Ministers decided to concentrate on simultaneous work on general and complete disarmament, confidence building (collateral) measures, and the discontinuance of nuclear weapon tests.[87]

The major documents before the conference during the first session in 1962 were the "Draft Treaty on General and Complete Disarmament Under Strict International Control," submitted by the Soviet Union on March 15, 1962, and the United States' "Outline of Basic Provisions of a Treaty on General and Complete Disarmament in a Peaceful World," submitted on April 18 of the same year. These two documents, amended during the following three years, remained the basis for negotiations at Geneva on general and complete disarmament.[88]

Chapter 4

Escalation of the Nuclear Arms Race and the Détente Legal Process (1963–1975)

The Development of the Superpower Law of Détente and Arms Control (1963–1975)

Both superpowers continued to increase their nuclear weapon arsenals form 1963 to 1975.[89] China also, on October 17, 1964, announced that it had successfully exploded its own atomic bomb.[90] Thus, the acquisition of nuclear weapon capability by China increased the size of the Nuclear Club, which in 1964 included both superpowers, Britain, France, and now China. The increase in the number of nuclear powers since the advent of the atomic age clearly demonstrated that proliferation of nuclear weapons had created new legal issues in nuclear disarmament. The nuclear arms race between the superpowers and the proliferation of nuclear weapons appeared to have become an uncontrollably evolving process, which had, in fact, overtaken any effective international legal process aimed at the elimination or nonproliferation of nuclear weapons.

Nevertheless, the political principle of détente, which was designed to improve superpower relations through negotiation and by avoiding confrontation, had a profound impact on the normative regulation of the superpower relationship. Détente evolved into a legal principle of importance in arms control and regulation. The experiment with superpower détente, which began with the opening of the SALT negotiations on November 17, 1969, produced a cluster of agreements signed at Moscow in 1972 (SALT I).

Before proceeding with an analysis of the SALT I Accords, it is important to note the détente and its legal aspects were not suddenly introduced in the superpower relations in 1969. On the contrary, superpower détente began to emerge almost immediately after the resolution of the Cuban Missile Crisis. As an aftermath, the near-nuclear war persuaded both nations to consciously seek a limited détente. Similarly, it was realized that, unless both sides agreed to legally manage their relationship, they would find themselves at nuclear war. In particular, both sides realized that their nuclear arsenals and rivalry had transformed the nature of their competition, and that they needed to place legal limits on the range of their permissible behavior to guard against the possibility that their failure to communicate and jointly manage their relationship could lead to a nuclear war.

As a result of the emerging, albeit limited détente, on June 20, 1963, the superpowers signed at Geneva a Memorandum of Understanding regarding the establishment of a Direct Communications Link, commonly referred to as the Hot Line Agreement.[91] Although this agreement was designed to prevent nuclear war arising through accident or miscalculation, it was of little legal significance to nuclear arms control, particularly in nuclear disarmament.

Limited détente greatly facilitated negotiations, which resulted in the conclusion of the Limited Test Ban Treaty (LTBT) signed at Moscow on August 5, 1963, by the superpowers and Britain.[92] Although the LTBT is a multilateral treaty later signed and ratified by more than a hundred countries (although not France or China),[93] it was essentially the product of the limited détente between the superpowers during the Kennedy and Khrushchev years.[94]

The LTBT, which bans nuclear weapon tests and explosions in the atmosphere, in outer space and under water,[95] removes a dangerous threat posed to human health by radioactivity released by nuclear weapon tests and explosions in those areas.[96] It is a legal instrument intended to exercise a positive influence in the prevention of nuclear proliferation, in the curbing of the superpower nuclear arms race, and ultimately in the facilitation of nuclear disarmament.

Despite the LTBT's failure to prohibit underground nuclear weapon tests and explosions, which would, in essence, have completely outlawed such tests,[97] it was in principle a positive step in the legal regulation of nuclear weapons tests and generally in the field of arms control. The LTBT was the first international agreement of worldwide scope in regulating the arms race and nuclear proliferation.[98] Its principal purpose, however, was the protection of the human environment, not arms control.

Unfortunately, a critical appraisal of the LTBT leads to the conclusion that it has essentially failed to achieve its legal objectives. By the time it was concluded, the two main testing states, the United States and Soviet Union, had already carried out an extensive series of nuclear explosions in the atmosphere. Both nations knew that this activity could be continued underground. Accordingly, the superpowers legally continued their underground nuclear tests and explosions, which provided most of the information required for further weapon development. In fact, since 1963 both superpowers have carried out considerably more nuclear explosions than they did before the signing of the LTBT. This testing enabled them to develop new generations of nuclear warheads and related delivery vehicles. Essentially, the superpower nuclear arms race was allowed to continue unhampered,[99] and thus the underlying legal objective of the treaty to prevent a continuing superpower arms race was not achieved. Furthermore, the LTBT failed to prevent the proliferation of nuclear weapons.[100]

Limited détente proved to be of norm-creating dynamism in that it led to the conclusion of the Hot Line Agreement and the LTBT; it also created the necessary environment for the conclusion of the SALT I Accords — for which negotiations started in 1969 — and was itself transformed into a legal principle regarding the management of superpower conflict. It proved to be a progressive legal force facilitating the continuation of superpower efforts to regulate their arms race and nuclear arsenals through bilateral treaties.

The détente legal process not only produced the SALT ABM Treaty and the SALT I Interim Agreement of May 26, 1972, which are strictly related to the regulation and control of the arms race, but also resulted in the conclusion of a series of agreements primarily designed to prevent a nuclear war. These agreements are the following:

1. The Agreement on Measures to Improve the U.S.–USSR Direct Communications Links, the so-called Hot Line Modernization Agreement, was signed on September 30, 1971, and entered into force on the same date. This treaty added satellite communications to earlier communication links between the parties.[101]
2. On September 30, 1971, the superpowers also signed the Agreement on Measures to Reduce the Risk of Outbreak of Nuclear War Between the Two Nations, the so-called Nuclear Accidents Agreement, which entered into force on the same date. This agreement requires each party to provide: immediate notification and to take preventive action regarding any unauthorized incident involving possible detonation of a nuclear weapon; immediate notification of the detection of an unidentified object by their respective missile warning systems or of interference with the warning systems; and advance notification of planned missile launches beyond borders in the direction of the other party.[102]
3. The U.S.–USSR Agreement on the Prevention of Incidents On and Over the High Seas was signed on May 25, 1972, and entered into force on the same date. This agreement established rules of conduct between the parties with respect to military ships and aircraft in international waters and airspace. It also requires notification of situations of danger and the exchange of factual information regarding incidents or damage suffered by ships and aircraft involving the other party.[103]
4. The Agreement on Basic Principles of Relations Between the U.S. and USSR was signed on May 29, 1972, and entered into force on the same date. This major agreement, which constitutes the legalization of the principle of superpower détente, established principles for the conduct of the parties toward each other, such as the principle of peaceful coexistence on the basis of equality; avoidance of military confrontation and nuclear war; limitation of strategic arms, preferably in the form of concrete agreements, and the ultimate objective of general and complete disarmament.[104]

This treaty not only specified the legal content of the principle of détente, but also attributed to it legal merit and instrumental value. In essence, this agreement provided a legal foundation on which to ease superpower Cold War relations. It was legally designed to substitute such relations with the principle of peaceful coexistence and thus create those confidence building measures which were further required to achieve the legal goal of final denuclearization.

5. The U.S.–USSR Memorandum of Understanding Regarding the Establishment of a Standing Consultative Commission, the so-called SCC Agreement, was signed and entered into force on December 21, 1972. This agreement established a Standing Consultative Commission with the task of promoting the implementation of the Nuclear Accident Agreement, the SALT ABM Treaty, and the SALT I Interim Agreement.[105]
6. The U.S.–USSR Agreement on the Prevention of Nuclear War was signed and entered into force on June 22, 1973. This treaty enjoins the parties not to threaten or use force against each other or their allies in circumstances endangering international peace, and requires them to hold urgent consultations in situations involving risk of nuclear war.[106]
7. The U.S.–USSR Treaty on the Limitation of Underground Nuclear Weapon Tests, the so-called Threshold Test Ban Treaty (TTBT), was signed on July 3, 1974, and entered into force on March 31, 1976. This treaty prohibits underground nuclear weapon tests producing yields in excess of 150 kilotons; the parties pledged to keep the number of underground tests to a minimum. It also provides for exchanges of data to assist verification by National Technical Means (NTM). However, the TTBT excluded from consideration the prohibition of underground nuclear tests for peaceful purposes.[107]

These bilateral treaties concluded between the United States and the Soviet Union, including also the SALT ABM Treaty and the SALT Interim Agreement, were the ultimate result of the superpower détente process. They created a law of détente.[108]

In conclusion, détente created the required legal environment and provided positive norms and principles for arms control and nuclear disarmament. The law of détente led the superpowers from the era of Cold War relations to a new epoch of peaceful coexistence and to the beginning of the legal regulation of their nuclear armaments. It served in a positive manner the establishment and promotion of confidence building measures which, in the legal sphere of arms control and most importantly nuclear disarmament, are a sine qua non.

The ABM Treaty (May 26, 1972)

Content and Objectives. After tortuous negotiations,[109] the Anti-Ballistic Missile (ABM) Treaty entered into force on October 3, 1972.[110] The treaty was designed to safeguard the doctrine of nuclear deterrence based particularly on the logic of mutual assured destruction. Its underlying rationale was to achieve that end by legally limiting and preventing the further development and deployment of defenses aimed at the interception and destruction of ballistic missiles.[111]

The ABM Treaty codified the mutuality of nuclear deterrence in the logic of assured destruction.[112] It constitutes the most comprehensive and detailed legal instrument of the SALT I Accords which for the first time established severe quantitative, qualitative, and geographical legal constraints and limits on superpower anti-ballistic missile defense systems.[113]

The key legal provisions of the ABM Treaty are Articles I and V. However, Article III of the treaty contains an exception to the general prohibition of ABM defense systems provided by the above articles. Both the United States and the Soviet Union reserved the right under Article III to have two deployment areas of ABM systems; One protects the state's capital, the other protects ICBM silos.[114] In accordance with this exception, the Soviets were allowed to deploy an ABM system around Moscow, and a second ABM system in defense of ICBM silos east of the Ural Mountains. The United States had the right to deploy an ABM system around Washington, D.C., and another to defend its ICBM silo site west of the Mississippi.[115]

Another key legal provision is Article V(1), which prohibits both contracting parties from developing, testing or deploying ABM systems or components which are sea-based, space-based, or mobile land-based. Immobile land-based ABM defense systems and components are legally authorized under the treaty. But mobile land-based ABM defense systems and components that are temporarily immobilized are also prohibited under Common Understanding C. Additionally, ABM launchers and radars which are not permanent fixed types are considered mobile and are, therefore, prohibited.[116]

Not surprisingly, the scope of the prohibitions imposed by Article V has raised questions of interpretation. Controversy over interpretation first arose at the time of the ratification of the treaty and during the U.S. Senate Hearings on the SALT II Agreement. It resurfaced during the negotiation process of the Strategic Arms Reduction Talks (START),[117] particularly regarding the decision of the United States to proceed with the development, testing, and final deployment of its Strategic Defense Initiative (SDI) program.[118] In fact the American-Soviet difference of opinion over the compatibility of the SDI program with the ABM Treaty is a significant question of interpretation in its own right. America's determination to proceed with its SDI project was a strategic and legal obstacle to superpower negotiations for the conclusion of a bilateral treaty, which would provide the partial reduction and the final elimination of their nuclear arms.

Implementation. Effective implementation of the treaty was to be achieved by using national technical means (NTM) of verification. The parties agreed not to interfere with each other's national means of verification and not to deliberately conceal information relevant to compliance with the treaty. Although the

NTM of verification are not defined by the treaty, they are to be used in a manner consistent with generally recognized principles of international law. Unfortunately, such principles are notoriously imprecise and are subject to varying interpretations. In essence, the nature and the extent of information gathered by NTM of verification depend on each party's technological ability to verify the other's effective compliance with its legal obligations imposed by the treaty.[119]

While some verification techniques are established and well known, others are secret and thus are unavailable.[120] Such national technical means concerning the verification of the observance of the ABM Treaty include primarily space satellites, space shuttles and platforms, high-flying airplanes, and radars. In particular, both superpowers have stressed reliance on satellite technologies, which are sufficient to verify the existence of various objects such as bombers, missile sites, submarines leaving ports, factories producing means of delivering nuclear weapons, tank brigades, and armies on the march.[121]

The NTM of verification are considered nonintrusive, at least in the sense that verification is conducted from outside the territory of the subject party[122] and on the legal basis of a treaty right. In particular, space satellites that can overfly and photograph most territories in a few minutes, and which are not considered, at least by common consent, to violate national sovereignty, have become the cornerstone of the superpowers' national technical means of verification techniques not only in verifying their compliance with the provisions of the ABM Treaty, but also in verifying their other arms control agreements discussed below.[123]

The NTM of verification, particularly in the form of space-based spy satellite technologies, do not always guarantee effective verification: The party subjected to such measures can technically interfere in an active or passive manner and thus prevent effective verification and therefore implementation of treaty obligations. More specifically, a state subject to verification procedures by NTM can resort to active interference, which connotes any countermeasures that interrupt or degrade the reconnaissance vehicle or facility itself. It may also undertake passive interference, which means concealments and deception activities that prevent verification or are designed to permit undetected circumvention of the specifics of a given treaty.[124]

To prevent active and passive interference with the NTM designed to effectively verify treaty compliance, Article XII (2) and (3) impose on the contracting parties an obligation not to interfere with the NTM of verification of the other party and not to use deliberate concealment measures which impede verification by NTM of compliance. Article XIII established a Standing Consultative Commission (SCC), which has been vested with the legal duty of ensuring the effective implementation of the treaty, assuring confidence in compliance with the obligations assumed, and considering questions involving unintended interference with NTM of verification. Similarly the preamble of the treaty states the superpowers' desire to strengthen their mutual trust and confidence.[125] Thus, the effective implementation of the provisions of this treaty, beyond the use of NTM of verification, depends also on the promotion of confidence building measures between the two parties.

THE INTERIM AGREEMENT (MAY 26, 1972)

After the BMD defense systems were legally regulated by the ABM Treaty, both superpowers on May 26, 1972, signed the Interim Agreement on the Limitation of Strategic Offensive Arms. It entered into force on October 3, 1972.[126] This agreement was limited in both time and scope. It was intended to remain in force for five years, unless replaced earlier by an agreement on more complete measures limiting strategic arms.[127] Its objective was to provide a provisional accord limiting certain strategic offensive arms, pending further negotiations on the conclusion of a more comprehensive treaty.[128] At this point, one must remember that both superpowers initially failed to conclude a bilateral treaty directly regulating the limitations of their strategic offensive arms: They failed to agree on a legal and technical description of a "strategic weapon."[129] Additionally, the parties were unable to resolve the problem of "unequal force aggregates," the exclusion of strategic bombers, and the lack of precision concerning permissible ICBM modernization.[130] Thus the interim agreement was limited only to the regulation of two central strategic offensive arms, the ICBMs and the SLBMs.[131]

Before proceeding to a legal analysis of some central provisions of this agreement, one must note that, although at the inception of the SALT I negotiations the superpowers had achieved numerical parity in their ICBMs, the Soviet Union had indeed overtaken the United States both in ICBMs and SLBMs at the conclusion of the above agreement. At the conclusion of the interim agreement, the Soviets had constructed and deployed 1,618 ICBMs and 740 SLBMs, while the United States had deployed only 1,054 ICBMs and 656 SLBMs.[132]

The interim agreement aimed at maintaining and legally safeguarding on a provisional basis the U.S.–Soviet strategic balance, until a more comprehensive and complete treaty could be concluded.[133] In the final analysis, the agreement symbolized an attenuation of the superpowers' rivalry and nuclear arms competition and confirmed their acceptance of the practicality of the doctrine of nuclear parity.[134]

The agreement imposed legal limitations on the future construction of fixed land-based ICBM launchers and on the construction of further SLBM launchers, under the specific conditions of these provisions.[135] Although these legal limits applied only to fixed land-based ICBM launchers and SLBM launchers, the construction of other nuclear weapon systems and delivery vehicles, which constitute strategic offensive arms, was not prohibited by the agreement. In effect, the interim agreement, even in the form of a provisional accord, did not limit the number or the payload of nuclear warheads, strategic bombers, missiles on warships, short and intermediate range ballistic missiles, land-based mobile ICBM launchers, air to surface ballistic missiles or American forward-based systems.[136]

On the contrary, the limits imposed by the agreement related only to fixed land-based ICBM launchers, to SLBM launchers, and modern ballistic missile submarines.[137] Yet even these limitations were not of a comprehensive nature. The agreement did not prohibit the completion of ICBM launchers under active construction at the time of its signature. Adversely, the completion of their construction was allowed by Agreed Statement I.[138] Additionally, Article IV of the agreement allowed the modernization and replacement of those strategic offensive ballistic missiles and launchers regulated by the agreement.[139]

Both parties had managed to agree only on the imposition of legal limitations on the above described strategic offensive arms, and that for two reasons. First, the nuclear weapons systems covered by the interim agreement could be verified on the basis of the use of their NTM of verification and compliance safeguards.[140] Second, the purpose of imposing legal limitations on these weapon systems was to maintain the strategic balance, which would further legally safeguard the nuclear deterrence doctrines.

The interim agreement and its protocol[141] did not have any substantial legal effect either on the reduction or the elimination of the nuclear weapon arsenals. On the contrary, it was drafted with the object of temporarily maintaining and safeguarding the strategic equilibrium, the nuclear deterrence doctrines, and eventually the prevention of a nuclear war between the superpowers. This objective confirmed the status quo; it was not aimed at the drastic reduction and further elimination of nuclear weapon arsenals as required by the legal goal of the concept of nuclear disarmament. In essence, the maintenance of the nuclear balance meant the maintenance of nuclear arsenals, a result that was inconsistent with the concept of nuclear disarmament and even of arms reductions.

It must be recognized, however, that the interim agreement represented a continuation of the process of détente. The agreement's legal parameters and guidelines were designed to further develop a legal framework for the conclusion of a more comprehensive bilateral treaty to be signed within prescribed time limits.

Renewed Superpower Tensions and the End of the SALT I Process (1973–1975)

President Richard Nixon was willing, after active negotiations, to proceed to the conclusion of a bilateral treaty which would implement the Interim Agreement on the Limitation of Strategic Offensive Arms.[142] But his resignation in mid–1974 due to the Watergate scandal prevented him from doing so. Although his successor, President Gerald Ford, continued his détente legacy, the legal environment created by the Nixon détente had begun to wane. Indeed, in 1973 Cold War relations between the two superpowers revived. In particular, the Arab-Israeli war of October 1973 led the superpowers to place their strategic nuclear forces on alert. In addition, the Kremlin's involvement in so-called wars of national liberation in Angola in 1974 and other regions negatively affected détente.[143]

With the revival of Cold War relations in 1973, the equilibrium which was to have been maintained by the interim agreement was challenged by the Soviet Union. In that year the Soviets began deploying a new generation of ICBMs with a greater payload capacity, each equipped with multiple warheads. The largest of these new Soviet MIRVed ICBMs, the SS-18, was armed with ten independently-targetable reentry vehicles. As a result of these deployments, the number of Soviet land-based ICBMs was further increased by a factor of four: from approximately 1,500 in 1972 to about 6,000 warheads in the early 1980s. Moreover, these new Soviet MIRVed intercontinental ballistic missile systems were of significantly improved accuracy. Beginning in 1974, the Kremlin also initiated procurement of a new strategic bomber, code-named "Backfire."[144]

Despite renewed tensions between the superpowers and the rapid increase of the Soviet strategic nuclear forces, the superpowers continued the spirit and process of détente in their bilateral approach to arms control. As a result, the summit meeting between Secretary Leonid Brezhnev and President Ford in Vladivostok on November 23, 1974, produced the Joint American-Soviet Statement on the Limitation of Strategic Offensive Arms, known as the Vladivostok Declaration. Although the Vladivostok Declaration announced a general agreement which signaled a new stage in their negotiations on the limitations of their strategic offensive arms, it did not reduce the nuclear arsenals of the parties.[145] It only outlined the elements of a further proposed SALT Treaty on the limitation of the superpowers' strategic offensive nuclear weapons.[146]

The Vladivostok Declaration did not provide any specific figures: It merely forecast limitations on the total numbers of strategic vectors, ICBMs and SLBMs equipped with MIRVs. However, the figures which President Ford made public on December 2, 1974, revealed that each party would be limited to a total of 2,400 strategic vectors, of which 1,320 ICBMs and SLBMs would be allowed to be loaded with MIRVs. It was also agreed that both parties would be left free within the above limits to determine the distribution of the various weapons systems of their strategic forces.[147]

In retrospect one sees that the Vladivostok Declaration constituted a positive legal measure designed to further promote the bilateral approach to the regulation and imposition of specific limitations on nuclear armaments. It was intended to continue the step-by-step approach to arms control. Importantly, the Vladivostok Declaration also provided a legal basis and framework for future negotiations, which led to the conclusion of the SALT II Agreement on June 18, 1979.[148]

Chapter 5

United Nations Nuclear Disarmament Legal Initiatives and the Development of the United Nations Law of Regional and Global Nuclear Weapons Nonproliferation (1963–1975)

The UN Multilateral Legal Approach to Nuclear Disarmament

FAILURE OF THE UN AGENDA ON GENERAL AND COMPLETE DISARMAMENT

The period 1963–1975 was one of active UN negotiations on a number of legal proposals aimed at general and complete disarmament.[149] The Eighteen-Nation Disarmament Committee, enlarged to include 26 member states in 1969, became known as the Conference of the Committee on Disarmament. Its representation was further increased to 31 members in 1974. Finally, in 1978, it was renamed the Committee on Disarmament and its membership increased to 40, including the five permanent members of the UN Security Council.[150]

Nevertheless, by the mid–1960s, the escalation of the nuclear arms race and competition, and the increase in size of the club of nuclear powers had convinced even the most ardent of UN disarmament activists of the impossibility of achieving general and complete disarmament by means of a single sweeping and comprehensive plan. Indeed, by the mid–1960s it was realized both inside and outside the UN that general and complete disarmament, including nuclear disarmament, was a very long-term legal goal. Although the General Assembly, in 1969, turned to the Conference on Disarmament and directed it to draft a comprehensive program for the cessation of the nuclear arms race with a view to general and complete disarmament, this initiative did not produce any positive legal results, at least regarding comprehensive and global nuclear disarmament.[151]

Despite its failure to achieve general and complete disarmament during the

1960s, the General Assembly, still determined to pursue that objective during the 1970s, proclaimed that decade as the First Disarmament Decade. The decade was designed to be a period during which nations and governments were required to intensify their efforts to achieve effective measures relating to the cessation of the nuclear arms race.[152]

Unfortunately, the First Disarmament Decade failed to meet its objective of ending the nuclear arms race. While it produced a series of conferences and pronouncements by various world leaders on the imperative need to slow down and finally reverse the nuclear arms race, it did not generate any legal results in nuclear disarmament. During the decade, both nuclear superpowers not only failed to reduce their nuclear arsenals by the elimination of even one nuclear warhead, they expanded their nuclear weapons systems and warheads. Unfortunately, the First Disarmament Decade also failed to prevent nuclear proliferation, as shown by the case of India.[153]

Failure to Outlaw the Use of Nuclear Weapons for War

During the period in review the United Nations failed to conclude a multilateral treaty proscribing the unlawfulness and prohibiting the use of nuclear weapons as a means of warfare. In 1967 the Soviet Union had submitted a draft convention to the General Assembly under which the parties would agree to refrain from using or from threatening to use nuclear weapons and from inciting other states to use them. This Soviet draft provided that the parties would also undertake to reach an early agreement on ceasing production and destroying stockpiles of nuclear weapons in conformity with a treaty on general and complete disarmament.[154]

Although the Soviet draft, which called on member states to undertake negotiations for the conclusion of a convention banning the use of nuclear weapons for war, was adopted by General Assembly resolution 2289 (XXII) in December 1967, the matter received no significant attention at the Conference of the Eighteen-Nation Committee on Disarmament; the Western powers rejected the draft convention.[155] One now sees that the UN failure to absolutely ban the use of nuclear weapons by means of an international agreement had a negative impact on UN efforts to eliminate nuclear weapons. If the United Nations had, at that particular time, outlawed nuclear weapons by adopting the Soviet draft convention, it would have promoted attempts to conclude an international agreement on the elimination of nuclear weapons on a comprehensive and global basis through an effective process of nuclear disarmament.

Failure to Adopt a Comprehensive Test Ban Treaty (CTBT)

During 1963–1975, the United Nations repeatedly, but with no success, attempted to conclude a CTBT. This failure owed primarily to American-Soviet disagreement on accepting a total nuclear test ban. In 1974 Soviet leader Brezhnev had renewed previous Soviet proposals and proposed the conclusion of a CTBT imposing a total ban on underground weapons tests and their complete cessation in accordance with an agreed-upon timetable. The United States rejected that proposal because it continued to insist that the verification of such a treaty had to be conducted on the basis of on-site inspection. The Soviets rejected on-site inspection techniques; they accepted only NTM of verification.[156]

As discussed above, both superpowers (and the United Kingdom) had concluded the Limited Test Ban Treaty (LTBT) in 1963, which allowed them to carry out only underground nuclear weapon tests. They also had concluded the Threshold Test Ban Treaty (TTBT) in 1974, which prohibited underground nuclear weapon tests having a yield greater than 150 kilotons. These treaties, which were acceded to by other member states of the United Nations, became the subject of a prolonged ratification process, particularly in the U.S. Senate. In 1990 both superpowers ratified these treaties, but both have conducted numerous nuclear weapon tests in contravention of them.[157]

Importantly, both the LTBT and TTBT were drafted with a view to allowing the nuclear superpowers to legally conduct nuclear weapon tests, sufficient for the development of new generations of nuclear weapons and the modernization of their older nuclear arsenals. In addition, the restrictions imposed by these treaties on the conduct of nuclear weapon tests did not have any effect in preventing nuclear proliferation, as was clearly shown by the underground nuclear explosion conducted by India in 1974, a party to the LTBT.

In view of the inadequacies of the LTBT and the TTBT to prohibit nuclear weapon tests, the conclusion of a CTBT under the auspices of a United Nations ban on all forms of nuclear weapon tests would have legally prevented both superpowers from further expanding their nuclear arsenals and also from modernizing their older nuclear weapons. Similarly, it would have made a positive contribution to the legal effort to prevent non-nuclear weapon states, non-parties to the NPT, from acquiring nuclear weapon capabilities, since the testing of such weapons would have been prohibited.

The UN Legal Approach to Regional Nuclear Weapons Nonproliferation

The UN efforts to prevent the spread of nuclear weapons on a regional basis as a collateral measure for achieving a comprehensive and global nuclear disarmament on a region-by-region basis produced a body of international law, namely: 1) The Treaty of Principles Governing the Activities of States in the Exploration and Use of Outer Space, Including the Moon, and Other Celestial Bodies, known as the Outer Space Treaty, which was concluded on January 27, 1967; 2) The Treaty for the Prohibition of Nuclear Weapons in Latin America, known as the

Treaty of Tlatelolco, signed on February 14, 1967; and 3) The Treaty on the Prohibition of the Emplacement of Nuclear Weapons and Other Weapons of Mass Destruction on the Seabed and Ocean Floor and in the Subsoil Thereof. This treaty was concluded on February 11, 1971, and is known as the Seabed Treaty.

These treaties have generated a set of positive principles and norms which can be termed the UN Law of Regional Nuclear Weapons Nonproliferation. They seek to prevent the nuclearization of entire regions and geographic areas. They represent significant legal breakthrough and the starting point of the UN process to work toward comprehensive nuclear disarmament by following a step-by-step approach as part of an overall legal strategy to achieve global and comprehensive denuclearization.

The Outer Space Treaty (January 1967) and the Prevention of the Nuclearization of Outer Space

Content and Objectives. The Outer Space Treaty, concluded under United Nations auspices on January 27, 1967, entered into force on October 10 of the same year. This treaty has been ratified by both nuclear superpowers and by a large number of other UN member states. Its conclusion under the aegis of the United Nations was due to widespread fear that the nuclear arms race would be extended to outer space.[158]

A review of the Outer Space Treaty shows that it was designed to promote and regulate the peaceful exploration and uses of outer space generally, including the moon and other celestial bodies. It was drafted with a view to promoting scientific, economic and peaceful cooperation among states party to the treaty with respect to their space activities. It restated the general legal principle of the peaceful uses of its subject-matter, which was first codified by the Antarctic Treaty for its own purposes.[159]

Article IV is the key legal provision on the prevention and prohibition of the militarization and nuclearization of outer space. It imposes a duty to refrain from placing in orbit around the earth objects carrying nuclear weapons or any other weapons of mass destruction. It also prohibits installation of nuclear weapons and weapons of mass destruction on celestial bodies or stationing such weapons in any other manner. Article IV explicitly states that the moon and other celestial bodies must be used exclusively for peaceful purposes. Thus the establishment of military bases, installations and fortifications, the testing of any type of weapons, and the conduct of military maneuvers generally in outer space is forbidden.[160]

Reduced to its essence, Article IV was drafted to prevent the militarization, particularly the nuclearization of outer space in general. Indeed, this article explicitly prohibits the militarization of the entire outer space region by any military means, particularly by nuclear weapons and weapons of mass destruction.

Implementation. Despite the absence of an international verification system, some provisions of the treaty are designed to play a role in safeguarding compliance, particularly regarding obligations to refrain from any attempt to nuclearize outer space, the moon and other celestial bodies. Article XI of the treaty provides that, to promote international cooperation in the peaceful exploration and use of outer space, the contracting parties conducting activities in outer space, including on the moon and other celestial bodies, agree to inform the Secretary-General as well as the public and the international scientific community of the nature, conduct, locations and results of such activities.[161]

Article XI can play a legal role in ensuring effective compliance with Article IV. Article XI could be interpreted to mean that states have the legal obligation to inform the Secretary-General of any activity in outer space which is not compatible with the content of Article IV. On this interpretation, those contracting parties involved in activities in outer space, including the moon and other celestial bodies, have a legal obligation in good faith, and by avoiding any sort of collaboration, to monitor and verify by their NTM of verification that other states party to the treaty do not violate Article IV.

Article XII provides that all installations, stations, equipment, and space vehicles on the moon and other celestial bodies must be open to representatives of other contracting parties on a basis of reciprocity. Such representatives must give reasonable advance notice of their projected visit. This provision adopts a form of on-site inspection (on the basis of reciprocity) by which contracting parties have the legal right to visit the stations, installations, equipment, and space vehicles of other contracting parties on the moon and other celestial bodies, but not in outer space in general. By virtue of Article XII, contracting parties can verify that stations, installations, equipment, and space vehicles on the moon and other celestial bodies are not in violation of Article IV. If they find that there are violations of Article IV, they are under a legal obligation to report it to the Secretary-General in accordance with Article XI.

Nonetheless, such on-site inspections and visits may be rendered impossible because of the legal obstacle posed by the reciprocity clause in Article XII. Since on-site inspections and visits are not unconditional but can be effected only on a basis of reciprocity, a contracting party involved in activities incompatible with Article IV may deliberately and on various grounds refuse to agree to such on-site inspections and visits to conceal military activities in violation of Article IV.[162]

Nuclear Weapon–Free Zones (NWFZs)

The formulation of the legal concept of NWFZs began to take place in the United Nations during the 1950s. Supporters of the establishment of such zones argued that NWFZs (a) constitute a measure for achieving general disarmament; (b) contribute to global peace and security; (c) reduce nuclear proliferation; and (d) assist the reorientation of foreign policies, particularly for smaller states.[163]

The first legal plan, which gave concrete content to the concept of NWFZs and which was submitted to the United Nations in 1957, was the Rapacki Plan for an NWFZ in Central Europe. The proposal was rejected. Nevertheless, since the 1950s the United Nations has witnessed the submission and discussion of various proposals for the creation of NWFZs in different regions of the globe. In the 1950s, Bulgaria conceived and advanced the idea for the creation of an NWFZ in the Balkans, which zone would have included Albania, Bulgaria, Greece, Romania, Turkey and Yugoslavia.[164] With the exception of the Latin American NWFZ established in 1967, during the 1960s and the first half of the 1970s the United Nations received proposals for the creation of NWFZs in several other regions of the world, including a Nordic zone,[165] an African zone,[166] a Central European zone,[167] and a Near East zone.[168]

THE LATIN AMERICAN NWFZ AND THE TREATY OF TLATELOLCO (FEBRUARY 14, 1967)

Treaty Content and Objectives. After complex negotiations among the Latin American states concerned, The Treaty for the Prohibition of Nuclear Weapons in Latin America, which established the Latin American NWFZ, was signed on February 14, 1967 at Tlatelolco in Mexico City. This treaty, known as the Treaty of Tlatelolco, entered into force on April 22, 1968. Its conclusion was characterized by General Assembly Resolution 2286 (XXII) as an event of historic significance.[169]

The Treaty of Tlatelolco constitutes a significant starting point in the evolutionary development of the international law of regional nuclear weapons nonproliferation. This treaty is the first multilateral regional treaty to give legal substance to the concept of NWFZ in a heavily populated region of the globe. In contrast, the Antarctic and Outer space treaties apply to vast but unpopulated regions.[170]

The treaty has been ratified by 32 Latin American nations, and has entered into force for all but three states: Guyana, St. Kitts and Nevis, and St. Lucia. The treaty has entered into force for Argentina, Brazil and Chile, which are militarily significant countries in the region, and with advanced nuclear programs.[171] Cuba, which is involved in the construction of a nuclear power plant, has signed the treaty, but the treaty has not entered into force for Cuba.[172]

The object of the treaty is to prevent and prohibit the nuclearization of the Latin American NWFZ. To serve this objective, Article 1 (1) imposes on the contracting parties the obligation to prohibit and prevent in their respective territories: "(a) the testing, use, manufacture, production or acquisition by any means or type of nuclear weapons by the participating states themselves, directly or indirectly, on behalf of anyone else or in any other way, and (b) the receipt, installation, storage, deployment and any form of possession of any type of nuclear weapons in the same manner as above." Under paragraph 2 of Article 1, the contracting parties are obliged to refrain from engaging in, encouraging or authorizing, directly or indirectly, or in any way participating in the testing, use, manufacture, production, possession or control of any nuclear weapon.[173]

Although, in accordance with Article 1 (1), the contracting parties have undertaken to use exclusively for peaceful purposes the nuclear material and facilities which are under their jurisdiction, Article 17 provides that participating states have the right to use nuclear energy for peaceful purposes, particularly for their economic development and social progress, but in conformity with the treaty. In addition, Article 18 provides that the contracting parties are allowed to carry out explosions of nuclear devices for peaceful purposes, including explosions which involve devices similar to those used in nuclear weapons: The same article allows the contracting parties to collaborate with third parties in carrying out nuclear tests and explosions for peaceful purposes.[174]

Article 5 defines "nuclear weapon" as any device which is capable of releasing nuclear energy in an uncontrolled manner and which has a group of characteristics that are appropriate for use for warlike purposes. However, this article fails to prohibit the contracting parties from developing and building launchers and other delivery vehicles for nuclear weapons. On the contrary, Article 5 provides that the contracting parties have the right to build instruments for the transport or propulsion of a nuclear device on condition that such instruments are separable from the nuclear device and are not an indivisible part of them.

Because Article 5 allows contracting parties to develop and construct ballistic missile delivery systems or any delivery vehicles that can be used for the delivery of nuclear weapons, this permission represents a substantial defect and failure in relation to the treaty's overall aims and objectives. Indeed, Article 5 may not only impede the realization of the treaty's objective to maintain the Latin American region free from nuclear weapons on a permanent basis, but may also interfere with the prevention of the proliferation of nuclear weapons delivery systems and, consequently, with the nonproliferation of nuclear weapons in general. Although both Argentina and Brazil possess ballistic missile capabilities, they have agreed to ban the production of nuclear-capable ballistic missiles.[175]

Treaty Implementation. The treaty has created a specific control system and machinery vested with power to ensure the implementation of the treaty's legal objectives through a system of verification techniques and procedures. Articles 7 and 8 create the Treaty Agency for the Prohibition of Nuclear Weapons in Latin America, known as the OPANAL. This agency, which comprises the General Conference, the Council and the Secretariat, constitutes the control machinery.[176]

Each of the agency's principal organs has been vested with power and responsibility to ensure the effective compliance of the contracting parties with their treaty obligations. The General Conference, as the supreme organ of the Treaty Agency, has the authority to supervise compliance with the treaty by the contracting parties, to establish procedures for the control system of the treaty to ensure the observance of the treaty provisions, and to receive and consider biennial and special reports submitted to it by the Council and the General Secretary.[177]

The Council has also been vested with power and responsibility to ensure the operation of the treaty's control system and safeguards for effective implementation. The Secretary-General enjoys discretionary power to request any of the contracting parties to provide the agency with complementary or supplementary information regarding any event or circumstance connected with treaty compliance. The parties are obligated to cooperate fully and promptly with requests for complementary and supplementary reports concerning conformity with the treaty.[178]

Although the Treaty of Tlatelolco created its own control machinery, it also saw fit to link itself to the international control system of the IAEA. Under Article 13, the contracting parties agreed to allow the IAEA to be involved in the implementation of the treaty indirectly and subject to conditions. The IAEA may apply its international control system and safeguards on condition that prior agreements have been signed on an individual basis between the IAEA and the contracting parties to the Treaty of Tlatelolco. In particular, since the Treaty of Tlatelolco can be in full force for the participating states without the conclusion of a prior agreement between the IAEA and the contracting parties, the involvement and the legal role of IAEA in the international control over the verification and implementation of the treaty appears to be limited.[179]

In accordance with Article 12, the control system established by the treaty serves the objective of verifying: (a) that nuclear devices, services and facilities of the contracting parties are only used for peaceful purposes and applications and are not used in the testing or manufacture of nuclear weapons; (b) that none of the nuclear activities prohibited by Article 1 of the treaty are carried out in the territory of the participating states with nuclear materials or weapons introduced from abroad; and (c) that explosions for peaceful purposes are compatible with Article 18 of the treaty.

The Treaty of Tlatelolco authorizes both the IAEA and the Council to carry out special on-site inspections designed to verify effective compliance with the treaty. Article 16 (1) (a) provides the IAEA with the right to carry out on-site inspections apparently on the nuclear facilities and installations of the contracting parties. Nevertheless, as has been explained, the IAEA has no direct right to carry out on-site inspections and apply its atomic safeguards by virtue of this treaty. The IAEA may carry out on-site inspections only on the basis of separate agreements concluded between states party to the treaty and the IAEA and in accordance with Article 13 of the treaty.

Article 18 (2) of the treaty requires the contracting parties which intend to carry out or to cooperate in carrying out permissible nuclear tests and explosions to notify the Treaty Agency and the IAEA of the date of the explosion. Such parties must supply both the IAEA and the Treaty Agency with the following information: (a) the nature of the nuclear device and the source from which it was obtained; (b) the place and purpose of the planned explosion; (c) the expected force of the device; and, (e) the fullest possible information on any radioactive fallout which may result from the planned explosion or explosions, and the measures taken to avoid danger to the population, flora, fauna and territories of any of the other contracting parties.

Article 18 (3) provides the General Secretary of the Treaty Agency, the technical personnel designated by the Council, and the IAEA with the legal right, whose exercise is discretionary, to observe the preparations and the detonation of the nuclear device. If these organs decide to exercise their right of observation they are allowed unrestricted access to any area in the vicinity of the site of the scheduled nuclear explosion. The purpose served by this provision is to ascertain whether the nuclear device used and the information supplied by the contracting party or parties concerned conforms to the required procedures and purposes of the treaty.

Article 24 provides for the judicial settlement of disputes and questions concerning the interpretation or application of the treaty by reference to the International Court of Justice. Article 24 is the first legal provision of an international treaty pertaining to the prevention of the proliferation of nuclear weapons and generally to the legal issue of nuclear disarmament, which provides directly for judicial settlement.

External Guarantees to the Latin American NWFZ: Additional Protocols I and II. Notwithstanding that the treaty prohibits the production or acquisition, deployment or stockpiling, use or threat of use of nuclear weapons by its Latin American participants, maintaining the Latin American region as an NWFZ on a permanent basis significantly depends also on the respect of the zone as such by outside nuclear weapon states and outside states having de facto or de jure control and possession over territories included in the zone established by the treaty. Thus there was a need for such outside states to legally guarantee that their behavior and involvement in this zone would be consistent with the objectives of the treaty.

To this end, the treaty has been accompanied by Additional Protocols I and II. Protocol I was designed to ensure the effective implementation of the objectives and purposes of the treaty by those extra-continental states which, de facto or de jure, are internationally responsible for territories lying within the limits of the geographical zone established by the treaty.[180] According to Article 1 of this protocol, the extra-continental states, upon becoming parties to Protocol I, agree to apply the statute of denuclearization in respect of warlike purposes as defined in Articles 1, 3, 5 and 13 of the treaty to such territories. Protocol I has been signed and ratified by the United States, the United Kingdom, France and the Netherlands. This protocol, like the Treaty of Tlatelolco itself, is of unlimited duration, and it has entered into full force.[181]

Additional Protocol II is aimed at securing legal guarantees from nuclear weapon states that: "(i) they will respect in all its express aims and provisions the statute of denuclearization of the Latin American region in respect of warlike purposes, as defined, delimited and set forth in the Treaty of Tlatelolco; (ii) they will not contribute in any manner to the performance of acts in violation of the prohibitions and obligations of Article 1 of the treaty with respect to the established Latin American NWFZ; and, (iii) they will not use or threaten to use nuclear weapons against the states party to the treaty.[182] This protocol has been signed and ratified by China, the United Kingdom, the United States, France and the Soviet Union."[183]

The legal guarantee given by the nuclear weapon states shows that they can play a significant role in the recognition and preservation of NWFZs as such. Of particular legal significance is the obligation undertaken by the nuclear weapon states (under Protocol II) that they will not contribute in any way to the acquisition of nuclear weapon capabilities by states party to the Treaty of Tlatelolco. This guarantee can be an important contribution to the development of an international legal regime of nonproliferation on a regional basis and in the form of NWFZs. The legal obligation of the nuclear weapon states under Protocol II not to use or threaten to use nuclear weapons in the Latin American NWFZ also constitutes a positive legal step in the development of an international legal regime on the prohibition of the use of nuclear weapons against the states party to an NWFZ.

The Prevention of the Nuclearization of the Seabed, Ocean Floor and Subsoil and the Seabed Treaty (February 1971)

Content and Objectives. After extensive bilateral negotiations, the superpowers submitted on October 7, 1969, a joint draft treaty to the Eighteen-Nation Disarmament Committee, which agreed on the final text of the treaty. Thus, on December 7, 1970, the General Assembly by Resolution 2660 (XXV) adopted the Seabed Treaty, and expressed the hope for the widest possible adherence to it by the contracting parties. The treaty entered into force on May 18, 1972, when the Soviet Union, the United States, the United Kingdom and more than 22 other countries deposited their instruments of ratification.[184]

The fundamental legal provision of the Seabed Treaty is in Article I (1). In this provision, the contracting parties agree "not to emplant or emplace on the seabed and the ocean floor and their subsoil any nuclear weapons or any weapons of mass destruction, including structures, launching installations or any type and form of facilities specifically designed and constructed for storing, testing or using of nuclear weapons and weapons of mass destruction." The wording of Article I (1) suggests that this prohibition applies only to fixed objects and fixed installations of nuclear weapons and weapons of mass destruction and only in specified maritime spaces, namely, the seabed and the ocean floor and their subsoil. In accordance with Article II, these maritime regions are beyond the outer limit of a seabed zone, which is further defined as being coterminous with the 12-mile outer limit of the zone referred to in Part II of the Geneva Convention on the Territorial Sea and the Contiguous Zone of 1958.[185]

The treaty does not prohibit the installation of nuclear weapons in the superjacent waters.[186] States party to the treaty, while not allowed to emplant or emplace fixed nuclear weapon systems and fixed nuclear weapon installations in the seabed and the ocean floor and their subsoil, can achieve the same military ends by installing and building such systems and facilities exactly above the prohibited maritime spaces and in the superjacent waters, as well as in any other part of the hydrospace. Moreover, the prohibitions laid down by Article I (1) in relation to the prevention of the emplacement and emplanting of fixed nuclear weapon systems installations in those maritime spaces do not seem to be invulnerable to the activities of a state determined to nuclearize these regions. States party to the treaty, depending on their technological capabilities, without committing any treaty violation, can nuclearize the seabed and the ocean floor by placing in these areas mobile nuclear weapon systems. The placement of such systems on the seabed and the ocean floor would not violate Article I (1) since that article prohibits only fixed nuclear weapon systems and installations in these maritime zones.

The treaty fails to keep the seabed and the ocean floor completely free of nuclear weapons, and is susceptible to legal exploitations in the manner explained. The treaty fails to prohibit the placement of nuclear weapons and installations of such weapons in the superjacent waters of the prohibited maritime zones, and, most significantly, it fails to prohibit in any way the navigation of submarines and surface warships capable of carrying and delivering strategic and tactical nuclear warheads. The treaty surely does not apply to naval forces capable of carrying and delivering nuclear weapons or even conventional warheads.

Naval nuclear disarmament in the context of sea-based nuclear ballistic systems and their means of carriage and delivery, such as submarines and surface warships equipped with nuclear missiles, constitutes a substantial part of the problem of global and comprehensive nuclear disarmament. However, both nuclear superpowers, heavily relying on the strategic importance of their naval nuclear arsenals and machinery for maintaining nuclear deterrence and enhancing their nuclear war fighting capabilities, have failed to conclude any treaty specifically dealing with the reduction and gradual elimination of their naval nuclear arsenals and machinery.

Implementation. Article III deals with compliance. Article III (1) provides for a system of observation. Each contracting party has the right to verify through observations the activities of other contracting parties on the seabed and the ocean floor and their subsoil, provided such observations do not interfere with the activities in these maritime areas.

Paragraph 2 of Article III provides that if a contracting party has reasonable doubts that another contracting party has been involved in nuclear activities on the seabed and the ocean floor and their subsoil in violation of its obligations under the treaty, then the contracting parties must consult with each other to remove these doubts. If such doubts persist after consultations, then the state that continues to have doubts has the legal obligation to notify other states party to the treaty. Furthermore, the contracting parties concerned have the legal duty to cooperate on the determination of the verification techniques and procedures required for ensuring that the activities of the state party in the aforesaid specified maritime areas are in conformity and compliance with the treaty. Such verification techniques and procedures include inspection of objects, structures, installations or other facilities which are reasonably expected to violate the provisions of Article I of the Treaty.

Paragraph 3 of Article III provides that if the contracting party responsible for the activities in the aforesaid maritime spaces, and whose activities gave rise to the reasonable doubts of violating the treaty, is not identifiable by the aforesaid verification procedures and techniques, then the contracting party having the doubts must notify and make appropriate inquiries of the activities of the contracting states in the region concerned and of any other party. If, after such notification and inquiries, the state responsible cannot be identified, the contracting party having the doubts and making the inquiries may exercise the right of verification measures, including inspection. Such a contracting party must invite the other parties in the region to participate in identifying the party responsible for the activities, whose conformity with the treaty raised reasonable doubts.

If this consultation and cooperation, as provided by paragraphs 2 and 3 of Article III, have not removed the doubts and there remains a serious question concerning the treaty compliance of the responsible party concerning its activities in the seabed and the ocean floor and their subsoil, then any state party may refer the matter to the Security Council, which may act in accordance with the UN Charter. The verification measures and activities allowed to ensure the effective implementation of the treaty by its contracting parties must not interfere with the legitimate activities of other contracting parties and must be conducted with respect for the rights of such parties as recognized by international law, which include such matters as the freedom of the high seas and the rights of the coastal states in relation to the exploration and exploitation of their continental shelves.

It is important to emphasize that pursuant to Article III (5), the verification of the effective implementation of the treaty by its contracting parties may be conducted by any contracting state using its own means of verification or with the full or partial assistance of any other contracting party, or through appropriate procedures within the framework of the UN and in accordance with the UN Charter. It is clear that the Seabed Treaty does not create a treaty organ or authority which, vested with appropriate legal powers and technological capabilities, would be able to ensure the effective implementation of the treaty.

Instead, the treaty entrusts its effective function and compliance upon the desire and discretionary right of its parties to check on each other's conformity with their obligations under the treaty.

The Development of the UN Legal Regime on Global and Comprehensive Nuclear Weapons Nonproliferation and the Treaty on the Nonproliferation of Nuclear Weapons (NPT) (July 1, 1968)

The problem of preventing the proliferation of nuclear weapons is as old as nuclear weapons. The question of how to enable the world community to enjoy the benefits derived from the peaceful applications and uses of fissionable nuclear materials and nuclear technology without spreading the technological capability of developing nuclear weapons has been a primary legal concern at the United Nations since the advent of the nuclear age.[187]

The superpower nuclear arms race and the proliferation of nuclear weapons among other powers increased the danger of a nuclear war.[188] In addition, earlier assumptions about the scarcity of nuclear materials and the difficulty of mastering nuclear technology for the development of nuclear weapons by additional states were inaccurate. In the early 1960s the search for peaceful applications of nuclear energy had brought technological advances in nuclear reactors for the generation of electric power, and had also increased the fears of using such technologies for the development of nuclear weapons.[189]

The international community realized that if the diversion of nuclear materials from peaceful purposes and uses was not prevented by an international system of safeguards, and if a growing number of states were involved in the proliferation of nuclear weapons, the danger of nuclear war as a result of accident, unauthorized use, or escalation of regional conflict would be greatly increased. It was realized that the uncontrolled spread of nuclear weapons would increase the difficulties of legal control and the ultimate elimination of nuclear weapons through effective nuclear disarmament.[190]

On November 23, 1965, the General Assembly adopted Resolution 2028 (XX), which called for the conclusion of a nuclear nonproliferation treaty and asked the Eighteen-Nation Disarmament Committee to assume and carry out this legal task. This resolution also provided the legal framework for an NPT on the basis of the following five principles: (i) The treaty should be devoid of any loopholes which might permit nuclear or non-nuclear weapon states to proliferate, directly or indirectly, nuclear weapons in any form; (ii) the treaty must incorporate an acceptable balance of mutual responsibilities and obligations of the nuclear and non-nuclear weapon states; (iii) the treaty should be a step toward the achievement of general and complete disarmament and, more particularly, nuclear disarmament; (iv) there should be devised acceptable and workable provisions to ensure the effective implementation of the treaty; and (v) the treaty must not adversely affect the right of any group of states to conclude regional treaties to achieve and ensure the total absence of nuclear weapons in their respective territories.[191]

These five principles promulgated by the General Assembly Resolution 2028 (XX) were to become the fundamental legal objectives of the nuclear nonproliferation treaty regime. After extensive negotiations the two superpowers filed a joint and agreed-upon draft treaty with the Eighteen-Nation Disarmament Committee on March 1, 1968. This joint draft was submitted to the General Assembly which, on June 12, 1968, adopted it by a 95–4 vote with 21 abstentions. This was the first time in the UN history of disarmament that a resolution sponsored by the nuclear superpowers failed to gain the unanimous approval of the General Assembly. Although the four states which voted against the adoption of the final text of the NPT were of minor rank and military importance, the 21 abstentions included France, which was a nuclear weapon state at the time of the conclusion of the NPT, and other states approaching the nuclear threshold, such as India and Brazil. The NPT was opened for signature on July 1, 1968, and entered into force on March 5, 1970.[192]

Articles I and II of the NPT serve to prevent and prohibit horizontal proliferation of nuclear weapons, that is, proliferation of nuclear weapons among non-nuclear states.[193] To achieve this aim, Article I provides that

> Each nuclear-weapon State Party to the Treaty undertakes not to transfer to any recipient whatsoever nuclear weapons or other nuclear explosive devices or control over such weapons or explosive devices directly, or indirectly; and not in any way to assist, encourage, or induce any non-nuclear weapon State to manufacture or otherwise acquire nuclear weapons or other nuclear explosive devices, or control over such weapons or explosive devices.

Article II provides that

> Each non-nuclear-weapon State Party to the Treaty undertakes not to receive the transfer from any transferor whatsoever of nuclear weapons or other nuclear explosive devices or of control over such weapons or explosive devices directly, or indirectly; not to manufacture or otherwise acquire nuclear weapons or other nuclear explosive devices; and not to seek or receive any assistance in the manufacture of nuclear weapons or other explosive devices.

The NPT Division Between Nuclear and Non-Nuclear Weapon States and the Implications of Their Imbalanced Obligations

Although the horizontal nuclear nonproliferation legal regime created by Articles I and II of the NPT constitutes a positive legal step toward the nonproliferation of nuclear weapons, these two articles nevertheless create a juridical division between the member states of the United Nations into nuclear and non-nuclear weapon states. This division results from the differential treatment of these two categories of states with respect to their legal right and obligations under the NPT. In this regard, Article IX (3) of the NPT defines a nuclear weapon state as one which had manufactured and exploded a nuclear weapon or other nuclear explosive device before January 1, 1967. Based on this article, the nuclear weapon states established as such before that date are the United States, the Soviet Union, the United Kingdom, France and China. All the other states were categorized as non-nuclear weapon states by application of Article IX (3) of the NPT; by acceding to this treaty they are legally obliged to maintain their legal status as such.

However, the legal division of member states of the United Nations into nuclear and non-nuclear weapon states by the NPT has become an issue. It is increasingly observed that it would be rational and legitimate to expect the NPT to serve the objective of global and comprehensive nuclear disarmament by equally requiring non-nuclear weapon states to maintain their legal status as such and at the same time requiring nuclear weapon states to eliminate their nuclear weapons within a concrete time frame.

The distinction between nuclear and non-nuclear weapon states by the NPT gives the impression that the treaty legitimizes the de facto status of those states which acquired nuclear weapons before January 1, 1967. Thus, the treaty represents a form of legal discrimination against states which did not acquire nuclear weapons before the above date, since these states on the basis of the NPT are legally prohibited from any form of horizontal nuclear proliferation. The NPT gives the impression that it has been drafted with the implied objective of legitimizing the nuclear hegemony and monopoly of the nuclear weapon states while prohibiting the non-nuclear weapon states from acquiring nuclear weapons and requiring them to maintain their non-nuclear status.

A literal interpretation of Article VI suggests that the NPT fails to impose concrete legal obligations on the nuclear weapon states to refrain from any further vertical nuclear proliferation through further development, production and deployment of nuclear weapons. Article VI and, generally speaking, the NPT legal regime also fail to impose on the nuclear weapon states a concrete legal obligation to eliminate or at least drastically reduce their nuclear arsenals through nuclear disarmament within a specified timetable.

On the contrary, Article VI imposes on all states party to the treaty, not specifically on the nuclear weapon states, the obligation to pursue negotiations in good faith on the effective cessation of the nuclear arms race and on nuclear disarmament. This provision particularly applies to the nuclear weapon states, but it is, nevertheless, obvious that the NPT fails to refer specifically to the obligation of the nuclear powers to cease their vertical nuclear proliferation and actively pursue denuclearization. Thus the NPT fails to create a specific and dynamic legal regime requiring nuclear weapons states to eliminate their nuclear weapons. In clear violation of Article VI, both superpowers increased six-fold their nuclear arsenals. On the other hand, regarding the prohibition of horizontal nuclear proliferation, the treaty imposes clear and categorical legal obligations on the non-nuclear weapon states and unconditionally requires them to maintain their legal status as such.

The demand of the non-nuclear weapon states to establish an effective direct and conditional legal link between their obligation to renounce the acquisition of nuclear weapon capabilities themselves, and the commitment of the nuclear weapon states to cease their nuclear arms race and achieve their nuclear disarmament, do not seem to have been legally recognized by the NPT. Indeed, the NPT fails to create balanced legal obligations between these two categories of states. The treaty fails to embody an acceptable balance of mutual responsibilities and obligations between the nuclear and non-nuclear weapon states in relation to the ultimate goal of the nuclear disarmament of the nuclear powers and the preservation of the non-nuclear status of the non-nuclear weapon states. In any case, the non-nuclear weapon states, on the basis of their legal obligations under Article II as compared to the obligations of the nuclear powers under Article IV, are at a legal disadvantage.

The Security Council has attempted to provide a legal assurance for the security of the non-nuclear weapon states against nuclear attack by the nuclear weapon states. Specifically, the Soviet Union, the United States and the United Kingdom sponsored Resolution 255 of the Security Council on June 19, 1968, before the signature of the NPT; this resolution provides that the Security Council welcomes the intention expressed by the above three nuclear powers that they will provide or support immediate assistance, in accordance with the UN Charter, to any non-nuclear weapon state party to the NPT which is a victim of an act or an object of a threat of aggression in which nuclear weapons are used.[194]

It is evident that the NPT fails to incorporate in itself any provision which would directly provide the legal pledge and guarantee of the nuclear weapon states not to use or threaten to use nuclear weapons against non-nuclear weapon states party to this treaty. One should recall that Soviet Premier Aleksei Kosygin had proposed the inclusion of a security guarantee in the treaty, which would have forbidden the use of nuclear weapons against non-nuclear powers which signed the treaty, on the condition that such states held no nuclear weapons in their territories. However, this Soviet proposal, which is known as the no-use proposal or the Kosygin Clause, was rejected by the NATO allies and was not incorporated in the NPT.[195]

Despite the failure of the NPT to embody a security guarantee prohibiting the use or the threat of use of nuclear weapons by the nuclear powers against the non-nuclear weapon states party to the NPT, Security Council Resolution 255 could have developed binding legal effect on the above three nuclear powers on the basis of their parallel declarations. The International Court of Justice, in its judgment on the nuclear test cases (Australia v. France) of December 20, 1974, held that unilateral declarations of a state's intention can have binding legal effects on that particular state.[196]

The NPT reflects a form of legal inequality between the nuclear and non-nuclear powers in their respective obligations on vertical and horizontal nuclear nonproliferation. Furthermore, although Article II was specifically designed to prevent and prohibit any form and in any manner the horizontal proliferation of nuclear weapons among non-nuclear weapon states, a literal interpretation of Article I clearly suggests that the nuclear powers reserved for themselves legal rights which cannot be compatible with the legal principle of state equality and with the legal objectives of nuclear disarmament and international security. Unlike non-nuclear weapon states, the nuclear powers are not barred from transferring nuclear weapon technology among themselves. They may also receive assistance in the manufacture and testing of nuclear weapons or other nuclear devices. Moreover, they are not subject to safeguards on any of their nuclear activities.

While, by virtue of the NPT, the non-nuclear weapon states must not acquire any nuclear weapons, the treaty fails to prohibit the nuclear powers from installing nuclear weapons in the territories of the non-nuclear weapon states party to the NPT. It thus seems that the NPT is an international legal instrument characterized by a dose of legal irony and contradiction in relation to its legal objectives. While the non-nuclear weapon states are obliged by the treaty to remain non-nuclearized, the nuclear powers are not prevented from the nuclearization of non-nuclear weapons states. As a result, the nuclearization of non-nuclear weapon states, as has been the case of the nuclearization of the respective allies of the superpowers, does not assist the NPT in imposing an effective and dynamic legal regime of vertical and horizontal nuclear nonproliferation with the ultimate objective of achieving global and comprehensive denuclearization.

Despite these defects and inadequacies, Article IX recognized the legal role of NWFZs in the prevention of horizontal nuclear proliferation on a regional basis. This article recognizes and also favors the right of the contracting parties to establish NWFZs in their respective regions. The feasibility of the establishment of NWFZs by non-nuclear weapon states in their respective regions has generally been hindered, however, by the fact that a large number of such states, being members of the superpower military alliances and blocs, have been nuclearized by the nuclear superpowers.

Although 188 member states of the United Nations have become parties to the NPT,[197] the comprehensiveness and effectiveness of the nuclear nonproliferation regime established by the NPT have been challenged since the treaty entered into force. Key non-nuclear weapon states have become de facto nuclear weapons states. By the mid–1970s, both India and Israel, which are not parties to the NPT, acquired nuclear weapons. The acquisition of nuclear weapons by these two countries marked the beginning of a new nuclear age.[198]

The IAEA and the NPT Verification System

Article III of the NPT imposes on each of the non-nuclear weapon states party to the treaty an obligation to accept safeguards on the basis of a separate agreement between each of the non-nuclear weapon states and the IAEA. The aim of the agreement is to prevent diversion of nuclear energy from peaceful uses to nuclear weapons or other nuclear explosive devices. Article III also imposes on each contracting party, either nuclear or non-nuclear, an obligation not to provide source or special fissionable material, or equipment or material especially designed or prepared for the processing, use or production of special fissionable material, to any non-nuclear weapon state for peaceful purposes, unless the source or special fissionable material is subjected to the nuclear safeguards of the IAEA. The application of the nuclear safeguards by the IAEA must be carried out in a manner designed to ensure the prevention of any form of horizontal nuclear proliferation of nuclear weapons and not to hamper the peaceful uses of nuclear energy.

The IAEA has become the central institutional machinery for the implementation of the NPT. It has emerged as a cornerstone of the nuclear nonproliferation international legal regime. A few weeks after the entry into force of the NPT, the Board of Governors of the IAEA established a safeguards committee. This committee drafted the model nuclear safeguards agreement INFCIRC/153, known as the Blue Book, which constitutes the basis of the nuclear safeguards applied to states party to the treaty. It sets out the content of comprehensive, full scope safeguards agreements covering all nuclear material in peaceful nuclear activities or under control of a contracting state.[199]

The IAEA inspectors have the legal task of proving the absence of nuclear material diversion to military uses by a contracting state. For this purpose they use various accounting and surveillance measures and procedures. Thus movement of nuclear material into and out of each nuclear plant and as it goes through various plant processes must be accounted for by the plant's operator. The operating country is required to send reports to the IAEA indicating any changes in the quantities of nuclear materials possessed. Inspectors at IAEA Headquarters audit these reports and verify their validity by on-site inspections of each facility in question.[200]

Furthermore, auditing inventory change reports, material balance reports (giving a physical inventory of nuclear material in a material balance area), and physical inventory listings (inventories of material by batch) are verified during on-site inspections to check for discrepancies. Occasionally the IAEA performs simultaneous physical inventory verifications. In addition, to verify the accuracy of the accounting reports, measurements are taken on the spot and samples are sent to IAEA Headquarters for analysis by the Agency's Safeguards Analytical Laboratory. During some inspections (30 percent in 1984), nuclear material is verified by nondestructive assay. However, new technologies are being developed and field tested by the IAEA that will make on-site analysis of nuclear materials possible on a wide scale in the near future.[201]

To carry out its task of overseeing the implementation of the NPT, the IAEA has developed the verificational technique of visual surveillance. It uses automatic cameras, television cameras and recorders to record material movements for several months at a time. After IAEA inspectors retrieve the filmed results, Agency inspectors use them to check the accuracy of accounting records covering the movement of nuclear materials, and to help in the analysis of any discrepancies. The Agency is now expanding the use of visual surveillance measures; since 1983 it has operated approximately 230 photo and television surveillance systems in the field.[202]

In addition, the IAEA uses tamper-proof seals as a verification technique. Between on-site inspections, such devices are used to seal off stores of nuclear materials and the reactor cores themselves. During inspection, these seals can be detached and later checked at IAEA Headquarters for tampering. Agency inspectors also check the functioning and calibration of plant instruments, accountability tanks, and other measuring and control equipment to verify that they have not been tampered with or modified. The IAEA publishes in its annual report a safeguards statement for the relevant year. The *Safeguards Implementation Report* summarizes the safeguards results for each type of facility on the basis of the latest state reports, agency inspections, and agency analyses of discrepancies.[203]

In brief, the verification measures designed to safeguard the implementation of the NPT, which have been developed by the IAEA and which have been included in individual agreements between the IAEA and the contacting states, include the following techniques: (a) the submission of reports by contracting parties to the IAEA on their nuclear materials and activities; (b) on-site inspection by IAEA inspectors for the auditing of inventory change reports, material balance reports, and physical inventory listings; (c) samples; (d) visual surveillance; (e) tamper-proof seals; (f) maintenance; and (g) results and publication.[204] These techniques focus particularly on the prevention of the diversion of nuclear materials intended for peaceful purposes to the development of nuclear weapons.

Chapter 6

Continuation of the Superpowers' Nuclear Arms Race and Their Arms Control and Disarmament Legal Process (1976–1985)

Expansion of the Superpower Treaty Law of Nuclear Weapon Test Limitations

The Peaceful Nuclear Explosions Treaty (PNET) (May 1976)

Content and Objectives. During 1976–1985, the superpowers continued their nuclear arms race.[205] Nevertheless, détente proved a dynamic force in the Soviet-American step-by-step treaty lawmaking to regulate their nuclear relationship. It also proved a substantial force in the bilateral adoption of legal regulations and measures in nuclear weapon tests. Indeed, the détente legal process contributed to the adoption of both the LTBT and the TTBT, both of which represent positive measures in the development of an international legal regime on the control and regulation of nuclear weapon tests.

While implementing their undertaking in Article II of the TTBT, the United States and the Soviet Union, after intensive negotiations for approximately 18 months, concluded the Treaty on Underground Nuclear Explosions for Peaceful Purposes (PNET) on May 28, 1976. The PNET was supplemented by a protocol and an agreed statement.[206]

Although the PNET was submitted to the U.S. Senate on July 29, 1976, Senate debate on its ratification, and that of the TTBT, was prolonged. The main obstacle was assuring effective verification and implementation. In the end, the Senate on September 25, 1990, consented to ratification of both the TTBT and the PNET but with the addition of a long resolution of effective verification of both treaties. The Supreme Soviet unanimously ratified both treaties on October 9, 1990. Thus, after approximately 25 years from the time of signature, both the TTBT and PNET entered into full force for both parties.[207]

The PNET was drafted to permit the development of the atom and its peaceful applications through appropriate testing procedures. While the TTBT allows underground testing of nuclear weapons not exceeding a yield of 150 kilotons for each exploded nuclear weapon or device, the PNET was designed to ensure that underground nuclear tests by the contracting parties would not be used for military purposes and applications. The fundamental objective of the PNET is to draw a legal boundary between permissible underground nuclear tests for military and peaceful purposes, and thus ensure that such nuclear tests by the contracting parties, except those allowed for nuclear weapons purposes by the TTBT, would only be used for the further development and peaceful applications of the atom.

To achieve this objective, the PNET imposes certain controls and limits. Article III (1) (a) of the treaty requires the parties, in exercising their reserved right, to carry out underground nuclear explosions outside the geographical boundaries of test sites designated for the testing of nuclear weapons under the TTBT. This geographical separation of the underground test sites for peaceful purposes from test sites for military nuclear explosions is intended to ensure that the same nuclear test sites are not used for both military and peaceful purposes.

Article III (2) imposes a ceiling on the yield of underground nuclear explosions for peaceful purposes. It requires that any individual underground nuclear explosion of any nuclear device, mechanism or system conducted by the contracting parties must not exceed a yield of 150 kilotons. This yield limit imposed by the PNET is the same as that permitted by the TTBT for the underground tests of nuclear weapons.

Article III (2) does not allow underground nuclear testing of any group explosion of any nuclear devices having an aggregate yield in excess of 150 kilotons. But such a group explosion, even if it has a yield exceeding 150 kilotons, is legally permissible if it allows identification of each individual explosion in the group, in accordance with Article IV of the PNET and in accordance with the provisions of its protocol. Both Article IV and the provisions of the protocol require the verification of the effective compliance of the contracting parties with their treaty obligations by both NTM and on-site inspections.

While the LTBT and TTBT adopted certain legal measures and imposed certain legal limitations on the testing of nuclear weapons, the PNET attempted to resolve the issue of safeguarding peaceful versus military applications of the atom derived by the testing of nuclear devices and systems. The legal problem of drawing a boundary between peaceful and military applications of the atom is as old as the beginning of the nuclear age. The PNET, however, laid down certain important rules designed to ensure the development and promotion of the peaceful application of atomic energy by allowing nuclear tests within legal parameters.

Implementation. Effective compliance is a major legal issue in relation to this treaty. Since there is no essential distinction between the technology and the nuclear materials tested for peaceful and military applications, the PNET is inherently vulnerable to circumventions by its contracting parties.

Even if the contracting parties test for peaceful purposes in full compliance with the PNET, they still test nuclear explosive devices, which tests can be useful for the development of nuclear weapons. Because there is one nuclear testing for both peaceful and military applications of the atom, legal permission to test for peaceful purposes paves the way for the prior testing of nuclear devices and mechanisms. India, which in 1974 successfully exploded a nuclear device and thus acquired nuclear weapon capabilities, has argued that it had exploded a peaceful nuclear device.[208]

In addition, even though the PNET outlaws nuclear tests which do not entail any peaceful application, and although the treaty imposes a ceiling of 150 kilotons on each individual nuclear test explosion, the 150 kiloton limit for peaceful nuclear explosions can still help non-nuclear weapons states develop weapons that could be far more destructive than the atomic bomb dropped on Hiroshima.

Article IV of the treaty provides two verification techniques: the use of NTM and on-site inspections. In both arms control and the limitation of the nuclear tests by the superpowers, NTM was becoming a consolidated verification system. The permissibility and use of NTM of verification was not only incorporated in SALT I but also was agreed upon and accepted as a fundamental legal method of the verification of both TTBT and PNET.

On-site inspection under PNET was for the first time adopted by both superpowers. The approval and adoption of on-site inspection, at least for the implementation of the PNET, constituted a significant legal breakthrough.[209]

Article IV (2) of the treaty obliges both parties to provide full information, access and assistance to the inspection teams to carry out their task. Additionally, the Protocol to the PNET deals with rules on the designation of on-site inspection teams, their rights and functions, and their privileges and immunities in carrying out their task of ensuring effective compliance.

Article V provides for the establishment of a Joint Consultative Commission to coordinate and promote the objectives of the PNET, vested with the legal power to assure confidence in compliance with the obligations assumed by the contracting parties. This commission has authority to consider questions regarding ambiguous issues of compliance with the treaty, to consider and resolve issues concerning the unintended interference of the contracting parties with the verification means of the treaty, and to consider changes in technology which bear on the treaty.

The legal acceptance and adoption by the PNET of NTM and on-site inspections constituted a positive legal development in the formulation of the verification system of the treaty. In particular, the adoption of on-site inspections constituted a breakthrough in the development of superpower lawmaking in verification.

The SALT II Agreement (June 18, 1979) and Its Nonratification

During 1975–1980, the superpowers continued the modernization and the production of more powerful and sophisticated strategic nuclear weapon systems.

In addition, both the United States and the Soviet Union proceeded in an uncontrolled manner with the modernization and the introduction of new INF and TNF (Tactical Nuclear Forces) missiles in Europe.[210] Notwithstanding the continuation of the superpower nuclear arms race during the mid–1970s, the superpowers continued their political and legal détente, and through their negotiations sought to impose limits and restrictions on their strategic nuclear forces and generally on their nuclear arms race.

Although bilateral relations of the superpowers had been characterized to some extent by the revival of their Cold War rivalries, they were negotiating to limit and control their offensive strategic nuclear forces. After extensive and complicated negotiations,[211] they concluded the SALT II Agreement on the limitation of their strategic offensive arms on June 18, 1979. This was accompanied by a protocol and a number of agreed statements and common understandings.[212]

The parties failed to finally ratify SALT II. Although President Jimmy Carter had heralded the SALT II Agreement as a national accomplishment,[213] the majority of U.S. senators were skeptical of its terms. Many were not inclined to ratify it without attaching to its terms on verification procedures conditions and changes that would have amounted to a substantial legal restructuring of the agreement requiring, in essence, its renegotiation.[214]

The Reagan SDI Program: Its Strategic and Legal Implications

On March 23, 1983, President Ronald Reagan announced his decision to embark on a program to counter the awesome Soviet nuclear missile threat with measures of a defensive nature. This program, which became known as the Strategic Defense Initiative (SDI), or the so-called Star Wars program, would be designed to intercept and destroy strategic ballistic missiles before they reached America's soil or that of its allies.[215] President Reagan asserted that U.S. strategic thinking, technological research and weapons development in the future would focus on systems which would give the United States the means of rendering offensive nuclear weapons impotent and obsolete.[216]

The SDI program focused on three areas of research and technology. The first, and probably most critical, aims to develop sensors for detecting the launching of nuclear warheads of enemy missiles, tracking them during flight, discriminating nuclear warheads from nonthreatening objects, such as decoys, and providing intercept guidance to the managers of the various defensive weapons systems. Development of the actual weapons for use in the space battle is the goal of the other areas. Two kinds of such weapons are being explored. Kinetic energy weapons would be ground or space based and would be launched by chemical rocket boosters or projected by hypervelocity electromagnetic or electrothermal guns. According to the Pentagon, this is the most mature SDI technology. But the technological development of directed energy weapons for SDI purposes is far behind.[217]

The efforts to build an SDI system bring together four basic concepts identified as promising to the needs of such a multitiered anti-ballistic missile system: space-based lasers, ground-based lasers, space-based particle beams, and nuclear directed energy weapons.[218] Phase I of the program, code named Brilliant Pebbles and which was expected to be deployed in late 1993, would have involved space-based lasers and a particle beam anti-ballistic missile defense system.[219]

The SDI system as announced by President Reagan obstructed the superpowers' nuclear disarmament process.[220] It also created a major controversy between the United States and the Soviet Union over its legality. The implementation of the SDI system would violate the ABM Treaty and other applicable legal rules and principles of international law.[221] President Bill Clinton announced his decision to abandon the development and deployment of a space-based SDI program, but the United States has not abandoned work on ABM defenses. In 1996, it spent $3.7 billion on that weapon system.[222]

Chapter 7

United Nations Nuclear Disarmament Efforts and the Expansion of the United Nations Law of Arms Control and Regional Nuclear Weapon Nonproliferation (1975–1985)

The UN and Its Legal Strategy for Global Nuclear Disarmament (1975–1985)

THE UN FINAL DOCUMENT AND REPORT ON NUCLEAR WEAPONS AND THE UN PROGRAM ACTION FOR NUCLEAR DISARMAMENT (1975–1980)

By the beginning of the period 1975–1980, the United Nations was not only facing the issue of the arms race and its implications for international peace and security, but was also experiencing the first setbacks to the NPT of 1968. The acquisition of nuclear weapons by India and Israel (non-parties to the NPT) by the mid–1970s seemed to usher in a new nuclear age for the non-nuclear weapon states.

The nuclearization of both India and Israel showed the international community that the NPT had failed to provide effective legal safeguards against horizontal proliferation. In these circumstances, the United Nations began to play a more active role in nuclear disarmament. The General Assembly, aided by the Ad Hoc Committee on the World Disarmament Conference,[223] rendered nuclear disarmament an urgent priority. On June 30, 1978, the General Assembly adopted by consensus the so-called *Final Document,* which was incorporated in its Resolution S-10/2.[224] The *Final Document,* for the first time in the history of the United Nations, set out an agreed upon program of action on disarmament containing priorities and measures that states should undertake as a matter of urgency. It also established a disarmament commission comprising all UN member states.[225]

In the *Final Document*, the General Assembly placed particular emphasis on the need to eliminate nuclear weapons on a comprehensive and global basis through effective nuclear disarmament. Existing arsenals alone were more than sufficient to destroy all life on Earth.[226]

The General Assembly proposed a series of measures. It called on the nuclear weapon states, particularly the nuclear superpowers, to halt and reverse their nuclear arms race through effective disarmament agreements and verification measures. It urged the club of nuclear powers, especially the United States and the Soviet Union, to negotiate agreements to: (a) cease the qualitative improvement and development of nuclear weapon systems; (b) cease the production of all types of nuclear weapons and their means of delivery, and the production of fissionable material for weapons; (c) cease their nuclear weapons testing; and (d) agree on a comprehensive phased program with agreed upon time-frames for progressive and balanced reduction of stockpiles of nuclear weapons and their means of delivery, leading to their ultimate and complete elimination at the earliest possible time.[227]

The *Final Document* called on the nuclear weapon states to provide effective legal guarantees and thus assure non-nuclear weapon states against the use or threat of use of nuclear weapons. In this context, it was pointed out that the provision of such guarantees to the non-nuclear weapon states would strengthen the security of those states and also improve international peace and security. The *Final Document* called for the effective prevention of the horizontal proliferation of nuclear weapons and the strengthening of the NPT legal regime and its safeguards. At the same time, it pointed out the need for the peaceful uses and applications of nuclear material and technologies under effective international controls by the non-nuclear weapon states without discriminatory practices and preferences by the nuclear supplier countries. It was emphasized that, in light of the NPT, an acceptable balance of mutual responsibilities and obligations for nuclear and non-nuclear weapon states must be attained and strictly observed.[228]

The *Final Document* also dealt with the concept of NWFZs. It characterized the NWFZ approach to the prevention of regional proliferation of nuclear weapons as an important measure for regional nuclear disarmament. It called on the nuclear weapon states to fully respect and guarantee the nuclear weapons-free status of such established NWFZs, and it called on the nuclear weapon states to refrain from the use or threat of use of nuclear weapons against the states party to an NWFZ. At the end, the *Final Document* called for a World Disarmament Conference.[229]

In 1978, the General Assembly adopted Resolution 33/91 D, which requested the Secretary-General to carry out a comprehensive study on nuclear weapons. The study was to focus on a discussion of the factual information on nuclear weapon arsenals, the trends in the technological development of nuclear weapon systems, the effects of their use, and their implications for international peace and security. This study was also to assess the legal impact of nuclear disarmament and would further propose measures for a global nuclear disarmament.

In 1979, the General Assembly declared the 1980s the Second Disarmament Decade. Although the First Disarmament Decade (the 1970s) did not produce any essential results, the chief goals of the Second Disarmament Decade were to halt and reverse the nuclear arms race in particular, and to conclude disarmament agreements in accordance with the priorities and the proposals outlined in the *Final Document.*[230]

The 1980 report of the Secretary-General on nuclear weapons was a comprehensive study on all aspects of nuclear weapons, including their technical description, technological advances in the building of more powerful, sophisticated, and accurate nuclear weapon systems, and military implications of proliferation of nuclear weapons and their impact on the maintenance of world peace and security. Although the report pointed out the failure of the UN multilateral approach and, in particular, the failure of the superpowers to eliminate nuclear weapons on a global basis, of specific importance are its conclusions on the effects of a nuclear war and the measures that it recommended for the elimination of nuclear weapons on a global basis.[231]

The report reaffirmed that in view of the enormous power of destruction released by nuclear weapons, in a nuclear war the consequences in human casualties and physical destruction would be virtually incomprehensible. Radioactive contamination would continue to exist for tens or thousands of millions of years; it would have "late effects" on human beings and other living organisms, causing cancerous and other genetic diseases for a prolonged period. A superpower nuclear war would annihilate both countries' populations and material resources; it would not be restricted to the nuclear weapon states involved. Nuclear fallout from a large nuclear war would affect the entire world (although predominantly the hemisphere in which the war was fought). The same widespread effects could be anticipated from some other environmental factors, such as the dispersal of nitrous oxides and dust in the atmosphere.[232]

Of the global effects associated with nuclear warfare, that of radioactive fallout would prove the most dangerous and devastating. As an example, such fallout from a large nuclear war involving a total explosive yield of 10,000 megatons of nuclear weapons would cause several million deaths from cancer within 40 years. Genetic damage would appear in about as many instances as lethal cancers, half of which would appear in the following two generations and the rest in generations thereafter.[233]

The report pointed out that ionizing radiation could possibly also cause many mutations in plants and animals; some of these mutations might change the ecosystem in unpredictable ways. A sizable depletion of the ozone layer in the stratosphere would be caused within a few months from the time of a nuclear war. This would result in an increase of radiation at the surface of the Earth and cause serious biological implications for the ecosystem. In particular, the increase of ultraviolet radiation on Earth would cause skin cancer as well as mutations in plants and animals.[234]

The report pointed out that a large nuclear war would cause unprecedented economic, social and political effects on a global scale. The phenomenon of a nuclear winter, mainly caused by the fall in temperature as a result of atmospheric debris from a major nuclear war, would cause further changes in the Earth's climate detrimental to the production of grain and other agricultural products. This, in turn, would subject the entire world to famine. Since a nuclear war would destroy the industrial and agricultural infrastructure of developed countries, this would result in the destruction of all means that are required to sustain human life.[235]

A major nuclear war would bring the end of the present civilization; the remnants of that civilization would be a primitive and archaic form of societal organization continuously subjected to the scourge of post-nuclear war's effects. The report called for complete and comprehensive elimination of nuclear weapons on a global basis as the only sure way to prevent a nuclear holocaust.[236]

While the nature of verification methods and techniques varies with the particular disarmament measure under consideration, the report suggested that a significant example is the IAEA and its nuclear safeguards system to verify non-diversion of fissionable materials from peaceful uses to military purposes and thus effectively implement the NPT legal regime. The international community must be legally vested with the power, machinery, and means to verify reliable compliance with nuclear disarmament agreements and measures. In this context, the report suggested that the establishment of a disarmament organization, and of an international satellite monitoring agency, as well as other institutions based on similar proposals, is extremely relevant.[237]

With respect to the superpowers' nuclear arms race and the doctrinal foundation of their nuclear predicament, the report correctly suggested that if nuclear disarmament is to become a reality, the superpower commitment to mutual deterrence through a balance of nuclear terror must be discarded. It emphasized that the legal goal to maintain world peace and security, and especially the effective prevention of a nuclear war, clearly show that superpower nuclear balance through deterrence is perhaps the most dangerous collective fallacy that exists.[238]

As a result of the *Final Document* and the Secretary-General's 1980 report, the United Nations began to adopt a more specific agenda on global nuclear disarmament. Both these documents constitute the most detailed and comprehensive study on vertical and horizontal proliferation of nuclear weapons as well as global nuclear disarmament since 1945. The UN agenda on global nuclear disarmament, as defined by the *Final Document* and the Secretary-General's report, was also essentially a reflection of the conclusions reached and the proposals made during the 1975 NPT Review Conference.[239]

Failure of the UN Program Action for Global Nuclear Disarmament (1975–1980)

A critical review and evaluation of the United Nations role in the effort to promote the objectives and goals of global nuclear disarmament during 1975–1980 clearly shows its failure to adopt a comprehensive legal regime on such disarmament. The United Nations approach to the legal management of the issues connected with nuclear disarmament proved itself a failed and frustrating legal process.

During the above period the United Nations failed to adopt a body of rules of international law imposing an end to vertical and horizontal proliferation of nuclear weapons and requiring the nuclear weapon states, especially the nuclear superpowers, to proceed with the radical reduction of their nuclear stockpiles and their ultimate denuclearization within a strict timetable for a phased nuclear disarmament. Moreover, the United Nations failed to outlaw and ban by positive rules of international law the military use of nuclear weapons, including the production and possession of such weapons. It also failed to adopt a comprehensive test ban treaty.[240]

Despite the failure of the United Nations on these points, the organization managed to conclude in 1977 the Convention on the Prohibition of Military or Any Other Hostile Use of Environmental Modification Techniques. This convention entered into force on October 5, 1978, and was ratified by both superpowers as well as by other UN member states.[241]

The object of this convention is to prevent and prohibit the use of any environmental or geophysical modification activity as a weapon of war. To this end, Article I (1) obligates each participating state "not to engage in military or any other hostile use of environmental modification techniques having widespread, long-lasting or severe effects as the means of destruction, damage or injury to any other State Party." The convention declares the peaceful uses of the environment and its geographical structure. At the time of the conclusion of this convention the use of environmental modification techniques for hostile purposes did not play a major role in the military planning of the nuclear superpowers. However, in view of possible future development of techniques for using the environment for such purposes, the United Nations as a whole, and, in particular, the United States and the Soviet Union, undertook the legal initiative to ban the military use of the environment, which culminated in the signature of the convention.[242]

Although the United Nations prohibited the use of futuristic technologies capable of exploiting the environment itself as a military weapon, it failed to outlaw the use of nuclear weapons that are undoubtedly capable of destructive environmental effects. During 1975–1980, the United Nations also proved unable to expand and reinforce the NPT legal regime. In addition, in spite of the recommendations made by the 1975 NPT Review Conference on horizontal proliferation, it failed to adopt effective legal measures for the prevention and reversal of such proliferation. Of specific importance was the failure of the UN member states to strengthen and expand the IAEA's nuclear safeguards system.[243]

As we have already seen, however, during 1975–1980 some multilateral approaches to horizontal proliferation began to emerge. The Nuclear Suppliers

Group, known as the "London Club," which was formed in 1974, met in 1977. During this conference, the 15 participant countries agreed on a set of principles and guidelines to govern and regulate their nuclear exports in relation to the problem of the horizontal proliferation of nuclear weapons. The guidelines agreed on and adopted by the London Club are based on a list of equipment and materials whose transfer to a non-nuclear weapon state triggers the application of the nuclear safeguards of the IAEA.[244]

The International Nuclear Fuel Cycle Evaluation (INFCE) was also formed in 1977 with the participation of approximately 40 states. Its objective was to undertake a technical study on the nuclear fuel cycle and thus ensure that the export of nuclear materials and technologies to non-nuclear weapon states would serve only peaceful purposes and not be diverted into military applications.[245]

In 1980, the UN General Assembly Resolution 34/112 established a preparatory committee for the United Nations Conference for the Promotion of International Cooperation in the Peaceful Uses of Nuclear Energy. The objective of this conference was to ensure international cooperation in the promotion of peaceful and non-military uses of sensitive nuclear technologies and materials, but the conference ran into differences between developed and the developing countries as to its purpose. In the end, it failed to agree on the adoption of legal measures for international cooperation in the peaceful uses of nuclear energy.[246]

Notwithstanding the formation of these multilateral organs and their approaches to horizontal nonproliferation, their political guidelines were devoid of any legal nature or binding effect. Particularly in relation to the need to strengthen the role of the IAEA in the implementation of the NPT, and to expand the agency's safeguards system and verification techniques, the United Nations made no legal progress.[247]

During the 1980 General Conference of the IAEA, a series of positive measures and recommendations were made for the strengthening of the NPT legal regime and the role of the IAEA in the implementation of the NPT. These proposed measures included the technical improvement of the agency's nuclear safeguards system, the universal adherence to the NPT, the universal acceptance of the agency's nuclear safeguards system, the application of the agency's safeguards to all nuclear facilities of the non-nuclear weapon states, and the strict policies and multinational arrangements for the export of sensitive nuclear materials and technologies and for the sensitive stages of the nuclear fuel cycle.[248]

The Board of Governors of the IAEA proposed in 1980 the establishment of a Committee on Assurances of Supply to deal with: (a) ways and means by which supplies of nuclear materials, equipment, technology and fuel cycle services could be assured on a more predictable and long-term basis in accordance with mutually acceptable considerations on nonproliferation; and (b) the agency's role and responsibilities in relation to this issue. The IAEA proposed the adoption of a series of multilateral approaches to the prevention of horizontal proliferation, including the establishment of an international plutonium storage, an international spent fuel management system, and regional nuclear fuel cycle centers.[249]

Unfortunately, neither the agency's member states nor the members of the United Nations adopted the proposed measures. As a result, by the end of the 1970s, the United Nations had failed to achieve global and comprehensive nuclear disarmament. Indeed, the United Nations had failed to halt and reverse both vertical and horizontal proliferation of nuclear weapons. This conclusion had been reached by the 1980 NPT Review Conference.[250]

THE UN AGENDA ON GLOBAL NUCLEAR DISARMAMENT AND ITS FAILURE (1980–1985)

The General Assembly's agenda on global disarmament for the 1980s included halting vertical and horizontal proliferation of nuclear weapons and their ultimate elimination, and also the linkage between the obligation of non-nuclear weapon states party to the NPT not to acquire nuclear weapons and the obligation of the nuclear weapon states to begin their denuclearization. The issue of legal assurances and guarantees by the nuclear weapon states not to use or threaten to use nuclear weapons against the non-nuclear weapon states became a significant element of the UN agenda during this period. In addition, the conclusion of a CTBT, particularly by the nuclear weapons states, and the nondiscriminatory participation of the non-nuclear weapon states in the benefits and the peaceful uses of nuclear energy, became major aspects of the UN multilateral initiatives during the first half of the 1980s.

Although the UN agenda on global and comprehensive nuclear disarmament for the period 1980–1985 reaffirmed continuing concern to resolve this global issue, the legal environment, regarding both strategic relations between the superpowers and the United Nations in general, was not favorable for denuclearization. As we have seen, the end of SALT, the revival of Cold War rhetoric by President Reagan, the nuclear buildup of the United States, the proposed development of SDI, and plans to nuclearize Western European countries were major factors in preventing the superpowers from negotiating and concluding a SALT III treaty. In relation to horizontal proliferation, the situation had substantially deteriorated: By the beginning of the 1980s, in addition to the nuclearization of both Israel and India, a number of militarily significant states in various regions of the globe appeared to be at the threshold of acquiring nuclear weapons.

Although South Africa, Pakistan, Argentina, Spain and Brazil were classified as near-nuclear weapon countries, such nations as Iran, Iraq, Libya, Taiwan and North Korea were classified as nuclear problem states because of their efforts to expand their nuclear programs and thus enable themselves to acquire nuclear weapons.[251] In addition to this trend of potential horizontal proliferation of nuclear weapons during the 1980s, the spread of ballistic missile systems that could deliver nuclear warheads in various regions of the world added a more complicated dimension to the already difficult problem of horizontal proliferation.[252]

Of particular importance to the prevention of such proliferation was the Israeli destruction of the Iraqi Osirak research nuclear reactor in 1981. Notwithstanding the fact that the Security Council unanimously condemned the Israeli air attack on Osirak as an act of aggression violating the UN Charter, this attack underlined the need to adopt a more specific international legal regime to protect and safeguard the nuclear facilities of non-nuclear weapon states against military attacks.

The Failure to Conclude a CTBT (1980–1985). Despite the General Assembly resolutions on the conclusion of a CTBT, despite concrete efforts by the Committee on Disarmament and the Conference on Disarmament, and despite a 1982 suggestion that the formation of an international seismic monitoring system would play a significant role in the implementation of a CTBT, the UN failed to adopt a positive international legal regime banning all nuclear weapon tests. Although in 1982 the United States indicated that a comprehensive test ban was its ultimate goal, it announced that it was not prepared to resume negotiations with the Soviet Union and Britain to this end.[253]

The United States did not accept the view that a CTBT would be useful. The superpowers not only failed to conclude a CTBT but also failed to ratify the TTBT and the PNET, their bilateral agreements on the partial restriction of their nuclear weapons tests concluded in 1976. In addition, the Reagan administration's program to expand America's nuclear weapon arsenals in the 1980s essentially worked to prevent the conclusion of a CTBT.

The UN Nuclear Arms Freeze Proposal (1980–1985). In 1982 the General Assembly supported the idea of a nuclear arms freeze, a proposal sponsored by India, Mexico and Sweden. According to this proposal, all nuclear weapons states, particularly the nuclear superpowers, were to freeze the production of nuclear weapons at levels existing in 1982.[254]

The nuclear arms freeze proposal was fully adopted by a resolution of the UN General Assembly in 1982. Under the resolution, the General Assembly called, for the first time, for a general freeze on nuclear weapons and their delivery systems. It urged the United States and the Soviet Union to proclaim an immediate nuclear arms freeze, and called on all nuclear weapons states to cease the production of fissionable material for nuclear weapons.[255]

During the following two years, at the 1983 and 1984 sessions of the Conference on Disarmament, the Soviet Union and other socialist countries pointed out that a nuclear arms freeze might be carried out initially by the two nuclear superpowers, provided there was a commitment that other nuclear weapon states (France, Britain and China) would follow suit. Nevertheless, the United States (in the Conference on Disarmament) rejected the idea that a freeze on nuclear weapons and delivery systems would offer a sound basis for a more stable nuclear balance or for subsequent nuclear arms reductions. The United States added that

American and Western strategy viewed the function of nuclear weapons as a means for the prevention of war and the preservation of peace.[256]

Although during 1983 and 1984 the General Assembly adopted three resolutions calling for a nuclear arms freeze on the basis of proposals supported by the Soviet Union, India and Mexico, these resolutions, albeit approved by large majorities, were widely opposed and rejected by the Western military establishment.[257] As a result, the nuclear arms freeze proposal, as a means for the prevention of any further vertical proliferation of nuclear weapons in the 1980s, failed to produce positive legal results. A nuclear arms freeze would have halted vertical proliferation and the continuation of the nuclear arms race; it would have focused efforts of the international community on the gradual elimination of nuclear weapons on a global basis.

Notwithstanding the failure of the proposal for a nuclear arms freeze, the United Nations in 1980–1985 attempted to introduce an additional measure whose acceptance would have helped stop vertical proliferation. This proposal called for ending the production of fissionable material for weapons. The General Assembly justifiably called this measure a strategy of suffocation of the nuclear arms race.[258]

Despite General Assembly resolutions to this end, and although the Conference on Disarmament had been considering a verifiable halt and prohibition of the production of fissionable material for nuclear weapons and other nuclear explosive devices, the club of nuclear powers reacted negatively to this proposal. Although the Soviet Union initially rejected it, in 1984 it voted in favor. On the other hand, the United States, Britain, France and China abstained from voting for its adoption.[259]

The Popular World Movement and the Five Continent Peace Initiative for Nuclear Disarmament (1980–1985). By the beginning of the 1980s, the issue of nuclear disarmament had become a concern not only for governmental bodies but also for nongovernmental organizations, as well as most importantly for the peoples of the world. While by the beginning of the 1980s the public movement, particularly in the United States and Western Europe, was pressing for a nuclear arms freeze and for the elimination of nuclear weapons, a new player appeared on the scene in 1984. In that year, the so-called Five Continent Peace Initiative was formed by the leaders of India, Tanzania, Mexico, Argentina, Sweden and Greece (a NATO member). This Peace Initiative was designed to create a worldwide voice calling for a global solution to the problem of nuclear disarmament. In particular, it assumed the task of persuading both nuclear superpowers to end their uncontrolled nuclear arms race and immediately proceed with their denuclearization.[260]

Although India was a de facto nuclear weapon state, and Argentina was considered a near-nuclear weapon state, the Peace Initiative, which met in New Delhi in May 1984, issued a declaration. This declaration urged the United States and the Soviets, as well as France, Britain and China, to halt all nuclear testing, production and deployment of nuclear weapons and their delivery systems, and immediately follow with substantial reductions in their nuclear forces. It called both nuclear superpowers to focus especially on the prevention of an arms race in outer space and a comprehensive test ban treaty.[261] But the conclusion is all too familiar: during 1980–1985, neither the United Nations nor the Peace Initiative and the world-popular antinuclear movement produced any positive legal results.

The Horizontal Proliferation of Nuclear Weapons (1980–1985). By the beginning of the 1980s, the horizontal proliferation of nuclear weapons became a crucial and complicated issue which added a further difficult dimension to global nuclear disarmament. India and Israel, non-parties to the NPT, had become de facto nuclear weapon states by the 1970s. By the beginning of the 1980s a number of militarily significant states in various parts of the globe were classified as near-nuclear or nuclear problem states on the basis of the degree of their involvement and technological capabilities in relation to the acquisition of nuclear weapon capabilities. The United Nations expressed its deep concern over this issue.

The United Nations, in the early 1980s, began to examine seriously the problem of horizontal proliferation. A United Nations study (*South Africa's Plan and Capability in the Nuclear Field*) concluded that South Africa possessed the technical capability to manufacture nuclear weapons and their delivery systems. On December 12, 1980, the General Assembly adopted Resolution 35/146A by which it condemned this capability and South Africa's failure to accede to the NPT. The General Assembly called on South Africa to sign the NPT and accept the nuclear safeguards system of the IAEA.[262] It requested the Security Council to prohibit all forms of nuclear collaboration with South Africa, and to institute effective enforcement action against South Africa to prevent it from endangering international peace and security through its acquisition of nuclear weapons.[263] But in 1991 South Africa acceded to the NPT. In 1993, it confirmed that it had developed six nuclear weapons and had destroyed all of them. In 1993, intensive IAEA inspections in South Africa did not prove that it still had nuclear weapons.[264]

Similarly, the United Nations paid particular attention to Israeli nuclear weapons capability. In 1981 the United Nations conducted its *Study on Israeli Nuclear Armament*, and on December 9, 1982, it adopted Resolution 37/82, by a vote of 106–2 (Israel and the United States opposing), with 34 abstentions. This resolution, after having condemned the nuclear collaboration of Israel and South Africa, pointed out the grave consequences which would endanger international peace and security particularly as a result of Israel's nuclear weapon capability.

The General Assembly demanded that Israel renounce, without delay, any possession of nuclear weapons and place all of its nuclear facilities and activities under international safeguards. It called upon Israel to accede to the NPT and accept the IAEA's nuclear safeguards. It called upon all states and other parties and institutions to terminate forthwith all nuclear collaboration with Israel. The General Assembly condemned the Israeli air attack on the Iraqi Osirak nuclear facilities in 1981 as an act of sheer aggression and condemned Israel's officially declared intention to repeat its armed attack against nuclear facilities.[265] But Israel has not acceded to the NPT, and is reported to possess 100 to 200 nuclear weapons.[266]

Notwithstanding these resolutions on South Africa and Israel, the United Nations in 1980–1985 failed to expand and strengthen the NPT legal regime. It did attempt to create an international storage of fissionable material, which would undertake to supply interested non-nuclear weapon states on condition that the recipient states would agree to accept the nuclear safeguards system of the IAEA and thus open all of their nuclear programs and facilities to the on-site inspections of the agency.[267]

The United Nations failed to conclude a CTBT, which was demanded by the non-nuclear weapon states during the 1980 NPT Review Conference, and which would have made a positive contribution not only in the vertical, but also in the horizontal prevention of nuclear proliferation. It also failed to formulate and adopt a specific international legal regime explicitly banning the use or the threat of use of nuclear weapons by the club of nuclear powers against the non-nuclear weapon states.

Since 1968 the Nuclear Club through the Security Council has recognized that aggression using nuclear weapons, or the threat of doing so against non-nuclear weapon states party to the NPT would warrant immediate action by the council. Furthermore, at the 1978 special session on disarmament, the five nuclear weapon states individually declared, each in keeping with its specific perceived security requirements, their intention not to use, or threaten to use, nuclear weapons against non-nuclear weapon states. Since then, particularly during 1980–1985, the General Assembly has called for international legal arrangements that would further provide the non-nuclear weapon states with such security assurance. It has favored the formulation and adoption of an international treaty signed by the nuclear weapon states with the explicit obligation not to use, or threaten to use, their nuclear weapons against non-nuclear weapon states which have no nuclear weapons in their territories.[268]

Despite widespread support for such a convention, no legal progress has been made to this end. Although each year since 1979 the Conference on Disarmament has been engaged in the active negotiation and elaboration of proposals for effective international legal guarantees and arrangements that would assure non-nuclear weapon states against the use or threat of use of nuclear weapons by the Nuclear Club, the 1985 Disarmament Conference reported to the General Assembly that states' differing perceptions of national security interests continued to impede any progress on this issue.[269]

Although the aforesaid legal guarantee would protect non-nuclear weapon states against a direct nuclear attack by any of the nuclear weapon states, it would not protect non-nuclear weapon states from the various disastrous effects of a nuclear war. Nor would it reduce the nuclear weapon status of the nuclear weapon states, and, therefore, the ultimate danger of a nuclear war. However, the most effective legal guarantee for the protection of the nuclear weapon states and generally the entire world, including the Nuclear Club itself, is the elimination of all nuclear weapons on a global and comprehensive basis. Only global denuclearization can provide the ultimate guarantee.

In conclusion, the UN effort to prevent and reverse horizontal proliferation during 1980–1985 failed to produce results as far as the NPT and the emergence of the new nuclear age were concerned. Although by 1985 the NPT had been ratified by 130 countries, including the club of nuclear powers, except France and China, and although 78 non-nuclear weapon states with significant nuclear industries by 1985 had concluded safeguard agreements with the IAEA, the United Nations failed, unfortunately, to strengthen the NPT and the role of the IAEA in its implementation.[270]

The Israeli destruction of the Iraqi Osirak nuclear facilities in 1981 raised a significantly delicate issue concerning the effective legal protection of the nuclear facilities of non-nuclear weapon states against a military action by an enemy state. Although the Security Council and the IAEA condemned the Israeli action as an act of aggression in violation of the UN Charter, the United Nations was unable to follow up with a specific legal regime to protect nuclear facilities against such an action.[271]

Regional Nonproliferation: New NWFZ Proposals (1975–1985)

The Proposed Middle East NWFZ

In 1975 the Shah of Iran proposed the establishment of an NWFZ in the Middle East particularly because of the rapid diffusion of nuclear material and technology in the region.[272] Subsequently, Egypt cosponsored the proposal for a Middle East NWFZ including the Arab states, Israel and Iran. Although the General Assembly in 1975 by its resolution 128–0 supported the establishment of the proposed zone, and although the General Assembly has since then passed annual resolutions urging the Middle Eastern states to declare and maintain the region free from nuclear weapons, Israel has not cooperated in convening a Middle East conference that would elaborate and promote the establishment of an NWFZ in this region. In addition, the United States has not played a positive role in the effort to establish a Middle East NWFZ.[273]

After the bombing of the Osirak Iraqi nuclear reactor in 1981 by Israel, the attempt to convene a regional conference to discuss the legal and technical issues connected with the establishment of a Middle East NWFZ was intensified, but interest soon waned. By 1985, a number of countries in the region were reported to be nuclear problem countries due to their effort to acquire nuclear weapons. In particular, Iraq and Iran intensified their efforts to develop nuclear weapons.[274]

The Proposed South Asian NWFZ

After the nuclear test carried out by India in 1974, and in view of its acquisition of nuclear weapons by the mid–1970s, Pakistan proposed to the General Assembly the establishment of a South Asian NWFZ. Since 1976, the General Assembly has passed a string of resolutions calling for the establishment of an NWFZ in this region. Meanwhile, Pakistan's nuclear capacity was rapidly progressing.[275]

The proposed South Asian NWFZ would have, except India and Pakistan, included the other states of the region such as Afghanistan, Bangladesh, Nepal, Bhutan, Sri Lanka and the Maldives. Although since the late 1970s, Pakistan has proposed to India to jointly sign the NPT and agree to full-scope safeguards, or bilateral inspection, India has rejected not only these proposals, but also any effort to establish a South Asian NWFZ. However, in 1985, both India and Pakistan agreed not to attack each other's nuclear facilities.[276]

The Indian government has repeatedly maintained that, since China has already introduced nuclear weapons in the Asian region, it was inappropriate to consider the establishment of an NWFZ in South Asia. China's nuclear weapon capability and the unabated Indian-Chinese tensions prevent India from agreeing on the establishment of a South Asian NWFZ, which would result in the denuclearization of India while China's nuclear capability would be left intact. India favors a more global and comprehensive nuclear disarmament.[277]

During 1975–1985 regional and international efforts to prevent the nuclearization of South Asia by establishing an NWFZ were without results. By 1985, Pakistan was reported to be a near-nuclear weapon country.[278]

The Proposed Indian Ocean Zone of Peace

The proposal to declare and establish the Indian Ocean as a zone of peace was initially raised by Sri Lanka in October 1964 at the Non-Aligned Heads of State Conference in Cairo. This proposal was later made at the Conference of Non-Aligned States in September 1970. During the Singapore Conference of Commonwealth Heads of State in 1971, a Sri Lankan memorandum stated that British withdrawal from east of Suez had opened up an opportunity, which could be seized to create a peace zone to stabilize the Indian Ocean as a power vacuum. In view of these proposals for the adoption of an Indian Ocean peace zone, the General Assembly in 1971 declared the Indian Ocean, along with the air space and the ocean floor subjacent thereto, to be for all time a zone of peace.[279]

Nevertheless, the invasion of Afghanistan in 1979 by the Soviet Union and the eruption of the Iran-Iraq war in 1980 caused the United States to intensify its military buildup in the region, and to decrease its interest in the elaboration and establishment of the proposed Indian Ocean peace zone. Moreover, the Ad Hoc Committee, which had assumed the duty to convene a conference in 1981 to negotiate and legally establish the Indian Ocean as a zone of peace, proved unable to reach a consensus to hold such a conference because a number of the states concerned did not believe that the political and security climate in the region would favor such a conference for the exchange of views and proposals for the establishment of this peace zone.[280]

Although the nuclear superpowers during 1977–1978 held bilateral talks on demilitarizing the Indian Ocean, during 1980–1985, due to the revival of their Cold War relations and nuclear arms antagonism, they did not continue their negotiations toward demilitarizing the Indian Ocean. The Soviet Union, and generally the Eastern European countries, had favored a multilateral treaty through which the Indian Ocean would be established as a zone of peace, and an NWFZ, and generally a completely demilitarized region. In particular, the Soviet Union had firmly supported the convocation of the anticipated 1981 conference, and also proposed that all countries refrain from sending large naval formations to the Indian Ocean, from carrying out military exercises in the area, and from enlarging and modernizing bases by the non-littoral states having military in the Indian Ocean.[281]

The Soviet Union had also indicated its readiness to resume negotiations with the United States on the limitation and reduction of their military activity in the region, and had proposed the withdrawal of all foreign naval powers from the Persian Gulf and the creation of an international peacekeeping force and mechanism for the Persian Gulf.[282]

Despite the positive statements and proposals of the Soviet Union for the complete demilitarization of the Indian Ocean regarding both conventional and nuclear naval armaments, and despite the supportive efforts of the non-aligned states, the Western military establishment has played a negative role in the negotiating and legal process to this end. The United States, to defend its strategic interests in the region, is not willing to withdraw its naval and other military forces from the area. Similarly, both the United Kingdom and France, which maintain naval and other military forces in the region, have opposed the creation of the proposed Indian Ocean peace zone.[283]

In general terms, the Western military powers have attempted to justify their opposition to such a legal development by maintaining the rather fallacious view that the complete demilitarization of the Indian Ocean cannot be possible while regional conflicts in this area remain unresolved. Furthermore, although India favors the negotiating and legal process to achieve demilitarization of the Indian Ocean, the Indian political leadership has indicated that its priority is to pursue the removal of the bases and the presence of the great powers from the region. On the other hand, Sri Lanka, because of its conflict with India, is afraid that such a development would leave India as the only major power in the region.[284]

Any treaty for the demilitarization of the Indian Ocean, however, must include legal restrictions on India's naval and military power in the region so that India will not threaten the security of the region's other states. To this end, the formation and presence in the Indian Ocean of an international organ under the United Nations to maintain peace and monitor the compliance of states with legal obligations deriving from an international agreement on the demilitarization of the region would be a positive legal development.

The Proposed Southeast Asian NWFZ

In 1971, the Association of Southeast Asian Nations (ASEAN) declared Southeast Asia as a Zone of Peace, Freedom and Neutrality (ZOPFAN). Furthermore, Indonesia suggested at the UN Conference on Disarmament on April 12, 1983, that the states in the Southeast Asian region establish an NWFZ to enhance the declaration of ZOPFAN.[285]

Although in 1985 a working group was formed to look at the proposal for the legal establishment of a Southeast Asian NWFZ, by the end of 1985 the Southeast Asian nations had failed to proceed with the legal elaboration and negotiation of a draft treaty leading to the establishment of the proposed NWFZ. The establishment of this NWFZ would have declared the Southeast Asian region free of nuclear weapons. It would have also exercised a positive legal impact on superpower nuclear disengagement in this region.[286]

Although the Southeast Asian states, namely, the ASEAN countries of Brunei, Indonesia, Malaysia, the Philippines, Singapore and Thailand, the three socialist states of Laos, Cambodia and Vietnam, plus Burma, Australia and New Zealand, have favored the establishment of a Southeast Asian NWFZ, and although both the Soviet Union and China support such a zone, the United States opposes it.[287]

The Proposed Korean Nuclear-Free Peace Zone (NFPZ)

In 1981, the Japanese Socialist Party and North Korea proposed the establishment of an NFPZ in the Northeast Asian region. The North Korean government, by launching its anti-imperialism, antiwar and antinuclear campaign has made active efforts to establish such a zone in the above region. Although it signed the NPT in 1985, and announced that it would refrain from testing, producing, stockpiling, and introducing nuclear weapons on its soil, and that it would not permit any foreign military bases or the passage of foreign nuclear weapons through its land, air space and territorial water, North Korea has been reported since the mid–1980s as a nuclear problem state close to acquiring nuclear weapons.[288]

The division and the continuous conflict and distrust between North and South Korea have become negative factors in the adoption of a Korean NFPZ. Although South Korea has since 1975 signed the NPT, with respect to legal and negotiating efforts to adopt the NFPZ it has played a somewhat negative role. This can be attributed to America's political influence on the South Korean regime and America's military presence in this country.[289]

The South Korean government has proposed a disarmament plan for the region, which would include the building of confidence through contacts, the conclusion of a nonaggression pact, and the beginning of disarmament negotiations between the two Koreas, but it has refused to confirm or deny the presence of nuclear weapons on its soil. Nevertheless, its ships could deploy nuclear weapons in an emergency military situation. In addition, as of early 1985 the United States reportedly had deployed nuclear weapons on the soil of South Korea.[290]

China has expressed its support for a nuclear-free Korean peninsula, and also for an independent, peaceful and reunified Korea. China has further called the United States to withdraw its military presence from South Korea. The Soviet Union also advocated the adoption of a declaration of nonaggression between the two Koreas. Moreover, the Soviet Union, while under the leadership of Mikhail Gorbachev, since 1985 had supported the creation of a nuclear-free Korean peninsula. Gorbachev pointed out that such a development would contribute to the goal of preventing the proliferation and buildup of nuclear weapons in Asia and the Pacific.[291]

However, the United States, which maintains a strong military presence in South Korea and generally in the Northeast Asian region, has hindered the negotiations over the adoption of a Korean NFPZ. Although the United States has not officially stated its position on the proposed Northeast NFPZ, it has not indicated its desire to withdraw its military presence from the region, a move that would facilitate the legal process for the establishment of this NFPZ. Such a move by the United States would constitute a significant legal step toward a superpower nuclear disengagement and denuclearization in the Pacific Ocean. Regardless of any U.S. actions, the present efforts by North Korea to acquire nuclear weapons have had a particularly negative impact on the prospects of establishing a nuclear weapon-free Korean Peninsula.[292]

THE ESTABLISHMENT OF THE SOUTH PACIFIC NFZ AND THE TREATY OF RAROTONGA (AUGUST 1985)

Content and Objectives of the Rarotonga Treaty. The Rarotonga Treaty,[293] which in August 1985 established the South Pacific Nuclear-Free Zone, has been signed and ratified by Australia, New Zealand, the Cook Islands, Western Somoa, Kiribati, Fiji, Niue, Tuvalu, Nauru, the Solomon Islands and Tonga. The Marshall Islands have refused to sign the treaty.[294] The Rarotonga Treaty constitutes, after the Treaty of Tlatelolco that established the Latin American NWFZ, the second international legal instrument designed to declare and preserve, for unlimited time and duration, a populated and vast geographic region nuclear weapon free. Indeed, the South Pacific NFZ declares the entire South Pacific a denuclearized zone, including the application of this treaty to the internal waters, the territorial sea and archipelagic waters, the seabed and subsoil beneath, the land territory and the airspace above the states party to this treaty.[295]

The treaty has been primarily designed to serve the legal objective of the exclusion of nuclear weapons from the South Pacific. To achieve this legal end, it imposes the legal prohibition and obligation upon its participating states to refrain from the production or acquisition, deployment or stockpiling of nuclear weapons or nuclear explosive devices within the South Pacific NFZ. In addition, the treaty prohibits the use or the threat of use of nuclear weapons by the member states.[296]

Article 3 of the treaty requires each contracting party to undertake the legal obligations: (a) not to manufacture or otherwise acquire, possess or have control over any nuclear explosive device by any means anywhere inside or outside the South Pacific NFZ; (b) not to seek or receive any assistance in the manufacturing or acquisition of any nuclear explosive device; and (c) not to take any action to assist or encourage the manufacture or acquisition of any nuclear explosive device by any state.[297]

Pursuant to Article 5 of the treaty, each member state undertakes to prevent in its territory the stationing of any nuclear weapon and nuclear explosive devices.[298] However, in accordance with this article, each contracting party in the exercise of its sovereign rights and powers remains free to decide itself whether to allow visits by foreign ships or aircraft, some of which may be equipped with nuclear weapons, to its ports or airfields, to transit its airspace or navigate its territorial sea or archipelagic waters. In essence, the treaty's Article 5 leaves each contracting party free to decide itself whether to permit port visits and landings by nuclear-capable vessels and aircraft.[299]

Article 6 of the Rarotonga Treaty imposes the legal obligation upon the contracting parties to prevent in their territory the testing of any nuclear explosive device. This article also requires each member state not to assist or encourage the testing of any nuclear explosive device by any state.[300]

Notwithstanding the prohibitions imposed by this article and by the previously discussed provisions, the treaty does not prohibit the production and possession of ballistic missile systems and other systems capable of delivering nuclear weapons. Article 4 to the treaty apparently allows the member states to carry out peaceful nuclear activities and uses. It also requires each of them not to provide source or special fissionable material, or equipment or material especially designed or prepared for the processing, use or production of special fissionable material for peaceful purposes to any non-nuclear weapon state not subjected to the nuclear safeguards required by Article 3 of the NPT and the nuclear safeguards applied by the IAEA. Therefore, the legal objective of this article is to enhance the effectiveness of the international legal regime on the nonproliferation of nuclear weapon materials and technologies, which is provided by the NPT and which is to be implemented by the IAEA safeguards and verification system and techniques.[301]

The primary legal objective of the Rarotonga Treaty is to keep the South Pacific free from nuclear weapons, but the treaty by virtue of its Article 7 also imposes upon the member states the obligation not to dump radioactive waste and other radioactive material at sea anywhere within the South Pacific NFZ. In addition, each contracting party has assumed the legal obligation to prevent the dumping of such substances by anyone in its territorial sea and not to assist or encourage anyone to do so within the region covered by the treaty.[302]

Because the Rarotonga Treaty not only contains provisions aimed primarily at the exclusion of nuclear weapons from the South Pacific, but also includes provisions that affect the export of nuclear materials and technologies to non-nuclear weapon states, and prohibits the dumping of radioactive waste and other radioactive matter at sea within the affected region, the region is characterized as a nuclear-free zone rather than, more narrowly, a nuclear weapon-free zone.[303]

One must recognize that its prohibitions against the unsafeguarded export of nuclear materials to non-nuclear weapon states and its prohibitions against dumping radioactive materials within the South Pacific, with the exclusion of nuclear weapons from the region, constitute additional legal elements that elevate the Rarotonga Treaty to the status of establishing a nuclear-free zone, in contrast with the Treaty of Tlatelolco, which has only established a nuclear weapon-free zone in Latin America. Nevertheless, the use of the term "nuclear-free zone" is in a sense misleading because the Treaty of Rarotonga requires its member states to prohibit only the stationing of nuclear weapons and nuclear explosive devices in their territories. This means that the treaty is limited to prohibiting the permanent land-based presence of nuclear weapons.[304]

On the other hand, the treaty appears to fully respect international legal rights with respect to the passing of nuclear weapons aboard ships and planes in the high seas. In addition, in relation to permitting foreign nuclear-capable ships or aircraft to visit the ports and airfields of the member states, the treaty allows the contracting parties, in the exercise of their sovereign rights, to decide whether or not to allow such visits. Therefore, the South Pacific NFZ is not a fully nuclear-free zone; nevertheless, it constitutes a positive legal element toward halting further nuclearization of the South Pacific.[305]

Verification and Dispute Resolution Legal System. Regarding the effective implementation of its provisions, the Rarotonga Treaty, unlike the Treaty of Tlatelolco, does not establish a permanent secretariat to ensure the full and effective compliance of the contracting parties with their treaty obligations. Instead, it renders the Director of the South Pacific Bureau for Economic Cooperation responsible for verification under the control system established by Articles 8, 9 and 10 and its annexes.[306]

The control and verification system for ensuring the implementation of the treaty by its member states parties requires each state to submit reports to the director about any significant event within its jurisdiction affecting the implementation of the treaty, and also to exchange information on matters arising under or in relation to it. Moreover, the treaty has established the Consultative Committee to consider any matter arising in relation to this treaty or for reviewing its operation.[307]

The treaty also provides a complaints procedure system by which a member state can complain to the Consultative Committee against another party for which the complainant has grounds to believe that it has violated the treaty. Before such a complaint is brought to the director of this committee, the complainant must bring the matter to the attention of the party in alleged violation, and must allow it reasonable opportunity to explain and resolve the matter. If the matter is not resolved, then the Consultative Committee has the legal power to consider the complaint.[308]

If the committee decides that there is sufficient substance in the complaint to warrant a special inspection in the territory of the respondent party or elsewhere, it has the legal obligation and power to order an immediate on-site inspection. To facilitate the conduct of on-site inspections, paragraph 6 of Annex 4 of the treaty imposes the legal obligation upon the member states to grant full and free access to all information and places within their territories which may be relevant to enable the special inspection team to implement the directives given to it by the Consultative Committee.[309]

In addition, in accordance with paragraph 7 of Annex 4, the member states have undertaken the legal duty, whenever they are subject to on-site inspection, to take all appropriate actions and steps to facilitate the inspection. They also must grant to the members of the special inspection team privileges and immunities necessary for the performance of their functions for the on-site inspection, including inviolability for all papers and documents, and immunity from arrest, detention and legal process for acts done and words spoken and written during and with respect to the performance of the special inspection.

Paragraph 8 of Annex 4 establishes that after the on-site inspection team has completed its inspection, it must submit its findings in a written report as soon as possible to the Consultative Committee. This report must outline the activities of the inspectors, set out relevant factors and information as ascertained by them, with supporting evidence and documentation as appropriate, and state their conclusions. After receiving this report, the Consultative Committee must submit a full report to all member states of the South Pacific Forum, and also decide whether the party complained of is in violation of its legal obligations under the Rarotonga Treaty.

In accordance with paragraph 9 of Annex 4, if the Consultative Committee has decided that the alleged violator has breached its obligations under the treaty, then, at any time, at the request either of the complainant or the violator the two states must promptly attend a meeting of the South Pacific Forum. The Rarotonga Treaty does not, however, provide any specific legal regime and procedure for the measures and sanctions that would be imposed upon the treaty violator. Nevertheless, Article 13 (1) of the treaty provides that if a state violates a provision of the treaty which is essential to the achievement of its legal objectives and goals or of its spirit, then every other member state has the right to withdraw from the treaty. This peculiar remedy and resolution of the breach of the treaty apparently imposes upon all participating states the collective legal responsibility to comply with the treaty, or terminate it if any of them commits a material violation of the treaty. Concerning dispute settlement, moreover, the Rarotonga Treaty fails to involve any international authority or judicial mechanism to resolve the legal issues arising out of the interpretation and application of the provisions of the treaty. This situation is in contrast to the dispute settlement legal mechanism and resolution measures provided by the Treaty of Tlatelolco.[310]

The Rarotonga Treaty provides its own legal system and mechanisms to ensure the compliance of its members with the treaty, with respect to ensuring the use of nuclear material and technology only for peaceful purposes and applications, which is allowed under the treaty. Annex 2 of the treaty further accords upon the IAEA the right to apply its nuclear safeguards and verification procedures to the treaty participants in this respect. Annex 2 requires each member state to separately negotiate and conclude an agreement with the IAEA to ensure the state's compliance with the treaty's provisions against the diversion of nuclear material and technology to the development of nuclear weapons. Most importantly, Annex 2 renders compulsory the application of IAEA safeguards and verification measures to all treaty participants.[311]

This requirement constitutes a significant legal innovation and development of the legal role of the IAEA, as the appropriate international authority, to ensure through its verification techniques and procedures that the Rarotonga Treaty participants fully comply with their right to use, within their territories under their jurisdiction or anywhere under their control, nuclear material and technology only for peaceful activities and applications. Accordingly, by virtue of Annex 2 of the Rarotonga Treaty, the IAEA has become an essential player in ensuring through the application of its nuclear safeguards, including on-site inspections, the compliance of the member states with their treaty obligations.

External Legal Guarantees and the South Pacific NFZ. Its juridical nature gives a nuclear weapon-free zone a dual legal objective. The first is to ensure through effective verification measures and procedures that the parties to a treaty establishing such a zone will maintain themselves and therefore the zone free from nuclear weapons. The second legal objective of an NWFZ is to make sure that such a zone will be respected and guaranteed, particularly by the nuclear weapon states and that those states will not use or threaten to use nuclear weapons against any member state of an NWFZ, including their responsibility to refrain from any involvement resulting in the nuclearization of such a zone.

As has been previously explained, the Rarotonga Treaty provides the legal regime and control system for ensuring the implementation of its content by its signatories regarding its legal objective to maintain the South Pacific NFZ free from nuclear weapons in its internal context. Concerning the legal respect and guarantee of the nuclear-free status of the zone by non-signatory states, particularly the nuclear weapon states, the treaty incorporates three protocols designed to implement and achieve such effects.[312]

Protocol I has been opened to signature and ratification by the United States, France and Great Britain, since these states in addition to their nuclear weapon status also possess and control territories within the zone. Thus, these three states, in accordance with Article 1 of this protocol, are to undertake the legal obligation in respect of the territory situated within the zone and for which they are internationally responsible, to apply the prohibitions included in Articles 3, 5 and 6, insofar as they relate to the manufacture, stationing and testing of any nuclear explosive device within those territories. They are also obliged to apply the safeguards contained in Article 8 (2)(c) and Annex 2 of the treaty in relation to their territories situated within the South Pacific NFZ.[313]

Protocol II was addressed to the five nuclear weapon states: the United States, the Soviet Union, China, France and Great Britain. Pursuant to Article 1 of this protocol, each of the five nuclear powers is to undertake the legal obligation not to contribute to any act that would violate the Rarotonga Treaty and its protocols. Furthermore, Article 2 of these protocols imposes the legal duty and obligation upon each of the above nuclear weapon states not to use or threaten to use any nuclear explosive device against the signatories to the treaty, or against any territory within the South Pacific NFZ for which the state that has become a party to Protocol I is internationally responsible. Protocol III of the Rarotonga Treaty, which has been opened for signature and ratification by the five nuclear powers, also requires them not to test any nuclear explosive device anywhere within the zone.

China has since 1987 signed and ratified Protocols II and III. However, the Chinese government has reserved the right to reconsider its legal obligation under these protocols if other nuclear weapon states or treaty signatories have taken any action in gross violation of the Rarotonga Treaty and its protocols which changes the status of the South Pacific NFZ and endangers the security interests of China.[314] Notwithstanding its legal obligations under these protocols, China has used the international waters east of the Solomon Islands for missile tests.[315]

The Soviet Union, under the nuclear disarmament oriented leadership of Mikhail Gorbachev, on December 15, 1986, signed Protocols II and III of the Rarotonga Treaty, which were further ratified by the Soviet Union in May 1988.[316] The Soviet Union at the time of the signature of these protocols stated that the

> Soviet Union proceeds from the fact that the establishment of such a zone in the South Pacific will serve an important contribution to the formation of an effective system of security in the Asian Pacific region, will strengthen the international nuclear nonproliferation regime and will contribute to the realization of the task of doing away completely and forever with nuclear weapons on earth.[317]

The Soviet Union also declared that allowing transit of nuclear weapons through visits by ships and aircraft carrying such weapons would contradict the aims of the Rarotonga Treaty and would be inconsistent with the aims of a nuclear-free zone. This Soviet reservation was criticized in Apia, Western Samoa, at the 1987 Apia Forum, and in 1988 the Soviet Union ratified Protocols II and III without any reservations.[318] In the context of the positive Soviet legal reaction and unreserved acceptance of the above protocols for the South Pacific NFZ, in July 1986 Gorbachev urged the other nuclear weapon states to guarantee the Rarotonga Treaty. Moreover, the Soviet leadership proposed to the Western military establishment, and particularly to the United States, to impose legal limits, controls and reductions of their military activities in the Pacific.[319]

Although the Rarotonga Treaty and the Gorbachev proposals aimed at the gradual and ultimate denuclearization of the South Pacific and the Pacific in general, a region uncontrollably militarized and nuclearized primarily by the naval forces of the superpowers,[320] the Western military and nuclear establishment negatively reacted both to the treaty and to the Gorbachev proposals. In fact, the United States, France and Great Britain opposed the Rarotonga Treaty and initially failed to sign its protocols.[321]

In March 1996, however, after conducting in January of that year six nuclear weapon tests in the region, France, with the United States and Britain, finally signed all three protocols to the Rarotonga Treaty. This constituted significant development for the realization of the legal objectives of the treaty. In the past, the South Pacific had become a focus of concentration of strategic nuclear forces by the superpowers. It had also become the site of American, British and French nuclear weapon tests in the past and as recently as the January 1996 tests by France. It has been estimated that the nuclear weapon states have conducted 226 nuclear tests in the Pacific, including 89 atmospheric tests on the territory covered by the Rarotonga Treaty. The signature of the protocols to the treaty by all nuclear weapon states promotes the international legal process of regional denuclearization and disarmament.[322]

Expansion of the UN Treaty Law on Regional and Global Nuclear Disarmament Measures

The Moon Treaty (1979) and Its Legal Impact on Regional Nuclear Disarmament

The Moon Treaty, officially the Agreement Governing the Activities of States on the Moon and Other Celestial Bodies,[323] was signed in 1979. It constitutes the legal product of the East-West political détente and norm-creating dynamic process in expanding and solidifying the international legal regime for the uses of the Moon and the other celestial bodies. Unlike the Outer Space Treaty, the Moon Treaty does not require its acceptance by the United States, the Soviet Union and the United Kingdom to enter into force. That entrance occurred on July 11, 1984.[324] The United States has not signed this treaty.

The Moon Treaty serves the legal objective of preventing the Moon from becoming an area of international conflict. This treaty constitutes a multilateral legal instrument that not only promotes the norms and principles of the Outer Space Treaty of 1967, but also creates a more specific legal regime for the regulation of the exploration and uses of the Moon and other celestial bodies within our solar system.

The Moon Treaty not only embodies the legal principle of the exploration and use of the Moon for exclusively peaceful purposes in view of the precedent of the Outer Space Treaty, but also expressly declares the Moon and its natural resources to be the common heritage of mankind. This new principle adopted by the treaty clearly shows a new legal direction in the effort to safeguard the Moon and its natural resources in all of their aspects for the mutual benefit of humanity.[325]

Regarding the legal input and impact of this treaty on the denuclearization and demilitarization of the Moon, it is Article 3 of the treaty which clearly embodies the legal norm of these objectives. This article clearly and categorically prohibits any threat or use of force, or any other hostile act or threat of hostile act on the Moon. It also imposes the legal obligation upon the contracting parties not to use the Moon to commit any such act or to engage in any such threat in relation to the Earth, including the Moon itself, spacecraft, the personnel of spacecraft or man-made space objects.[326]

In accordance with the above article, the contracting parties have assumed the legal obligation to refrain from placing in orbit around or any other trajectory to or around the Moon objects carrying nuclear weapons or any other weapons of mass destruction, or placing or using such weapons on or in the Moon. The establishment of military bases, installations and fortifications, the testing of any type of weapons, and the conduct of military maneuvers on the Moon are explicitly prohibited by Article 3 of the Moon Treaty. The prohibitions of the nuclearization and militarization of the Moon apply equally to the other celestial bodies within our solar system by virtue of Article 1 of the Moon Treaty.[327]

There should be no doubt that through this treaty the Moon and other celestial bodies are to be exclusively used only for peaceful purposes, and that their exploration and uses must serve the common interests and benefits of humanity. It is also clear from the wording and the spirit of the provisions of the Moon Treaty that it creates a legal order which requires and imposes the complete denuclearization and demilitarization of the Moon and other celestial bodies, and bars from those places any weapons of mass destruction.[328] The regime established by the Moon Treaty imposes an additional legal restriction on the implementation of the American-proposed SDI system and the deployment of ASAT (anti-satellite) weapon systems on the Moon and on other celestial bodies.

Moon Treaty Verification. Respecting its effective implementation, the Moon Treaty, by virtue of its Article 15, provides each state party to this treaty with the right to ensure that the activities carried out by the other treaty signatories in the exploration and use of the Moon are compatible with the treaty. To this end, all space vehicles, equipment, facilities, stations and installations on the Moon must be open to on-site inspections of the other parties. For on-site inspections to be carried out, the inspecting state must give reasonable advanced notice to the party subject to such inspection.[329]

Furthermore, the parties concerned should consult with each other before such an on-site inspection takes place to ensure that maximum precautions are taken to assure safety, and to avoid interference with normal operations in the facility to be visited and inspected. In accordance with this article, the inspecting state may also act on its own behalf or with the full or partial assistance of any other signatory through appropriate international legal procedures and regulations.[330]

Moreover, if any signatory has reason to believe that another state does not fulfill its legal obligations under the Moon Treaty, in pursuance of Article 15 (2), the parties concerned must enter into consultations to peacefully resolve the controversy. The UN Secretary-General must also be informed of the results of the consultations and must transmit the information received to all states concerned. If such consultations fail to resolve the controversy, then Article 15 (3) gives any state the right to seek the assistance of the Secretary-General, without seeking the prior consent of any other party concerned, to resolve and settle the controversy.[331]

The Moon Treaty consolidates further the legal norm of on-site inspection for verification. It also provides a legal system of inter-party consultations for the resolution of any controversy involving the implementation of the treaty. Moreover, the UN Secretary-General may, upon the request of any signatory, offer his good offices for the peaceful resolution and settlement of any legal controversy concerning the implementation of the Moon Treaty.

The Convention on the Physical Protection of Nuclear Material (1980) and Its Legal Impact on the Prevention of the Spread of Such Material

The United Nations had an imperative concern to ensure that the horizontal proliferation of nuclear material and technology by the recipient states would be used only for peaceful purposes and applications and not for the development of nuclear weapons. The United Nations, and particularly the IAEA, began also to express their great interest in legally safeguarding the physical protection of nuclear material against its unlawful taking and use.[332] In particular, the legal need to ensure that terrorists not acquire nuclear material persuaded both the United Nations and the IAEA to enter negotiations to conclude a multilateral treaty to achieve such safeguarding purposes.

After active negotiations, which formally started in October 1977 under the auspices of the IAEA, by the end of 1979 the drafting of the Convention on the Physical Protection of Nuclear Material was completed and agreed upon by the participant states. The convention was concluded and opened to signature on March 3, 1980.[333] It entered into force on February 8, 1987. To date nearly 30 states have become parties to this convention, including the United States, the Soviet Union, China and other states engaged in the production and possession of nuclear material. However, several of these states have accepted the convention by filing their respective declarations and reservations.[334]

For the purposes of this convention, Article 1(a) and (b) define the nuclear material to be physically protected. According to these provisions, the term "nuclear material" means plutonium; uranium-233; uranium enriched in the isotopes 235 or 233; uranium containing the mixture of isotopes as occurring in nature other than in the form of ore or ore residue; and any material containing one or more of the foregoing. According to Article 1, paragraph b, the term "uranium enriched in the isotope 235 or 233" means "uranium containing the isotopes 235 or 233 or both in an amount such that the abundance ratio of the sum of these isotopes to the isotope 238 is greater than the ratio of the isotope 235 to the isotope occurring in nature."[335]

Since the fundamental legal objective of the convention is to safeguard against the potential dangers posed by the unlawful taking and use of nuclear material, the legal need to ensure the physical protection of this material requires not only its protection in domestic use and storage, but most importantly its safeguarding during international transfer and transportation. The international transport of nuclear material increases the potential dangers for its unlawful taking. To this end, and for the purposes of this convention, Article 1(c) defines "international nuclear transport" as the "carriage of a consignment of nuclear material by any means of transportation intended to go beyond the territory of the state where the shipment originates beginning with the departure from a facility of the shipper in that state and ending with the arrival at a facility of the receiver within the state of ultimate destination."[336]

Although the provisions of the convention apply to nuclear material used for peaceful purposes, which same material can be used under proper technologies for the development of nuclear explosive devices and weapons, the convention has been designed not to pose any obstacles and restrictions to the international transfer of such material. On the contrary, the convention has been drafted to ensure that nuclear material in domestic use or storage, or undergoing international transportation and transfer, will not be taken and used by any other entity than the responsible authorities.[337]

In view of the susceptibility of nuclear material to theft, robbery, embezzlement by individuals, corporate and even state agencies, and, in particular, in view of the potential danger that nuclear material could be used by terrorist groups with international networks and ramifications, the convention constitutes a positive international legal measure for its physical protection. The unlawful taking and use of nuclear material would contribute to the proliferation of such material outside the prohibitions and controls provided by the NPT international legal regime and the safeguards of the IAEA.

Due to these obvious, compelling and imperative reasons, the convention, by virtue of Article 7, has made punishable as criminal offenses at an international level the intentional commission of the following acts: "(a) an act without lawful authority which constitutes the receipt, possession, use, transfer, alteration, disposal or dispersal of nuclear material and which causes or is likely to cause death or serious injury to any person or substantial damage to property; (b) a theft or robbery of nuclear material; (c) an embezzlement or fraudulent obtaining of nuclear material; and (d) an act constituting a demand for nuclear material by threat or use of force or by any other form of intimidation." Article 7 renders a criminal offense the international use of nuclear material to cause death or serious injury to any person or substantial property damage or to commit any of the previous offenses to compel a natural or legal person, international organization or state to do or refrain from doing any act. Any attempt or participation in the commission of any of the previously described offenses constitutes a punishable act.[338]

Furthermore, in accordance with Article 7 each signatory has assumed the legal obligation to make punishable these criminal acts under its national law, and impose appropriate criminal penalties which take into account the grave nature of the offenses. The convention, to ensure the prosecution and criminal punishment of those responsible for such offenses, pursuant to Article 8, also requires its signatories to take the necessary legal measures to establish their criminal jurisdiction over the offenses set forth in Article 7 when the offense occurs in the territory of a member state or on board ship or aircraft registered in that state, and when the alleged offender is a national of that state.[339]

Paragraphs 2, 3 and 4 of Article 8 of the convention imposes on each signatory the legal obligation to take the necessary legal measures to establish its criminal jurisdiction over the offenses described by Article 7 in cases where the alleged offender is present in its territory and it does not extradite such an offender to the state of his nationality. The convention signatories have the legal obligation to establish their criminal jurisdiction over the offenses of Article 7 when they are involved in international nuclear transport either as exporting or importing states.[340]

With respect to facilitating the criminal prosecution and punishment of the perpetrators of the offenses of Article 7, the convention's Article 9 requires the member state in whose territory the alleged offender is present to take appropriate measures, including detention, under its national law and ensure that person's presence for prosecution or extradition. Article 10 provides that the member state in whose territory the alleged offender is present, if it does not extradite him, must submit the case, without exception and without undue delay, to its competent authorities for prosecution, through proceedings in accordance with the laws of that state. Article 11 of the convention, to facilitate and expedite the criminal prosecution and punishment of the offenders, provides that the offenses prescribed by the convention must be deemed to be included as extraditable offenses in any extradition treaty existing among signatories to the convention.[341]

In view of the preceding analysis of the fundamental legal objectives of the convention reflected by its provisions, this international instrument constitutes a positive legal measure for the prevention and the prohibition of the unlawful taking, use and spread of nuclear material which can also be used for the development of nuclear explosive devices and weapons. The convention is the first multilateral treaty in the history of nuclear arms control and disarmament that renders the unlawful taking and use of nuclear material an internationally punishable criminal offense. The convention constitutes a positive measure which strengthens the NPT legal regime.

Although the convention serves the legal objective of safeguarding nuclear material against any unlawful taking and use, it fails to criminalize the proliferation of nuclear material through clandestine and black market operations, which can be carried out by state authorities, and also by corporate and individual entities. The legal need for the criminalization of such a proliferation seems obvious in the post–Cold War era. Recent reports regarding the theft or illicit international trafficking of nuclear weapon grade material from the former Soviet Union clearly show the grave dangers of the uncontrolled spread of this material.[342] Therefore, it is an imperative legal need to expand the legal role of the convention by adding provisions criminalizing and further effectively sanctioning the clandestine transfer and proliferation of nuclear material.

Implementation of the Convention and Its Legal Mechanisms. The convention contains a number of provisions and measures designed to ensure the implementation of its legal objectives through the effective compliance of its signatories with their treaty obligations. Article 3 of the convention requires each member state to ensure as far as practicable that during international nuclear transport, nuclear material within its territory, or on board a ship or aircraft under its jurisdiction (insofar as such ship or aircraft is engaged in the transport to or from that state), is physically protected against any unlawful taking. Article 4 of the convention also imposes the legal obligation upon each member state not to export or authorize the export of nuclear material unless it has received assurances that such material will be protected during its international transport.[343]

Furthermore, in accordance with Article 5, the convention requires its signatories to identify and make known to each other directly or through the IAEA their central authority and point of contact having responsibility of the physical protection of nuclear material, and for coordinating recovery and response operations and actions in the event of any unauthorized removal, use or alteration of nuclear material, or in the event of a credible threat of such activity. Additionally, pursuant to Article 5, the signatories have assumed the legal obligation to provide cooperation and assistance to the maximum feasible extent in the recovery and the physical protection of nuclear material which has been unlawfully taken.[344] In accordance with Article 5 (2), the convention provides that the means of implementation of the required cooperation in the physical protection and recovery of unlawfully taken nuclear material must be agreed upon and determined by the states concerned. This provision also requires the member states concerned to exchange information with each other or international organizations to help protect threatened nuclear material, verify the integrity of the shipping containers, or recover unlawfully taken material. Article 5 (3) requires cooperation and consultation as appropriate, directly between states or through international organizations, to obtain guidance on the design, maintenance and improvement of systems to protect nuclear material in international transport. Pursuant to Article 5 (2) (iii), the member states must ensure the return of nuclear material stolen or missing as a consequence of the previously described criminal offenses.[345]

In relation to its implementation, the convention, according to Article 17, provides the legal mechanisms for the settlement of a dispute among signatories concerning the interpretation or application of this convention. In accordance with this article, the states concerned must consult with a view to the settlement of any dispute concerning the interpretation or application of the content of the convention by negotiation, or by any other peaceful means acceptable to all parties. If a dispute of this nature cannot be settled in the legal manner prescribed, then, at the request of any party concerned, the dispute must be submitted to arbitration or referred to the International Court of Justice for decision.[346]

Article 17 of the convention, by providing for the peaceful and judicial resolution of disputes concerning the interpretation and application of this convention, constitutes a positive step toward legal settlement of such disputes. Since the convention, on the basis of its legal objectives, exercises a positive legal impact on the control and physical protection of nuclear material, the legal mechanisms of Article 17 for the peaceful and, in particular, for the judicial settlement of the disputes previously described are of significant legal value in the judicial settlement of controversies and disputes arising from multilateral treaty arrangements dealing with the regulation and control of nuclear material.

Although the Russian government is reassuring the world about the control and safety of its nuclear material, the potential danger of the unauthorized possession and clandestine transfer of nuclear weapon grade material from the former Soviet Union raises grave global concerns. It is estimated that there is enough nuclear weapon grade material spread across the former Soviet Union to make 100,000 nuclear weapons. Although the end of the Cold War has essentially ended the threat of nuclear confrontation between Russia and the United States, the potential danger of the spread of nuclear weapon material from the former Soviet Union, and acquisition of that material by terrorist groups and states involved in the quest to acquire nuclear weapons, poses new dangers of uncontrolled and clandestine international nuclear proliferation. These dangers pose a new threat of nuclear anarchy to the international community's security.[347]

Chapter 8

The End of the Cold War, the End of the Soviet Union, and the Beginning of Superpower Nuclear Disarmament (1986–1997): The INF and START Treaties

The Gorbachev-Reagan Summitry and NST Negotiations (1986–1988)

THE U.S.–SOVIET NST NEGOTIATIONS AND THE GORBACHEV-REAGAN GENEVA SUMMIT MEETING (NOVEMBER 1985)

After walking out of the Intermediate Nuclear Forces (INF) negotiations and the Strategic Arms Reductions Talks (START) by the end of 1983 in protest of American deployment of new INF nuclear missiles in Western Europe, the Soviet Union refused to return to the negotiating table in Geneva throughout 1984. In January 1985, the superpowers agreed to resume their negotiations. Their overall negotiations, falling under the umbrella of Nuclear and Space Talks (NST), covered separate negotiations on START, INF and defensive weapons in space.[348] The START and INF negotiations were facing their own difficulties and complexities; the announcement of the Strategic Defense Initiative (SDI) by President Reagan in March 1983 and the determination of his administration to proceed with its developmental testing and final deployment in outer space, in contravention of the ABM Treaty, became a major obstacle that further complicated the START and INF negotiations.[349]

Nevertheless, almost immediately after his rise to the leadership of the Soviet Union in March 1985, Mikhail Gorbachev began to introduce not only to the United States and generally to the Western nuclear military and capitalist establishment, but also to the entire world, his revolutionary and radical thinking and changes concerning the military and foreign policies of the Soviet Union, with which he hoped to build a new system of global peace and common security in the nuclear age. Regarding the U.S.–Soviet nuclear arms race and the superpowers' constant nuclear tensions, the Soviet leader introduced a new strategic thinking and a dynamic and radical nuclear disarmament-oriented leadership.[350]

To this end, in March 1985 Gorbachev stated the readiness of the Soviet Union not to continue the nuclear arms race. He also proposed to the United States to agree on ending that race, and offered a freeze of nuclear arsenals and an end to deployment of more nuclear missiles. Additionally, Gorbachev in his address to the French Parliament on October 3, 1985, stressed the need to cease immediately the "infernal train" of the nuclear arms race before it was too late, and to start the reduction of nuclear arms.[351]

Particularly with respect to the NST negotiations in Geneva, Gorbachev, in April 1985, announced his unilateral decision to cease the deployment of SS-20s in Europe until November of that year. He also offered to reduce the SS-20 INF missiles already deployed in Europe to 243, a number equal to the level prior to the breaking off of the INF negotiations. In Fall 1985, the Soviet Union made a comprehensive proposal for the entire range of nuclear weapon systems dealt with in Geneva. In return for a settlement on the ban of development, testing and deployment of space weapons and especially the U.S.–proposed SDI system, the Soviets were prepared to agree on the reduction of their strategic nuclear forces by 50 percent.[352] Because of the U.S.–Soviet legal controversy over the SDI program, and because of the negative implications of the SDI in the superpowers' strategic balance, the superpowers had failed to make any substantial legal progress of breakthroughs in their NST Geneva negotiations.[353]

In spite of these failures, Gorbachev and Reagan agreed to a summit meeting, which was held in Geneva in November 1985.[354] In accordance with the joint U.S.–Soviet communiqué released after this summit meeting, both leaders set out the principles underlying their intentions to cooperate in the prevention of a U.S.–Soviet nuclear war, and to accelerate the legal process for their nuclear disarmament through gradual but radical reduction in their nuclear arms. Both sides agreed that a nuclear war cannot be won and must never be fought. They also recognized that a U.S.–Soviet nuclear war would have catastrophic consequences for the entire human race. In addition to their agreement to accelerate their NST negotiations toward terminating their nuclear arms race on Earth and preventing an arms race in space, both leaders expressed their willingness to reduce their countries' nuclear arms by half, and to negotiate an interim INF agreement. Gorbachev and Reagan also agreed to study the question of establishing joint centers to reduce nuclear risk, and agreed to modernize the already existing U.S.–Soviet hotline communications system.[355]

Continuation of the U.S.–Soviet NST Negotiations and the Gorbachev-Reagan Reykjavik Summit Meeting (October 1986)

On the basis of the principles agreed upon between the United States and the Soviet Union during the Geneva summit meeting with respect to making legal progress in their NST negotiations held in Geneva, Gorbachev by the beginning of 1986 assumed a revolutionary and radical leadership in superpower nuclear disarmament. On January 15, 1986, the Soviet leader in an address known as "The Year 2000 Nuclear Disarmament Speech" proposed a step-by-step, consistent process for ridding the earth of nuclear weapons, to be undertaken and completed within the next 15 years, before the end of the century, and pointed out the need for the third millennium to begin without nuclear weapons.[356]

The Gorbachev proposal to free the world of all nuclear weapons by the year 2000 contained new aspects and detailed steps. The Gorbachev Plan for a global nuclear disarmament included two stages for its implementation. In the first stage, which would take five to eight years, all ground-launched long-range intermediate nuclear forces (LRINF) in Europe had to be eliminated. Within this period the superpowers would be prohibited from transferring LRINF's to third parties. In the first stage, a freeze would also be imposed on the French and British nuclear weapon arsenals at their existing levels.[357]

According to the second stage, as of 1990 while both the United States and the Soviet Union would continue with the total elimination of their INF weapons, including the imposition of a freeze on their remaining tactical nuclear weapons, the other nuclear powers would participate in nuclear disarmament. During the second stage a global elimination of tactical nuclear weapons with ranges below 1,000 kilometers would take place. By the year 2000, all nuclear weapons would be eliminated.[358]

In addition to his radical proposal for a global and comprehensive nuclear disarmament by the year 2000, Gorbachev, in his address to the Soviet Communist Party Congress on February 25, 1986, stated that it was time to realize to the full extent the harsh reality that nuclear weapons could produce a hurricane that would sweep the human race from the face of the Earth. He also added that continuation of the nuclear arms race on Earth, let alone its spread to outer space, would accelerate the already critically high rate of stockpiling and perfecting of nuclear weapons.[359]

Although the United States and its Western allies failed to react positively to the Gorbachev proposal for world nuclear disarmament by the year 2000, the Reagan administration found some positive elements in the Soviet proposal for the elimination of INF nuclear missiles, particularly in Europe. In light of this common ground, the United States and the Soviet Union accelerated their negotiations in Geneva with the objective of removing the remaining obstacles and eventually concluding an agreement requiring the elimination of all U.S. and Soviet INF nuclear missiles in Europe.[360]

As a result of their breakthrough INF negotiations, by September 1986 the nuclear superpowers had managed to remove some substantial obstacles preventing legal progress toward an INF treaty. Gorbachev had since 1985 insisted that the Soviet Union would conclude such treaty only if both the French and British nuclear systems were included in the agreement. Because this Soviet condition was firmly rejected by the Western allies, it became a major obstacle to an INF agreement. On September 19, 1986, Gorbachev made a unilateral concession, and finally agreed to drop his condition that French and British nuclear systems be included in an INF agreement.[361]

By September 1986 both the United States and the Soviet Union had made substantial legal progress concerning the effective implementation of an INF agreement. They had agreed in principle that the verification system of such a treaty would, among other points, include on-site inspection.[362] In essence, the adoption of on-site inspection for the INF agreement not only constitutes a significant breakthrough in verifying nuclear disarmament agreements, but also constitutes a dynamic and innovative legal measure for the effective implementation of such agreements.

In spite of the failure of the nuclear superpowers to make any substantial legal progress in their negotiations in space defense weapons or reductions in their strategic nuclear arms, the legal progress and breakthroughs made by fall 1986 in relation to the INF negotiations increased the expectations that an INF agreement could be signed by Gorbachev and Reagan during their forthcoming summit meeting, to take place in Reykjavik in October 1986.[363] Nevertheless, the Gorbachev-Reagan summit failed to produce any positive legal results in the superpowers' NST negotiations in general, and particularly in the conclusion of an INF agreement.[364]

The Reykjavik summit was dominated by the U.S.–Soviet legal controversy over the SDI system and its conflict with the ABM Treaty. President Reagan's lack of flexibility and his insistence on proceeding with the developmental testing and deployment of the SDI system in outer space, albeit in a clear violation of the ABM Treaty, prevented the superpowers from making any legal progress in the elimination of their INF missiles in Europe, and in reductions of their strategic nuclear arms. Reagan's inflexibility concerning his SDI system led the Reykjavik summit to failure notwithstanding Gorbachev's readiness for making legal progress in disarmament both in INF and strategic nuclear arms.[365]

In Reykjavik Gorbachev stated his readiness to sign an INF agreement by which both the U.S. and Soviet INF nuclear missiles would be eliminated in Europe.[366] The Soviet leader also proposed to the American side the conclusion of an agreement by which the U.S.–Soviet strategic nuclear armaments would be reduced by half, so that these most deadly nuclear weapons would be abolished by the turn of the century. Gorbachev also stated his intention to extend his moratorium on any nuclear weapons tests and explosions.[367]

Gorbachev pointed out that the Soviet Union would proceed with the conclusion of an INF Treaty and a START treaty on the basis of his proposals if the United States would agree to adhere to its ABM Treaty obligations and make an official commitment not to proceed with the developmental research, testing and deployment of its SDI program.[368] The implementation of the SDI program by the United States would have provided it with a strategic superiority over the

Soviet Union.[369] Nevertheless, President Reagan showed no flexibility or compromise on the SDI system.[370]

After Reykjavik: The Gorbachev-Reagan Washington Summit Meeting and the INF Treaty (December 1987)

After intensive negotiations in a breakthrough mode in February 1987, Gorbachev made a major unilateral announcement that the Soviet Union would delink INF from the SDI and START.[371] Based on this significant Soviet concession, a new legal impetus was provided for the conclusion of an INF treaty. Finally, at a Moscow meeting in September 1987, U.S. Secretary of State George Shultz and Soviet Foreign Minister Eduard Shevardnadze announced that they had agreed in principle to conclude an INF treaty which was to be formally signed by Gorbachev and Reagan at a special summit meeting to be held in Washington by the end of fall 1987.[372]

In view of the Shevardnadze-Shultz Moscow agreement in principle on the elimination of all American and Soviet INF nuclear missiles, the INF Treaty was finally signed during the Gorbachev-Reagan summit meeting held in Washington in December 1987.[373] Both leaders characterized the INF Treaty as an historic achievement both for its objective, namely, the complete elimination of an entire class of American and Soviet nuclear arms, and for the innovative character and scope of its verification system.[374] The conclusion of the INF Treaty should be primarily attributed to Gorbachev, who by his unilateral concessions made possible the conclusion of this agreement.

INF Treaty Content and Objectives. The INF Treaty, formally the Treaty on the Elimination of Intermediate-Range and Shorter-Range Missiles, consists of: (a) the text of the treaty; (b) a memorandum of understanding concerning the establishment of the database which contains all the information given in the first data exchange on respective Soviet and American intermediate and shorter-range missiles, including missile numbers, technical characteristics and locations; (c) a protocol on procedures governing the elimination of missile systems, which provides a detailed outline of the procedures to be followed in eliminating each element of a given missile system; and (d) a protocol concerning inspections giving procedural guidelines to be followed during the inspection process.[375]

Additionally, to improve the viability and effectiveness of the treaty and to resolve questions of compliance, the Soviet Union and the United States signed a memorandum of agreement in December 1989 concerning the application of verification provisions to the INF Treaty.[376] The treaty, which according to its Article XV (1) is of unlimited duration, was ratified by both parties in May 1988 when they exchanged their instruments of ratification by signing the required protocol, and since then the INF Treaty has been in force.[377]

In accordance with the preamble to the INF Treaty, both parties state that nuclear war would have devastating consequences for all humanity. Both parties, guided by the objective of strengthening strategic stability, also express their conviction that the measures set forth in the INF Treaty are designed to help reduce the risk of outbreak of war and strengthen international peace and security. Moreover, both the United States and the Soviet Union point out that the conclusion of the treaty is consistent with their legal obligations under Article VI of the NPT Treaty to proceed with the legal process of their denuclearization.[378]

Article I of the INF Treaty states in succinct terms that each party must eliminate its INF ballistic nuclear missiles and must not have such systems thereafter. According to Article II of the treaty, the INF nuclear missile systems which must be eliminated include intermediate-range ground-launched cruise and ballistic missiles having a range exceeding 1,000 kilometers up to 5,500 kilometers, and shorter-range ground-launched cruise and ballistic missiles have a range of 500–1,000 kilometers. Article II also provides legal-technical definitions of the missiles, their operating bases and support facilities as well as a legal description of other elements related to the INF missiles to be eliminated under the treaty.[379]

Article III of the treaty lists the Soviet and American INF systems to be eliminated. On the American side, the list includes the Pershing II, the BGM-109G cruise missile, and the Pershing IA. The Soviet list includes the SS-20, SS-4, SS-5, SS-12 and SS-23. Pursuant to Article X (6) of the treaty, the Soviet cruise missile SSC-X-4 and the American Pershing IB, which both had been tested but not yet deployed, have been added to the list of the INF missiles to be eliminated.[380]

Based on the data exchanged between the two parties, 846 American and 1,846 Soviet intermediate and shorter range delivery vehicles then deployed in Europe and elsewhere had to be eliminated under the INF Treaty. On the American side, this involved the elimination of 846 nuclear warheads form the European theater; the treaty required elimination of 3,154 Soviet nuclear warheads worldwide.[381]

In accordance with Article IV (1) of the treaty, each party assumed the obligation to eliminate all its intermediate-range missiles and launchers of such missiles, and all support structures and support equipment of the categories listed in the memorandum of understanding associated with such missiles and launchers, within three years after entry into force of the INF Treaty; thereafter, no such missiles, launchers, support structures of support equipment could be possessed by either party. Based on Article IV (2), the two parties assumed the legal obligation to eliminate all their intermediate-range missile systems in a two-stage process, to be completed within three years after the INF Treaty entered into force. Since the treaty entered into force in May 1988, the parties must have completed the process for the elimination of all their intermediate-range nuclear missiles and launchers, and all support structures and support equipment by approximately mid–1991.[382]

With respect to the elimination of all their already deployed shorter-range missiles and launchers of such missiles, and all support equipment for these missile systems, Article V of the treaty provided that the elimination of these missile systems was to take place in two stages and to be completely implemented within 18 months after the treaty's entry into force. Thus, the complete elimination of all U.S. and Soviet shorter-range missile systems must have been implemented by approximately the end of fall 1989. Article V provided that each party, no later than 12 months after the treaty's entry into force, must have completed the removal of all its nondeployed shorter-range missiles to elimination facilities.[383]

The INF Treaty prohibited both parties from the production or flight-test of new INF missile systems upon its entry into force. Thus, upon the Treaty's entry into force and thereafter, while the parties had assumed the legal obligation to begin the elimination of all their INF nuclear missile systems, Article VI required the parties not to produce or flight-test any intermediate-range missile or produce any stages of such missiles or any launchers of such missiles; or produce, flight-test or launch any shorter-range missiles or produce any stages or launchers of such missiles.[384]

Concerning the elimination of all U.S. and Soviet INF missile systems, the INF Treaty provided a specific legal regime to this end. In addition to Article X of the treaty, which sets out the processes for the elimination of all such missile systems, the Protocol on Procedures Governing the Elimination of the INF missile systems that constitutes an integral part of the treaty provides a very lengthy and detailed process aimed at eliminating these nuclear weapons.[385]

In accordance with Article X of the treaty and particularly with its protocol on elimination, distinctions should be made among the specific arrangements for the elimination of the missiles, launches and reentry vehicles of the INF systems covered by the treaty. Regarding the elimination of the missiles, the treaty required that first the reentry vehicles (the warhead-bearing components) be removed. Rocket stages could be burned or exploded. The airframe of the cruise missiles had to be cut in two pieces lengthwise.[386]

Launcher erector mechanisms were to be dismantled form the launcher chassis and cut into two pieces, as was the chassis. Reentry vehicles were to be crushed following removal of the nuclear warheads and parts of the guidance system. These parts were to be returned to the parties' nuclear arsenals, for reuse for either military or civilian purposes.[387] Both parties were to destroy all of their support structures and support equipment associated with the INF missile systems.[388]

In view of the preceding discussion of the treaty's legal regime for the elimination of the INF missile systems through appropriate processes and technical procedures, there should be no doubt that these legal measures greatly assisted in ensuring the elimination of these systems, so that they could not be reassembled and used in the future. With respect to the elimination of the INF missile systems, both parties in conformity with their treaty obligations and particularly with the treaty timetable by the end of 1989 successfully completed the elimination of their shorter-range INF missile systems.[389] It has been reported that both parties by mid–1991 completed the legal process for the elimination of all of their intermediate-range INF missile systems.[390]

Nevertheless, the term "elimination" used by the INF Treaty to denote the complete destruction of the INF missile systems does not seem to correspond literally to its legal and technical meaning. Since both parties have the right to retain the nuclear warheads and the guidance systems from their destroyed INF systems and further reuse them for military purposes, this clearly shows that the term "elimination" rather means the destructive dismantling of INF missile systems.[391] It would be more consistent with the legal and technical meaning of the term "elimination" employed by the INF Treaty and generally with the juridical concept of nuclear disarmament if both parties had agreed either to completely destroy the nuclear warheads and guidance systems taken out of their dismantled INF missile systems, or to use them exclusively for peaceful civilian purposes.

INF Treaty Verification Regime and System. To ensure the effective compliance of the parties with their treaty obligations, the INF Treaty by its main text and by its protocol on inspections provides a detailed and significant verification system.[392] The treaty allows the parties to use their NTM of verification, and allows them to conduct on-site inspections to ensure their effective compliance with the treaty. In particular, the adoption of on-site inspection by the treaty, which the parties accepted for the first time in their legal history of nuclear arms control in the pre–INF Treaty period, constitutes an innovative and dynamic legal breakthrough and approach in relation to verification efforts.

Article XII of the INF Treaty provides each party with the right to use NTM of verification at its disposal and in a manner consistent with generally recognized principles of international law. The NTM used by the parties to ensure their compliance with their treaty obligations to eliminate all of their INF missile systems include such means as high and low-orbiting satellites employed to collect images and signals from space, submarines used for tapping into undersea communications lines, aircraft patrolling outside monitored borders, ships at sea and a variety of ground-based sensors, including over-the-horizon radar for aircraft and missile detection systems.[393] At the time of the treaty's conclusion, both parties had made significant advances in their NTM of verification which substantially increased their technological ability to verify treaty compliance.

Article XXII of the treaty guarantees transparency of the territory of each party to be checked by their NTM by prohibiting interference with such verification systems, and also by prohibiting each party from using concealment measures which impede verification by such means. Additionally, to enhance observation of what is to be verified under the treaty by NTM, Article XII (3) requires the parties to carry out the following cooperative measures: (a) The party whose base is to be observed by NTM within six hours after such a request has been made by the other party must open the roofs of all fixed structures for launchers located at the base, remove completely all missiles on launchers from such fixed structures for launchers, and display such missiles on launchers in the open without using concealment measures; and (b) such a party must leave the roofs open and the missiles on launchers in place until 12 hours have elapsed from the time of the receipt of a request for such an observation.[394]

Both superpowers traditionally relied heavily on the use of the NTM for the verification of their nuclear arms control agreements in the pre–INF Treaty years. The INF Treaty, based on the preceding analysis, has adopted specific legal measures designed to guarantee transparency of the territory of each party for the use of NTM verification to ensure the effective compliance of the parties with their treaty obligations. Moreover, by the time of the conclusion of the INF Treaty both superpowers had made great technological advances in their NTM. Indeed, such an enhancement of the capabilities of their NTM combined with the treaty's provisions requiring each party to maintain the transparency of its territory has significantly increased the usefulness and the reliability of NTM to effectively verify compliance not only with the INF Treaty, but also with any other nuclear disarmament treaty between the two superpowers.[395]

In accordance with Article XI of the INF Treaty and the treaty's protocol on inspections, five different forms of on-site inspections are provided. They include: (1) baseline inspections to verify the accuracy of the initial data provided by the parties; (2) close-out inspections to be conducted after one of the parties declares a facility to be free of INF equipment and no longer supporting intermediate or shorter-range missile operations; the other party has the right to visit the facility to confirm its new status within 60 days of the declared close-out date; (3) quota inspections to be carried out in a way similar to baseline inspections, with only minor differences. All facilities listed in the memorandum of understanding are subject to these inspections for the entire 13-year period. Each party is permitted a total of 185 inspections during this period: 20 per year for the first three years, 15 per year for the next five, and 10 per year for the last five years; (4) elimination inspections for on-site monitoring of the elimination of certain treaty-limited items, namely missiles, launchers and associated support equipment; and (5) portal monitoring that allows a continuous, long-term monitoring for a period of up to 14 years. Based on this type of on-site inspection, a U.S. inspection team is monitoring the Soviet Votkinsk plant near the Urals that formerly assembled INF missile systems. A Soviet inspection team is also monitoring the Hercules Corporation's Bacchus Works near Salt Lake City, Utah, which used to produce rocket motors for the U.S. Pershing II INF missiles.[396]

An overview of the conduct of both parties' on-site inspections, which have been taking place since 30 days after the INF Treaty entered into force, involving 200 inspectors for each party, clearly shows that these on-site inspections are carried out smoothly and in conformity with the provisions of Article XI and the protocol on inspections of the INF Treaty. In addition to the U.S. and Soviet inspection teams respectively at the Votkinsk and Hercules INF missile plants, other Soviet and American inspection teams have been conducting on-site inspections on each other's territories, thus making sure that the INF missile systems are eliminated in accordance with the treaty.[397]

In addition to the above on-site inspections, 19 American and 77 Soviet sites associated with the deployment, launcher production facilities, testing, repair, training sites, storage facilities and missile elimination sites have been the subject of on-site inspection.[398] Although the INF Treaty is a bilateral agreement by which the United States and the Soviet Union are subject to on-site inspections, the nuclear weapon systems affected were deployed by the superpowers in Eastern and Western European states after consultations with the states concerned. The territories of such third states, then, are affected by the elimination measures and by verification procedures involved under the INF Treaty.[399] This means that the treaty develops a third party legal effect in some manner.

Aside from the verification legal system of the treaty involving both NTM and on-site inspections, the verification structure and mechanism of the treaty includes the creation by the parties of a Special Verification Commission (SVC). In accordance with Article XIII, the SVC has generally assumed the responsibility to promote the objectives and the effective implementation of the INF Treaty. It also has undertaken the legal duty to resolve compliance questions with the obligations assumed by the parties, and further to agree upon the adoption of measures which may be necessary to improve the viability and effectiveness of the INF Treaty. Furthermore, pursuant to the above article, the Nuclear Risk Reduction Centers, which were created by the superpowers in summer 1987, have assumed the task of dealing with the exchange of data and the announcement of dates for the elimination of the INF missile systems.[400]

It is of particular significance that both parties have proceeded with the INF Treaty's implementation in a successful and effective manner. Indeed by the end of 1989, both had eliminated all their shorter-range INF missile systems.[401] Also, it has been reported that by mid–1991 both parties had eliminated all their long-range INF missile systems.[402]

Although both parties have proceeded with the elimination of all their INF missile systems in an effective manner in accordance with the INF Treaty, the United States has allegedly accused the Soviets of committing some violations against the treaty. These American allegations concern minor violations, and in any case the American side has not been able to substantiate and pursue them.[403] Both parties have successfully and effectively proceeded with their treaty obligation to eliminate all of their INF missile systems.[404]

The Legal Impact of INF Treaty on the U.S.–Soviet Nuclear Disarmament Process. The INF Treaty constitutes the first nuclear disarmament treaty[405] between the superpowers. There should be no doubt that the treaty has become the starting point in the superpowers' bilateral legal process for their gradual and ultimate denuclearization. Additionally, the INF Treaty constitutes an unprecedented legal breakthrough in making possible the superpowers' transition from the counterproductive model of nuclear arms control to that of gradual nuclear disarmament, which is consistent with the juridical concept and legal goal of nuclear disarmament.

Concerning the legal impact of the INF Treaty on the superpowers' bilateral legal process for their gradual and ultimate denuclearization, the INF Treaty is the first U.S.–Soviet bilateral treaty by which an entire class of their nuclear weapons and missile systems has been eliminated comprehensively, on a global basis. In pure arithmetical terms, the INF Treaty reduces the overall American and Soviet nuclear weapon arsenals by approximately 4,000 nuclear warheads. This represented only an eight percent reduction in the global total of American and Soviet strategic and tactical nuclear warheads, which at the time of the conclusion of the treaty numbered more than 50,000.[406]

Despite the recognition that the INF Treaty has been designed to reduce the superpowers' total nuclear weapon arsenal by a very small percentage, and despite the fact that such a reduction does not affect their first-strike capabilities, or generally their capabilities to destroy the entire world many times over,[407] even this small reduction in the U.S.–Soviet nuclear arsenals resulted in the elimination of the U.S.–Soviet INF missiles deployed in Europe. The United States still maintains in Europe tactical nuclear weapons,[408] some of which are deployed in U.S. bases in Greece and Turkey.[409]

Additionally, it is significant that the INF Treaty constitutes a positive legal development compared to the U.S.–Soviet failure in the pre–INF Treaty period to reduce their nuclear arsenals by at least one nuclear warhead. Their legal model of nuclear arms control and limitation, which ironically resulted in the continuous expansion of their nuclear arms race, proved counterproductive to the objective of their nuclear disarmament. Moreover, the INF Treaty provides the superpowers a dynamic new legal impetus for the reversal of their nuclear arms race and the promotion of the prospects for their gradual and ultimate nuclear disarmament on a comprehensive, global basis.

The conclusion of the INF Treaty, which President Reagan and the Soviet leader Gorbachev characterized as historic both for its objective, namely, the complete elimination of an entire class of U.S.–Soviet INF nuclear arms, and for the innovative character and scope of its verification structure and system,[410] became possible particularly due to Gorbachev's nuclear disarmament-oriented leadership, and generally because of his new strategic thinking for world peace and security. There must be no doubt that Gorbachev's flexibility and his unilateral concessions greatly facilitated the final signature of the INF Treaty. It is of particular significance that Gorbachev during the signature of the treaty called it the first step down the road leading to a nuclear-free world, and the start of nuclear disarmament.[411] The INF Treaty, both in political and legal terms, constitutes a dynamic legal instrument which marks the beginning of the superpowers' nuclear disarmament as well as the beginning of the end of their Cold War relations, their relentless nuclear arms race and the constant threat of their nuclear confrontation.

That both parties have eliminated their INF missile systems in an effective manner shows that the INF Treaty has been properly and successfully implemented, and that its innovative and dynamic system of verification has made that possible.

The effective implementation of the INF Treaty has already set a major legal precedent that has positively affected the creation of a new legal reality concerning the superpowers' new nuclear disarmament relationship through the instrumental value of the rule of international law. In the pre–INF Treaty period both superpowers, due to their Cold War relations, their nuclear arms race and constant threat of nuclear confrontation, and also because they did not legally adopt effective verification measures such as on-site inspections, failed to proceed with nuclear disarmament. However, the successful legal experience of the INF Treaty has clearly demonstrated its political and legal dynamism in the effort to overcome the Cold War and verification obstacles.

The INF Treaty's legal impact on the cause of the elimination of all American and Soviet nuclear weapons on a global basis is of enormous and extraordinary significance. In particular, the fact that both parties implemented their legal obligations under the INF Treaty in a successful and effective manner supports the argument forwarded by this study that, under international law, a total denuclearization of both nuclear superpowers can be legally feasible and effective, provided that there exists the required political will of the two parties to achieve this legal objective.

The Gorbachev-Bush Summitry, the End of the Cold War and the Road to the START I Treaty (1989–1991)

When George Bush assumed his presidential duties in January 1989, he decided to postpone the resumption of the START negotiations with the Soviets for seven months. To justify this delay, the Bush administration argued that it needed the time to conduct a comprehensive review of America's policy toward the Soviet Union. Nevertheless, Bush's speeches and statements during his first months in the White House clearly showed his Cold War posture and his nuclear strategies toward the Soviets.

In May 1989, U.S. Secretary of State James A. Baker and Soviet Foreign Minister Eduard Shevardnadze agreed to round 11 of their START negotiations in Geneva. Thus, in June of 1989, the superpowers began their negotiations with the objective of reaching an agreement on the reduction of their strategic offensive nuclear weapons. While during these negotiations the parties discussed a variety of issues associated with substantive verification and procedural questions, by the end of November 1989 they had failed to make any substantial legal progress toward a START I Treaty.[412]

In spite of this failure, the START negotiations became the dominant issue during the Gorbachev-Bush summit meeting held in Malta in December 1989. Although the two leaders did not resolve many substantive and technical issues preventing the conclusion of a START I Treaty, they agreed to accelerate their START negotiations in a breakthrough manner to resolve these issues, and thus to conclude the START Treaty during their next summit to be held in June 1990. Both sides agreed to complete work on the TTBT and the PNET for signature at their 1990 summit.[413]

The Signing of the START I Treaty (July 1991)

During their Moscow summit meeting on July 31, 1991, President Gorbachev and President Bush signed the START I Treaty, an event that became possible due to the end of the Cold War and the superpowers' entry into a new post–Cold War relationship of cooperation and security. It also constitutes the legal result of the decade-long START negotiations. The START I Treaty is the first treaty in the legal history of U.S.–Soviet nuclear arms control which requires the parties to make reductions in their strategic offensive nuclear arms.[414] The treaty entered into force in December 1994.[415]

START I Content and Objectives. The START I Treaty[416] consists of a complicated legal document of 700 pages. In addition to its main text, the treaty has been accompanied by the following: an annex on definitions; a protocol on notifications; a protocol on conversion or elimination; a protocol on ICBM and SLBM throw-weight; the protocol on the Joint Compliance and Inspection Commission; a protocol on telemetry; the protocol on Inspections and Continuous Monitoring (with 12 annexes); and a memorandum of understanding. The treaty is supplemented by a separate annex of agreed statements, related agreements, letters signed by U.S. and Soviet representatives, supporting documents, and declarations.

In accordance with the preamble to the treaty, both parties are conscious that nuclear war would have devastating consequences for all humanity, and that such a war cannot be won and must never be fought. The two superpowers state their conviction that the measures for the reduction and limitation of strategic offensive arms and the other obligations provided by the START I Treaty will assist in reducing the risk of outbreak of nuclear war, and strengthen international peace and security by recognizing that their interests and the interests of international security require the strengthening of strategic nuclear stability. Moreover, both parties note that the reduction and limitation of their strategic nuclear forces under the START I Treaty correspond to their commitments under Article VI of the NPT.[417]

In accordance with Article II of the treaty, the parties assumed the legal obligation to reduce and limit their ICBMs and ICBM launchers, SLBMs and SLBM launchers, heavy bombers, ICBM warheads, SLBM warheads and heavy bomber armaments. The same article requires implementing the reductions and limitations of these strategic nuclear weapon systems in three phases, with equal interim levels at the end of each phase. Thus, by the end of the third phase (no later than seven years after entry into force of the START I Treaty), the Soviet and American strategic offensive nuclear arms would be reduced and limited to 1,600 strategic nuclear delivery vehicles and 6,000 "accountable" nuclear warheads, including no more than 4,900 ballistic missile warheads, and in the Soviet case no more than 1,540 nuclear warheads on 154 heavy intercontinental ballistic missiles. In a side letter, the Soviets agreed to eliminate 22 SS-18 launchers every year for seven years to achieve this level.[418]

Each side agreed to deploy no more than 1,100 nuclear warheads on mobile ICBMs, and to limit the aggregate throw-weight of its deployed ICBMs and SLBMs so that seven years after the treaty's entry into force and thereafter such aggregate throw-weight must not exceed 3,600 metric tons. The treaty ceiling of 1,600 strategic nuclear delivery vehicles also includes deployed ICBMs and their associated launchers, deployed SLBMs and their launchers, and deployed heavy bombers. The "accountable" warhead ceiling of 6,000 includes the actual number of warheads on deployed ICBMs and SLBMs. The number of long-range, nuclear-armed, air-launched cruise missiles carried by heavy bombers would be adjusted by a formula that understates the actual number of weapons. Heavy bombers equipped only with nuclear-armed gravity bombs and short-range attack missiles (SRAMs) would be counted as single warheads, a decision that greatly discounted the number of nuclear weapons carried by such heavy bombers.[419]

The treaty provides that no missile type may be flight-tested with more than its existing number of nuclear warheads, and on-site inspections would verify that deployed ballistic missiles contain no more reentry vehicles than the number of nuclear warheads that have been attributed to them. Both parties also agreed not to deploy new or modified ICBMs and SLBMs that carry more than ten nuclear warheads.[420]

The START I Treaty specifies that the number of nuclear warheads on three existing categories of ballistic missiles may be reduced or "downloaded," but neither party may reduce accountable nuclear warheads by more than 1,250 through downloading. Each Soviet SS-N-18 SLBM (not to be confused with the Soviet SS-18 ICBM) is counted as having three warheads, although the SS-18 has been deployed with both a three- and seven-nuclear warhead platform; 896 SS-N-18 warheads would count toward the Soviet overall downloading limit. The American Minuteman III ICBMs could be downloaded by one or two nuclear warheads.[421]

With the 1,250 limit, up to 500 other reentry vehicles could be downloaded on two other existing ballistic missile types, but no missile could be downloaded by more than four reentry vehicles. In addition, new types of multiple-warhead missiles would not be developed and later downloaded, nor would either side develop new missiles designed to carry more nuclear warheads than on any downloaded type, with the exception of the Minuteman III and the SS-18. Any ICBM downloaded by more than two reentry vehicles would have to be equipped with a new front section platform, and all old platforms destroyed.[422]

The START I Treaty required both parties to reduce their deployed heavy ICBMs and their nuclear warheads by half. The Treaty also imposed other constraints on heavy ICBMs which included: no downloading; no increase in launch weight or throw weight; no mobile launchers for heavy ICBMs; and no new types of heavy missiles. New heavy ICBM silo construction is allowed, but only in exceptional cases, for relocation or to replace eliminated heavy ICBM silos in extraordinary circumstances. However, the number of such heavy ICBM silos may not exceed 154. Modernization and testing of existing heavy ICBMs may be continued by the parties. Other ICBMs or SLBMs will be considered new types if they exceed certain variances in size, weight and throw weight; the throw weight of existing types of ICBMs and SLBMs may not be increased by more than 21 percent.[423]

The treaty provided that heavy bombers equipped to carry only gravity nuclear bombs and SRAMs would be counted as signal nuclear warheads. In addition, an agreed number of heavy bombers could be removed form accountability, within the 1,600 delivery vehicle limit if they were converted to a non-nuclear capability. Heavy bombers equipped with long-range nuclear ALCMs had to be made distinguishable from other heavy bombers. In exchange for not including the Tupolev 22-M (Backfire) bomber in START, the Soviet Union declared that it would not deploy more than 300 air force and 200 naval Backfires, and that these bombers would not be given intercontinental capability.[424]

New long-range conventionally armed cruise missiles that are distinguishable from nuclear-armed ALCMs are not limited under the START I Treaty and may be deployed on any aircraft. But nuclear-armed ALCMs with a range in excess of 600 kilometers are affected by the treaty. Thus, each current and future U.S. heavy bomber equipped for long-range nuclear ALCMs would be counted as 10 nuclear warheads, but may actually carry up to 20. Each Soviet heavy bomber so equipped would be counted as carrying eight nuclear warheads, but may be equipped for up to 16. The United States can use the above counting rule in accounting for 150 heavy bombers; the Soviet Union could apply it to 180 heavy bombers. If the number of heavy bombers carrying long-range nuclear missiles exceeds these levels, they will be counted as carrying the number of missiles with which they are actually equipped. However, multiple-warhead long-range nuclear ALCMs are banned under the START I Treaty.[425]

Although Sea-Launched Cruise Missiles (SLCMs) are not constrained under the START I Treaty, each side provided the other with a declaration concerning long-range (over 600 kilometer) nuclear SLCMs. In accordance with these declarations, both parties declare annually the maximum number of SLCMs they will deploy in each of the following five years. The parties agreed not to deploy more than 880 nuclear SLCMs, and agreed that nuclear-armed SLCMs with a range of

300–600 kilometers will be the subject of confidential annual data exchanges. The sides also agreed not to produce or deploy nuclear SLCMs with multiple warheads.[426]

This treaty is the first between the superpowers in their more than four decades-old nuclear arms competition which imposes significant reductions in their strategic offensive nuclear arms, namely, ICBMs, SLBMs and ALBMs. With the implementation of the third and final phase of the reduction of the U.S. and Russian strategic nuclear arms under the START I Treaty by the end of 1999, the United States will have approximately 9,000 strategic nuclear warheads. At that time the Russian nuclear arsenal will consist of about 7,000 strategic warheads. By the end of 1999 the ballistic missile throw-weight capabilities for each party will be reduced to 3,600 metric tons.[427]

Since by the time of the signature of the START I Treaty the United States had deployed about 12,000 strategic nuclear warheads and the Soviet Union had deployed nearly 11,000, by the end of 1999 the treaty will reduce the U.S. strategic nuclear forces by 25 percent and the Russian strategic nuclear arms by 35 percent. Of course, these reductions in the superpowers' strategic nuclear arms constitute a significant step in their bilateral legal process for the elimination of their strategic nuclear weapons through gradual nuclear disarmament.[428]

Although both parties have failed by the START I Treaty to reduce their strategic offensive nuclear arms by half as they had agreed during the START negotiations, nevertheless, by virtue of the START I Treaty the superpowers' strategic nuclear warheads by the end of 1999 will be reduced by approximately 7,000. This reduction clearly means that the START I Treaty constitutes a significant international legal instrument in superpower nuclear disarmament. Furthermore, the treaty will reduce the ballistic missile throw-weight to 3,600 metric tons, which particularly considering Russia's missile throw-weight capability means a 50 percent reduction.[429]

It is of particular significance that, while the START I Treaty imposes reductions on the triad of the superpowers' strategic nuclear weapons, namely those land-based, sea-based and air-based, it also had a significant legal impact on the reduction in the Soviet land-based SS-18 ICBMs, which are the largest, most accurate and most destructive strategic nuclear weapons that have threatened the United States in a first-strike nuclear war scenario. In accordance with the treaty, the SS-18 ICBMs, which had 3,080 nuclear warheads at the time of the signature of the treaty, were to be reduced to 1,540. This means a 50 percent reduction in these lethal weapons, which are capable of annihilating the United States and the entire world in 30 minutes.[430]

START I Protocol on Elimination of Nuclear Arms. While Article VII of the START I Treaty generally regulates the conversion and elimination of the strategic offensive nuclear arms and weapon systems affected by the treaty, the treaty's protocol on conversion or elimination provides a specific legal procedural regime for this activity. Regarding mobile launchers of ICBMs and their launch canisters, Article I (2) of the protocol requires the parties to carry out the following actions: (a) They must remove the missile's reentry vehicle or vehicles; (b) they may remove the electronic and electromechanical devices of the missile's guidance and control system from the missile and its launcher canister; (c) they may remove the missile from its launch canister, remove the missile attachment devices from the launch canister, and disassemble the missile into stage; (d) they may remove propellant from stages; (e) they may remove or actuate auxiliary pyrotechnic devices installed on the missile and its launch canister; (f) they may remove penetration aids, including devices for their attachment and release; and, (g) they may remove propulsion units from the self-contained dispensing mechanism.

In accordance with Article I (4) to this protocol, the parties must also carry out the following actions: "(a) If solid fuel has not been removed from stages, the stages must be destroyed by explosive demolition or burned; (b) rocket nozzles and motor cases as well as the interstage skirts of a missile must be crushed, flattened, cut into two pieces of approximately equal size, or destroyed by explosion; and (c) the self-contained dispensing mechanism, as well as the front section, including the reentry vehicle platform and the front section shroud, must be crushed, flattened, cut into two pieces of approximately equal size, or destroyed by explosion."

Additionally, regarding the elimination process for mobile ICBM launch canisters, in accordance with Article I (5) the parties must crush, flatten, or destroy by explosion the body of the launch canister or, if the body of the launch canister is composed of segments, cut each of the segments into two pieces at a location that is not an assembly joint. If launcher canister's body is of unitary construction, it must be cut into two pieces of approximately equal size, or cut into three pieces so that pieces no less than 1.5 meters long are cut from the ends of its body. In accordance with Article I (1) and (2) of the protocol, the elimination of these systems must be carried out at the elimination facilities for ICBMs, and must be subject to on-site inspections by the parties' inspection teams.

Concerning silo launchers of ICBMs, silo training launchers and silo test launchers, Article II (1) of the protocol provides that elimination of these systems must be carried out in situ and be subject to verification by NTM. Pursuant to paragraph 2 of the above article, before the elimination process begins for silo launchers of ICBMs and silo test launchers, all missiles and shipping containers for ICBMs or ICBM stages, as well as all support equipment, must be removed at least 1,000 meters from each ICBM launcher to be eliminated.

Article II (6) of the protocol's elimination process for silo launchers of ICBMs or silo test launchers provides that: the silo door must be removed, dismantled or destroyed, and the silo headworks and the silo must be destroyed by excavation to a depth of no less than eight meters, or by explosion to a depth of no less than six meters; following the elimination of the ICBM silo, the silo may be filled to the level of the bottom of the hole created by excavation or explosion.

Paragraph 7 of the above article provides that the elimination of silo training ICBM launchers must be accomplished by removing, dismantling, or destroying the silo door and by destroying the silo headworks by excavation or explosion.

Article II (8) of the protocol requires that the elimination of a silo launcher of ICBMs, a silo training launcher, or a silo test launcher must be completed no later than 180 days after its initiation. This initiation, by virtue of paragraph 3 of the above article, commences as soon as the doors of the silo launchers of ICBMs, silo training launchers or silo test launchers have been opened. According to paragraph 9 of the above article, the ICBM silos must remain visible to national technical means of verification during the entire elimination process and for the following 90-day period, after which the silos may be filled with earth.

Article III (1) of the protocol provides that the elimination of road-mobile launchers of ICBMs, road-mobile training launchers, rail-mobile launchers of ICBMs, and rail-mobile training launchers must be carried out at conversion or elimination facilities for mobile launchers of ICBMs, and must be subject to on-site inspection. Article III (3) requires the parties to carry out the following actions with road-mobile and road-mobile training launchers: "(a) The erector-launcher mechanism and leveling supports must be removed from the launcher chassis; (b) framework of the erector-launcher mechanism on which the ICBM is mounted and erected must be cut at locations that are not assembly joints into two pieces of approximately equal size; (c) missile launch support equipment, including external instrumentation compartments, must be removed from the launcher chassis; (d) the mountings of the erector-launcher mechanism and of the launcher leveling supports must be cut off, and the launcher chassis and each mounting must be cut into two pieces of approximately equal size at a location that is not an assembly joint; (e) a portion of the self-propelled launcher chassis, at least 0.78 meters in length, must be cut off and that portion to the rear axle must be cut into two pieces of approximately equal size; and (f) if a road-mobile launcher of ICBMs is not mounted on a self-propelled launcher chassis, the trailer chassis must be cut into two pieces of approximately equal size and at a location that is not an assembly joint."

Considering rail-mobile launchers of ICBMs and rail-mobile training launchers, paragraph 4 of Article III provides that: "(a) The erector-launcher mechanism must be removed from the railcar (or flatcar); (b) the framework of the erector-launcher mechanism on which the ICBM is mounted and erected must be cut into two pieces of approximately equal size; (c) missile launch support equipment, including external instrumentation compartments, must be removed from the railcar (or flatcar); and (d) the railcar (or flatcar) must be cut into two pieces of approximately equal size." The elimination of fixed structures for mobile launchers of ICBMs, must, according to paragraph 7 of Article III, be carried out in situ and must be subject to NTM of verification. Paragraph 8 of the above article concerning the elimination of fixed structures for mobile launchers of ICBMs, requires that the superstructure of each fixed structure be dismantled or demolished and removed from its base or foundation, and that the base or foundation of each such structure be destroyed by excavation or explosion.

Article IV (1) of the protocol generally provides that the elimination of SLBM launchers must be carried out at conversion or elimination facilities for such launchers and must be subject to NTM of verification. Paragraph 2 of the same article provides that before beginning the elimination process for SLBM launchers, all missiles must be removed from such launchers. Paragraph 5 of Article IV requires for the elimination of SLBM launchers that the missile section be removed from the submarine, or that the missile launch tubes and all elements of their reinforcement, including hull liners and segments of circular structural members between the missile launch tubes, as well as the entire portion of the pressure hull, the entire portion of the outer hull, and the entire portion of the superstructure through which all the missile launch tubes pass and that contain all the missile launch-tube penetrations, be removed from the submarine. The missile launch tubes that have been removed must be cut into two pieces of approximately equal size and must remain in the open vicinity of the submarine until elimination is complete. Paragraph 7 of Article IV requires that a ballistic missile submarine must remain visible to NTM of verification during the entire elimination process for SLBM launchers.

Article V (1) of the protocol provides that the elimination of soft-site launchers must be carried out in situ and be verified by NTM. Pursuant to paragraph 2 of this article, before beginning the elimination of soft-site launchers, all missiles, launch canisters, and shipping containers for ICBMs or SLBMs or for their stages must be removed at least 1,000 meters from each soft-site launcher to be eliminated. Furthermore, in accordance with paragraph 4 of Article V, the elimination of soft-site launchers requires the following actions: "(a) All fixed launch and propellant-handling equipment, as well as erecting and handling equipment and fuel tanks associated with such a launcher must be removed at least 1,000 meters from the soft-site launcher to be eliminated; (b) the entire area, at least 20 meters in diameter and centered on the soft-site launchers, must be excavated or exploded to a depth of no less than two meters; and (c) to enhance safety, after the elimination is completed, the resultant hole may be filled with earth."

Article VI (1) and (2) of the protocol requires elimination or conversion of strategic bombers to be carried out at conversion or elimination facilities for such bombers and to be verified by NTM of verification and by on-site inspections. Furthermore, for the elimination of heavy bombers or former heavy bombers, paragraph 5 of the above article provides the following process: "(a) The tail section with tail surfaces must be severed from the fuselage at a location obviously not an assembly joint; (b) the wings must be separated from the fuselage at any location by any method; and (c) the remainder of the fuselage must be severed into two pieces, within the area of attachment of the wings to the fuselage, at a location obviously not an assembly joint." Article VI (6), (7) and (8) requires that during and upon the completion of their elimination strategic bombers must remain visible to NTM of verification and be subject to on-site inspections ensuring their elimination.

Paragraph 9 of Article VI provides a specific process for the conversion of strategic bombers, as follows: "(a) To convert a heavy bomber so that it is no longer equipped for long-range nuclear ALCMs, all weapons bays equipped to carry long-range nuclear ALCMs must be modified to render them incapable of doing so; all external attachment joints for long-range nuclear ALCMs and all external attachment joints for pylons for long-range nuclear ALCMs must be removed or modified to render them incapable of carrying long-range nuclear ALCMs; (b) to convert a heavy bomber so that it is no longer equipped for nuclear armaments, all weapons bays equipped to carry nuclear armaments must be modified to render them incapable of carrying them." In addition, all external attachment joints for nuclear armaments and all external attachment joints for pylons for nuclear armaments have to be modified or removed to render them incapable of carrying such armaments. In accordance with paragraph 13 Article VI, upon the completion of the conversion of heavy bombers, such converted bombers must not be flown, but must be moved directly to the viewing site at the conversion or elimination facility, where they will be inspected on-site.

Finally, Article IX of the protocol of conversion or elimination provides procedures for elimination of facilities, which, in accordance with paragraph 2 of Article XII of the inspection protocol to the START I Treaty, include: ICBM bases; submarine bases; ICBM loading facilities; SLBM loading facilities; repair facilities for ICBMs, SLBMs, or mobile launchers of ICBMs; storage facilities of ICBMs, SLBMs, mobile launchers of ICBMs, heavy nuclear weapons and their delivery systems so that they become inoperable for the purposes prohibited under the treaty.

The parties have failed to agree in this treaty on the complete destruction of their strategic nuclear warheads or the reuse of such nuclear warheads only for peaceful purposes. Thus, they may retain such nuclear warheads and they may reuse them on new nuclear weapon systems. Moreover, since the parties have primarily agreed to dismantle the delivery vehicles for their strategic nuclear weapons covered by the treaty, they may retain their launchers and boosters, and they may reuse them for new nuclear weapon systems not prohibited under the START I Treaty or for other purposes.[431]

START Verification System. To ensure the effective compliance of the parties with their legal obligations under the START I Treaty, the treaty has established a legal regime and verification system which consists of NTM of verification and on-site inspections. The verification structure created by the START I Treaty has been based upon the verification system of the INF Treaty, which has ensured the successful and effective implementation of that treaty. The verification legal regime of the INF Treaty, particularly in relation to on-site inspections, has provided both parties with the required legal experience and mutual trust showing that the implementation of their nuclear disarmament treaty arrangements is feasible and effective.[432]

Concerning the use of national technical means of verification, Article IX of the START I Treaty provides each party with the right to use its own NTM of verification in a manner consistent with generally recognized principles of international law. Article IX imposes upon the parties the legal obligation not to interfere with each other's NTM of verification of the implementation of the treaty. In particular, paragraph 3 of the above article requires both parties not to use concealment measures that impeded treaty verification. The parties' legal obligation not to use concealment measures includes the obligation not to use them at test ranges, including measures that result in the concealment of ICBMs, SLBMs, mobile launchers of ICBMs or SLBMs and their launchers during testing.[433]

According to Article X of the START I Treaty, during each flight test of an ICBM or SLBM, the parties have undertaken the legal obligation not to engage in any practice that denies full access to resulting telemetric information. In particular, both parties have assumed the legal duty to broadcast such information from test flights of ICBMs and SLBMs and not to engage in the use of encryption, jamming, or broadcasting telemetric information from an ICBM or SLBM using narrow directional beaming, and encapsulation of telemetric information, including the use of ejectable capsules or recoverable reentry vehicles. In addition, the parties have agreed to exchange telemetry tapes, interpretive data, and acceleration profiles for every flight test of a ballistic missile. This issue is specifically regulated by the protocol on telemetric information attached to the START I Treaty.[434]

To reinforce and supplement the use of their NTM of verification of the treaty, both parties have agreed to provide each other with data exchange and notifications on their strategic systems covered by the treaty. Before the signature of the treaty, the sides exchanged data on numbers, locations, and the technical characteristics of START-accountable strategic nuclear weapon systems and facilities. Both parties have also assumed the legal obligation under the treaty to provide each other with regular notifications and data updates on the above strategic nuclear weapons systems. To enhance the effectiveness of their NTM used for the verification of their compliance with the treaty, in accordance with Article XII of the treaty each party must, if the other party makes a request pursuant to the Notification Protocol attached to this treaty, carry out several cooperative measures, which, among others include: "(a) a display in the open of the road-mobile launchers of ICBMs located within restricted areas specified by the requesting party; (b) a display in the open of the rail-mobile launchers of ICBMs located at parking sites specified by the requesting party; and (c) a display in the open of all heavy bombers and former heavy bombers located within an air base specified by the requesting party."[435]

The START I Treaty has established a detailed legal system of on-site inspections capable of ensuring the effective compliance of the parties with their obligations under the treaty. Article XI of the treaty provides each party the right to conduct on-site inspections and continuous monitoring activities to verify compliance with the treaty's provisions. The treaty's Protocol on Inspections and Continuous Monitoring Activities, which is supplemented by 12 annexes specifically regulating the conduct of on-site inspections and continuous monitoring activities, provides a detailed and dynamic system of on-site inspections designed to ensure that both parties effectively comply with their treaty obligation.

Article XI of the START I Treaty, its Protocol on Inspections and Continuous Monitoring Activities, and the annexes attached to this protocol entail 12 types of on-site inspections and exhibitions, including continuous monitoring at mobile ICBM final assembly facilities and other cooperative measures. These on-site inspections are: "(1) baseline data inspections; (2) data update inspections; (3) new facility inspections; (4) suspect site inspections; (5) reentry vehicle inspections, (6) post-exercise dispersal inspections; (7) conversion or elimination inspections; (8) close-out inspections; (9) formerly declared facility inspections; (10) technical characteristics exhibitions, (11) distinguishability exhibitions; and (12) heavy bomber baseline exhibitions."[436]

To carry out their on-site inspections and monitoring on each other's territory, the parties have agreed that such inspections and continuous monitoring to verify compliance with the START I Treaty be conducted by their own inspectors and monitors on each other's territory. The list of inspectors must not contain at any one time more than 400 individuals, and the list of monitors must not contain at any one time more than 300 individuals. To exercise their functions effectively to implement the START I Treaty, the inspectors and monitors, including their air crew members operating the airplanes transporting these functionaries are accorded the required immunities and privileges.[437]

The START I Treaty establishes a continuous monitoring at the perimeter and portals of each party's mobile ICBM assembly facilities. The treaty allows the United States to establish two monitoring facilities in the Soviet Union, including one at Votkinsk, which is the final assembly facility for the SS-25, and the other at Pavlograd, the final assembly facility for the SS-24. Similarly, Russia has the right to monitor the Thiokol strategic operations facility at Promontory, Utah, which is the final assembly facility for the accountable stage of the MX ICBM. Such monitoring will also be established at any future U.S. and Russian facilities at which mobile ICBM assembly takes palce.[438]

Under the START I Treaty each party has the right to carry out 15 on-site inspections per year to update data — at any identified aircraft, submarine, or ballistic missile base or deployment area for mobile ICBMs — by which each side can verify compliance with limits on numbers and physical properties. The treaty allows each party to carry out ten additional on-site inspections a year, which allow their inspectors to verify that the number of nuclear warheads deployed on their ballistic missiles does not exceed the treaty limits. These ten additional inspections are to be done on short notice. Specifically, within nine hours of the time the inspectors arrive in the country under inspection they are to be transported to the base they select. Upon arrival, they will designate the missile to be inspected, which must remain buttoned up until the inspectors can look at it. Inspection must begin within eight hours. In essence, these "challenge" inspections add confidence that the provisions on warhead numbers and on downloading are obeyed by the parties. These inspections also guard against uploading warheads and swapping old types of ballistic missiles for new ones.[439]

In addition to the use of NTM and on-site inspections and continuous monitoring activities designed to verify the parties' effective compliance with their legal obligations under the START I Treaty, to promote the treaty's objectives and its effective implementation, Article XV requires the parties to establish a Joint Compliance and Inspection Commission. The parties have agreed to meet, if either party so requests, within the framework of this commission to: "(a) resolve questions relating to compliance with the obligations assumed; (b) agree upon such additional measures as may be necessary to improve the viability and effectiveness of this treaty; and (c) resolve questions related to the application of relevant provisions of this treaty to a new kind of strategic offensive nuclear weapon." According to the Protocol on the Joint Compliance and Inspection Commission attached to the START I Treaty, within 30 days of treaty's signature, the above commission was to begin to meet to start implementing verification measures, such as the review of site diagrams and the details of the exchange of telemetry tapes.[440]

Of importance to the beginning of the treaty's implementation soon after its signature was the requirement, according to documents associated with the treaty, that the following actions occur before the treaty's ratification: "(a) lists of inspectors exchanged and approved; (b) exhibitions of strategic nuclear delivery vehicles; (c) photographs of certain equipment exchanged; (d) engineering data provided to facilitate establishment of the continuous monitoring sites, and (e) telemetry issues addressed, including demonstration tapes and equipment, exchange of examples of interpretive data and acceleration profiles." Additionally, 120 days after the signature of the treaty, both parties were obliged to cease encryption and jamming practices with respect to their strategic nuclear arms and systems covered by the treaty. Both parties have already carried out practice inspections.[441]

In addition to its verification system of NTM and on-site inspections intended to ensure its effective implementation and to enhance the viability and effectiveness of the START I Treaty, Article XVI of the treaty requires both parties not to assume any international obligations or undertakings that would conflict with treaty provisions. Both parties have also agreed to hold consultations within the framework of the Joint Compliance and Inspection Commission to resolve any ambiguities that may arise in this regard. Furthermore, in the interest of the viability and effectiveness of the treaty, in their First Agreed Statement attached to it, both parties agreed not to transfer strategic offensive arms to third states subject to the limitations of the treaty.

In view of the preceding legal analysis of the verification structure and system adopted by the START I Treaty, the treaty's verification system, consisting of the use of NTM of verification and on-site inspections, can ensure the effective compliance of the parties with their treaty obligations. The use of advanced NTM of verification possessed by both parties, such as satellite surveillance systems, ensures the effective implementation of the START I Treaty; the conduct of on-site inspections and continuous monitoring activities by the parties on each other's territories provides a dynamic verification system capable of further guarding against violations of the treaty. The verification regime created by the START I Treaty, which has been essentially built on the verification system of the INF Treaty and its legal experience and success, is capable of ensuring the transparency of the parties to verification, and the permission of on-site inspections in particular provides both parties with intrusive and dynamic verification means for the effective implementation of the START I Treaty.[442]

The Legal Impact of the START I Treaty on the U.S.–Soviet Nuclear Disarmament Process. A legal evaluation of its impact on U.S.–Soviet bilateral nuclear disarmament clearly shows that the START I Treaty constitutes a significant development to this end. Indeed, the fact that both parties are obliged to reduce through elimination and conversion their lethal strategic offensive nuclear arms by approximately 7,000 strategic nuclear warheads, which at the time of the signature of the treaty numbered about 23,000, leads to the conclusion that the START I Treaty requires a substantial reduction in the U.S.–Soviet strategic nuclear arsenals. Despite these reductions, both parties will still have deployed nearly 16,000 strategic nuclear warheads, which are more than enough to destroy not only themselves, but civilization itself many times over in a U.S.–Soviet nuclear war.[443]

The end of the Cold War has reduced the likelihood of a direct and intentional nuclear war between the nuclear superpowers. Reduced tensions in this regard have greatly facilitated the legal process for the conclusion of the START I Treaty. The United States and Russia through this treaty are moving in the right legal direction to reduce the strategic offensive nuclear weapon systems that have enabled them to have a first-strike nuclear capability against each other. In essence, the START I Treaty is designed to serve the legal objective to enhance its signatories' security against a nuclear first strike by reducing such strategic weapons in a gradual and balanced manner. The strategic nuclear weapons covered by the START I Treaty constitute the most destabilizing weapons in relation to superpower security against a nuclear first strike. These weapons, particularly the land-based ICBM, present the principal threat to the survivability of a nuclear retaliatory deterrent.[444]

Although verification of nuclear disarmament treaties cannot be absolute, the legal regime of verification measures established by this treaty not only ensures its effective implementation, but also, if one party covertly violates its treaty obligations on a scale and in a way that could threaten the security of the other by acquiring a significant strategic advantage, the other party by virtue of the treaty's verification system could promptly discover such a violation.[445]

The international law created by the START I Treaty provides the required legal framework and background for the facilitation of the easier and quicker conclusion of further superpower treaty arrangements requiring deeper reductions in their strategic nuclear arsenals, including the total elimination of those arsenals. The international law embodied in the START I Treaty supports the legal argument forwarded by this study that, in view of the end of the Cold War which has deflated the mutual threat of nuclear war between the nuclear superpowers, and which has established a more cooperative and friendly relationship, in terms of international law, the total and comprehensive elimination of all types of American and Russian nuclear weapons is both feasible and effective.

Although the START I Treaty generally had a positive legal impact on U.S.–Soviet denuclearization, the treaty has some shortcomings which could undermine its role in reversing the superpower arms race and its legal objective to reduce strategic nuclear weapons to the extent that it does, including its general legal impact on superpower denuclearization. Some of these shortcomings have been noted earlier. The treaty also requires reductions in strategic nuclear weapons already deployed. Except the prohibition on the development and deployment of future mobile ICBMs, the treaty does not impose a ban on the production and deployment of nuclear weapon systems under development at the time of its signature, or on newer ones to be developed in the future. The treaty has also failed to prohibit the modernization of strategic nuclear arms remaining after their reductions in accord with the treaty.[446] As a result of these failures, by the time of the completion of the final stage of the elimination of the strategic nuclear weapons covered by the treaty, namely, by the end of 1999, the structure of the superpower strategic nuclear forces will comprise more sophisticated nuclear weapon systems.[447]

According to its Article XVII (2), the START I Treaty will remain in force for 15 years unless superseded by an agreement requiring deeper reductions in superpower strategic offensive nuclear arms. Thus, the START I Treaty will probably remain in force until the year 2007. One year before the expiration of the 15-year period, the parties must meet to consider the extension of the treaty, which upon their relevant agreement can extend it for successive five-year periods if the treaty is not superseded by one further reducing their strategic nuclear forces.

During the START I Treaty, both parties have the right to alter it by their agreed amendments pursuant to its Article XVIII. Thus, the START I Treaty will remain flexible. Article XVII (3) provides each party with the right to withdraw from the START I Treaty if it decides that extraordinary events related to the treaty have jeopardized its supreme interests, provided that the withdrawing party notifies the other party six months before its final withdrawal, including a statement of those extraordinary events.

In connection with the above provision of the treaty, the Soviet side in its statement of June 13, 1991, which has been attached to the START I Treaty, declared that the START I Treaty may be effective and viable only under the conditions of compliance with the ABM Treaty of 1972. This statement added that the extraordinary events referred to in Article XVII (3) of the START I Treaty also include events related to withdrawal by one of the parties from the ABM Treaty, or related to its material breach. Thus, the Soviet side has linked the viability and success of the START I Treaty to the adherence of the United States to its legal obligations under the ABM Treaty, which prohibits the development, testing and the final deployment of the SDI program.[448]

The Bush-Yeltsin 1992–1993 Summitry and Its Impact on U.S.–Russian Denuclearization

The Bush Unilateral Nuclear Disarmament Initiatives and START II Proposals (January 28, 1992)

In September 1991, President George Bush and President Mikhail Gorbachev announced unilateral measures for the withdrawal of mainly tactical nuclear weapons.[449] By January 1992, the Soviet Union had legally and officially ceased to exist. Although Russia has emerged as a new nuclear superpower, Russia is facing severe economic problems. Its President, Boris Yeltsin, has on occasion demonstrated his willingness to be an ally and partner with the West and particularly with the United States. In view of this situation, President Bush, during his State of the Union address to Congress on January 18, 1992, announced a number of unilateral measures affecting U.S. strategic nuclear weapon systems in the post–Cold War era. He also proposed further, deeper reductions in the U.S. and former–Soviet strategic nuclear weapons in addition to those required by the START I Treaty.

President Bush announced that the United States would acquire only 20 B-2 nuclear-capable strategic bombers, although his administration had previously decided to acquire 75 such bombers. He further stated that his administration would cancel the Midgetman small ICBM program, and halt production of new strategic nuclear warheads for SLBMs, which refers to ceasing production of the Trident II D5/W88 MIRVed SLBM. Furthermore, President Bush announced his decision to cease all new production of the MX (Peacekeeper) MIRVed ICBM and not to acquire any additional advanced nuclear cruise missiles.[450]

In addition to these unilateral measures, President Bush made the following proposals on the reduction in the U.S. strategic nuclear weapons contingent on a Russian response: (1) The U.S. would eliminate all of its MX ICBMs, accounting for 500 strategic nuclear warheads; (2) it would reduce the number of nuclear warheads on its Minuteman ICBMs to one, thus eliminating another 500 strategic nuclear warheads; (3) it would reduce the number of nuclear warheads on its SLBMs by approximately one-third, a reduction of current sea-based strategic nuclear weapons by more than 1,300 nuclear warheads; and (4) the U.S. would convert a substantial portion of its strategic bombers to primarily conventional military use. President Bush pointed out that the United States would agree to make the above reductions if Russia agreed to eliminate all former Soviet land-based multiple-warhead ICBMs.[451]

The Bush proposals on the reduction in U.S. and former Soviet strategic nuclear weapons constituted a basis for the negotiation and conclusion of a START II Treaty. Their final adoption by such a treaty would mean that the U.S. and the former Soviet strategic nuclear weapons would be reduced to approximately 5,000 warheads for each side, in addition to reductions required by the START I Treaty. Such a legal development would mean the reduction of the superpowers' strategic nuclear arms by approximately half, in addition to reductions required by the START I Treaty.[452]

The Yeltsin Response: His Unilateral Nuclear Disarmament Initiatives and Start Treaty proposals (January 29, 1992)

Almost immediately after the announcement of the Bush proposals, Russian President Boris Yeltsin responded by announcing a number of initiatives and proposals, which can be considered more radical than those of President Bush. President Yeltsin announced that Russia had taken off alert about 600 land and sea-based strategic nuclear missiles carrying a total of 1,250 nuclear warheads. In addition, he stated that Russia was prepared to eliminate 130 land-based ICBM silos, and that it had already halted programs for developing or modernizing several types of offensive strategic nuclear weapons.[453]

Yeltsin also announced that he would halt the production of the TU-160 "Black Jack" and TU-95MS "Bear" heavy strategic bombers. Russia would also cease building long-range air and sea-based cruise nuclear missiles, would not design new cruise missiles and would destroy existing sea-based cruise nuclear missiles if the United States did the same. Yeltsin stated that the launching systems aboard six submarines armed with nuclear missiles would be dismantled, and that Russia had cut by half the number of nuclear missile submarines on combat patrols, and was prepared to stop such patrols altogether if the United States followed suit.[454]

Regarding reductions in strategic nuclear arsenals beyond those required by the START I Treaty, Yeltsin did not directly accept Bush's chief proposal, which called for elimination of all U.S. and former Soviet land-based, multiple-warhead ICBMs. Nevertheless, the Russian president stated that he would propose to President Bush during their meeting in Washington on February 1, 1992, an overall proposal for strategic nuclear arms reductions. In this regard, Yeltsin stated that, in accordance with his overall proposal, both the United States and

Russia would be required to reduce their strategic nuclear weapons to only 2,500 nuclear warheads each.[455] This Yeltsin proposal for a START II Treaty with the United States embraced a very drastic measure for the sharp reduction of strategic nuclear weapons. It was more far-reaching than that proposed by Bush, which would have left each side with about 5,000 strategic nuclear warheads.

The Russian leader reiterated his nation's adherence to the 1972 ABM Treaty. However, Yeltsin announced Russia's readiness to develop, create and jointly operate a global defense security system with the United States against a ballistic nuclear attack, a system which could be based on the U.S. SDI program. Although Yeltsin did not specify how such a system might work, he nevertheless made clear that such a system of global defense would only be deployed instead of the SDI program aimed at building a space-based defense system under American control. In view of this Yeltsin proposal for a global defense system against a ballistic missile nuclear attack, Russia seemed to be making a substantial policy shift on ballistic missile defenses, which the former Soviet Union viewed as an effort by the United States to gain strategic advantage.[456]

President Yeltsin also pointed out that Russia and the United States should no longer target each other with nuclear missiles. To this end, Yeltsin announced that Russia would no longer target American cities and military targets with its ICBMs.[457] Initially, the United States did not reciprocate. But in 1994 Russia and the United States signed an agreement on that point.[458] Yeltsin renewed his proposal to the United States to join Russia in ceasing all underground nuclear weapon testing, a significant step toward a U.S.–Russian CTBT that the Bush administration rejected. The Russian president also proposed the establishment of a new International Monitoring Agency to monitor nuclear disarmament as well as the production of nuclear weapon materials. In the end, Yeltsin stated that Russia would immediately ratify the START I Treaty and would implement it within three years, rather than in the seven years allowed by the treaty.[459]

The Yeltsin-Bush Moscow Summit Meeting (January 1993) and the Signature of the START II Treaty

START II Treaty Content and Objectives. After intensive negotiations, on January 3, 1993, during their Moscow summit meeting, Presidents Yeltsin and Bush signed the START II Treaty.[460] Although the United States has ratified the treaty, Russia has not. The treaty requires both parties to make deeper reductions in their strategic nuclear arsenals than those required by the START I Treaty of July 1991. In essence the START II Treaty constitutes a dynamic legal measure for nuclear disarmament between the two nuclear superpowers.[461]

Upon the entry into force of the START II Treaty, the United States and Russia will implement its legal terms in two stages. In the first stage, within the seven-year period following entry into force of the START II Treaty, and in combination with the ratification of the START I Treaty of 1991, both parties have assumed the legal obligation to reduce their strategic nuclear forces to no more than an overall total number of warheads for each between 3,800 and 4,250 (as each nation shall determine), or such lower number as each nation shall decide. Assuming the START II Treaty's ratification in 1993, the complete implementation of the first phase of the reductions required by the START II Treaty would have taken place in 2000. Accordingly, by 2000 each party would have reduced its strategic nuclear offensive arms to no more than 4,250 warheads. The reductions in strategic nuclear warheads during the first stage as required by the START II Treaty would have affected the triad of the parties' strategic nuclear forces.[462]

In accordance with the second stage of the implementation of the START II Treaty, which would be completed no later than January 1, 2003 (or by the end of the year 2000 if the United States could contribute to the financing of the destruction or elimination of strategic offensive arms in Russia), both parties would: (a) reduce their strategic nuclear warheads to between 3,000 and 3,500 each (as each nation would determine) or such lower number as each nation would decide; (b) eliminate all of their MIRVed ICBMs; and (c) reduce their SLBM warheads to between no more than 1,700–1,750 (as each nation would determine).[463]

To calculate the totals of strategic nuclear weapons on the basis of the reductions required by the START II Treaty, and particularly with respect to such weapons carried by heavy (strategic) bombers, the treaty provides the following procedures and measures: (a) The number of warheads for heavy bombers with nuclear roles would be the number of nuclear weapons which they are equipped to carry; and (b) under agreed procedures, heavy bombers, not to exceed 100, that were never equipped for long-range nuclear ALCMs and that are reoriented to conventional roles would not count against the overall total established by this agreement. The START II Treaty provides that: (1) Such heavy bombers would be based separately from heavy bombers with nuclear roles; (2) no nuclear weapons would be located at bases for heavy bombers with conventional roles; (3) such aircraft and crews would not train or exercise for nuclear missions; and (4) current inspection procedures already agreed on in the START I Treaty would help affirm that these bombers have conventional roles.[464]

The START II Treaty incorporates the verification procedures and means of NTM and on-site inspections already provided and described in detail by the START I Treaty.[465] It is of particular legal importance that effective verification of the implementation of nuclear disarmament agreements between the United States and the Soviet Union had been a major legal obstacle which prevented them from proceeding with their denuclearization. The end of the Cold War, the effective implementation of the INF Treaty, the mutual trust and confidence building between these nations, and above all their legal acceptance and openness to advanced national technical means of verification and particularly the adoption and permission of intrusive on-site inspections, have marked an unprecedented legal breakthrough in the effective verification of nuclear disarmament agreements between the nuclear superpowers. In essence, the issue of the effective verification of nuclear disarmament agreements between the nuclear superpowers is no longer a major legal obstacle to their denuclearization.

This conclusion can be safely supported by the fact that during the negotiation of the START II Treaty, the issue of the effective verification of the treaty did not even become a focus of contention. The new international law of verification procedures consisting primarily of advanced NTM and intrusive on-site inspections, which has been developed by the nuclear disarmament treaty law-making of the nuclear superpowers, clearly supports the legal argument that under the new international law of nuclear disarmament not only a superpower total nuclear disarmament, but also comprehensive global nuclear disarmament is both legally possible and effective.

The START II Treaty, in conjunction with the START I Treaty, constitutes a major legal breakthrough in the U.S.–Russian legal process of denuclearization. Even though the START II Treaty is separate from but builds upon the START I Treaty of 1991,[466] both treaties, assuming their entry into force by their prompt ratification by the parties, would effect a dramatic reduction in the superpower strategic nuclear forces by the completion of their implementation by the end of the year 2003. While the United States possesses 11,602 strategic nuclear warheads, and Russia (including those deployed in the former Soviet Republics of Ukraine, Kazakhstan and Belarus) possesses 10,877, after the implementation of the START I Treaty, the United States and Russia will be left with 8,592 strategic nuclear weapons each.[467] By the end of the year 2003 in the final phase of the implementation of the START II Treaty, the United States and Russian would each possess no more than 3,500 strategic nuclear weapons.[468]

The START II Treaty by the time of the completion of its implementation in the year 2003 would eliminate all multiple-warhead and land-based ICBMs on both sides. Russia would eliminate its SS-18 and SS-24 land-based multiple-warhead ICBMs. The United States would eliminate its MX and Minuteman II land-based ICBMs. The United States by the end of the year 2003 would have downloaded its 500 Minuteman III land-based ICBMs from three strategic nuclear warheads each to one each. Similarly, Russia by the end of the year 2003 would retain only 500 single-warhead land-based mobile SS-25 ICBMs.[469]

In addition to reductions in both parties' air-based ICBMs and strategic bombers, the treaty requires the United States and Russia to reduce their respective sea-based ICBMs. Russia would retain 1,744 submarine-launched ICBMs, the United States would keep 1,728 such weapons. Thus the treaty calls for the United States to reduce by half its sea-based ICBMs; it would further reduce its D-5 Trident submarine-launched strategic missiles from eight warheads to four.[470]

Impact of the START II Treaty on the U.S.–Russian Denuclearization Legal Process. Based on the preceding analysis, the START II Treaty in combination with the START I Treaty of 1991 constitutes a significant legal measure in the

U.S.–Russian bilateral nuclear disarmament process under the rule of international law. Indeed, the fact that the two nuclear superpowers by virtue of the two treaties, if fully implemented, would each be left with no more than 3,500 strategic nuclear warheads by the year 2003, means that both the United States and Russia would reduce their current strategic offensive nuclear arms by approximately 60 percent. Such a reduction and elimination of their strategic nuclear arsenals would clearly constitute an unprecedented and dramatic legal breakthrough in their bilateral nuclear disarmament process.

A critical evaluation of the legal impact of the START II Treaty on superpower disarmament clearly leads to the conclusion that by the end of the Cold War and by the beginning of the new post–Cold War era, these former nuclear rivals, whose constant nuclear competition and threatened confrontation had brought the entire world to the brink of its nuclear annihilation, have entered a new era of denuclearization under the rule of international law. This legal development shows that the evolving new Russo-American legal relationship in this sphere not only further diminishes the threat of a superpower nuclear war, but also enhances the prospects of world peace and security.

Notwithstanding the recognition that the START II Treaty calls for deep reductions in both nuclear superpowers' land-based, air-based and sea-based strategic nuclear weapons, it is of particular legal importance that the START II Treaty requires both parties to eliminate all of their land-based (silo-based) multiple-warhead ICBMs.

The elimination of all U.S.–Russian land-based multiple warhead MIRVed ICBMs under the START II Treaty would constitute an unprecedented legal breakthrough in the denuclearization of the nuclear superpowers. These strategic nuclear weapons have constituted the backbone of the superpowers' strategic offensive nuclear arms in their respective arsenals. These are the most accurate, sophisticated and destructive nuclear weapons which have been designed by the nuclear superpowers to initiate a preemptive nuclear first strike against each other.[471] The elimination of these multiple warhead MIRVed ICBMs would not only greatly reduce the superpowers' strategic nuclear forces, but would also radically reduce the possibility of a superpower nuclear war, regardless of who is in power in the Kremlin or Washington, since both nations would be deprived of the strategic nuclear arms required for a preemptive first strike.[472]

The START II Treaty would exercise a positive legal impact on the reduction of the superpowers' strategic nuclear arsenals, yet even if the treaty were fully implemented by the year 2003, both Russia and the United States would each still possess approximately 3,000–3,500 strategic nuclear weapons. Thus, under a fully implemented treaty, Russia and the United States would retain a combined total of 6,000–7,000 strategic nuclear weapons at the beginning of the 21st century.

Although a nuclear war between Russia and the United States as a political issue now appears remote, the possibility of a nuclear war between the two as a strictly technical military issue remains, even though it has been significantly reduced. In spite of the end of the Cold War and the evolving political cooperation and partnership between Russia and the United States, it cannot be precluded that uncertain and unforeseeable regional and international crises and most importantly leadership changes in Russia might again bring Russia and the United States on a collision course. If such a course evolved to a nuclear confrontation, both Russia and the United States would have several thousand strategic nuclear warheads, enough to destroy each other and the entire world many times over.

Although President Yeltsin proposed to President Bush to eliminate all of the Russian and American land-based and submarine-based strategic nuclear weapons by the conclusion of the START II Treaty, President Bush rejected this proposal. The START II Treaty also fails to prohibit both parties from developing new types of more advanced and sophisticated strategic nuclear weapons in the future.[473]

In spite of these failures of START II Treaty, it constitutes a major nuclear disarmament treaty between the nuclear superpowers. In particular, the conclusion of this treaty and its positive impact on the U.S.–Russian bilateral legal process for denuclearization shows that the new international law of nuclear disarmament has become a significantly valuable instrument and a positive force which can ensure that a U.S.–Russian total and comprehensive nuclear disarmament can be both possible and effective under international law.

The Yeltsin-Clinton Summitry and the Continuation of U.S.–Russian Nuclear Disarmament (1993–1997)

THE YELTSIN-CLINTON MOSCOW SUMMIT (JANUARY 1994) AND ITS RESULTS

President Bill Clinton has been actively involved in the continuation of nuclear disarmament between the United States and Russia since he took office in January 1993. The Clinton administration has focused its efforts on building more confidence measures and developing a new partnership for peace with Russia and the other former Soviet republics, including the former Warsaw Pact member states in the context of NATO.[474]

During their Moscow summit meeting in mid–January 1994, President Yeltsin and President Clinton issued a bilateral statement known as the Moscow Declaration. Based on the Moscow Declaration, both parties agreed to re-aim their strategic nuclear missiles at open ocean areas instead of at each other. The Moscow Declaration is a significant legal measure because for the first time since the dawn of the nuclear age and the eruption of the Cold War the United States and Russia will not operate their strategic nuclear forces in a manner targeting each other as adversaries. The two nuclear superpowers are able, by using their computer technology, to retarget each other with their nuclear missiles within minutes in a U.S.–Russian crisis. Nevertheless, the Moscow Declaration takes a positive legal step toward removing the threat of a U.S.–Russian nuclear war and its attendant global devastation. The Moscow Declaration also greatly assists in strengthening further the peaceful cooperation and existence between the nuclear superpowers.[475]

During their Moscow summit meeting, Presidents Clinton and Yeltsin agreed to a nuclear testing moratorium, and called on the other nuclear powers to refrain from carrying out underground nuclear explosions. They also called for the negotiation and conclusion of a comprehensive test ban treaty, preferably by March 1995, when the conference for the review and extension of the NPT would begin. Although the United States, Russia, France and Britain had accepted a moratorium on nuclear testing, in October 1993 China conducted an underground nuclear test.[476]

During the Yeltsin-Clinton Moscow summit, the parties began to negotiate an accord which would permit them to conduct on-site inspections of each other's facilities where they store the plutonium triggers from dismantled nuclear warheads. Such an accord would assist the nuclear superpowers in calculating how much plutonium has been removed from their dismantled warheads during the reduction of their nuclear arsenals. This accord was completed and signed in March 1994. It could represent the beginning of a new international control regime over plutonium, which is the basic building block of nuclear weapons.[477]

During the Moscow summit in January 1994, Russia, the United States and Ukraine, in conformity with the Lisbon Protocol of May 1992, signed a trilateral agreement that Ukraine would transfer all of its nuclear weapons to Russia within seven years, and as quickly as three years undertake legal obligation to be a nuclear weapons-free state. After the Moscow summit, the Ukraine Parliament ratified the START I Treaty and Ukraine acceded to the NPT. The former Soviet Republics of Belarus and Kazakhstan have ratified the START Treaty and have joined the NPT. Belarus and Kazakhstan have also agreed to transfer all of their nuclear weapons to Russia. Thus, Russia has become the sole heir to the former Soviet nuclear weapons, and thus a nuclear superpower. Russia has also stated that it has become the legal successor to the former Soviet Union's obligations and rights under international arms control and disarmament agreements.[478]

The Yeltsin-Clinton Moscow Summit (April 1996)

The Moscow summit meetings between President Yeltsin and President Clinton in April 1996 did not produce further nuclear arms reductions between the superpowers. This summit, and with the participation of the other members of the Group of Seven (France, Germany, Italy, Japan, Canada and Britain, in addition to the United States), dealt primarily with issues involving the nonproliferation of nuclear material. At the summit, the participants reached a common understanding on nuclear material accounting and control, and on the physical protection of nuclear material. They called for the urgent ratification by all states of the Convention on the Physical Protection of Nuclear Material. The participants also agreed on several measures to combat the illegal trafficking of nuclear material, and they endorsed various measures related to the production, storage and disposal of weapon-based fissile material.[479]

Legal Dynamics and Prospects for a U.S.–Russian Total Nuclear Disarmament in the post–Cold War Era

Due to their Cold War relations, their relentless nuclear arms race and the constant threat of their nuclear confrontation, by 1985 the nuclear superpowers possessed more than 50,000 nuclear weapons. For the first time in human history two nations possessed enough explosive power to destroy both themselves and all of human civilization many times over. Their uncontrolled nuclear arms race and the constant threat of nuclear confrontation had placed the superpowers on a collision course that brought the entire world to the brink of nuclear annihilation. In view of the superpowers' nuclear predicament, many experts, including the renowned Sovietologist, George Kennan, the architect of America's Cold War containment doctrine, had clearly expressed the fear that the deepening of the confrontation between the superpowers was leading to a global thermonuclear war.[480]

Although in the pre–1985 period the superpowers were deeply involved in their nuclear arms race, during that period the United States and the Soviet Union, to control and manage their nuclear behavior and adversarial relationship and most importantly to maintain their nuclear peace, resorted to the instrumental value of international law by developing and adopting the bilateral legal model of nuclear arms control. Notwithstanding the recognition that this legal model and approach have played a positive role in the management of their nuclear relationship, and might have prevented nuclear war, it apparently failed to promote the legal concept of nuclear disarmament between the superpowers, and thus materialized its legal objectives. As a result, by 1985 both superpowers had built more nuclear weapons with more sophisticated and destructive capabilities. By 1985 the United States and the Soviet Union had failed to eliminate even a single nuclear warhead from their vast nuclear arsenals. This failure clearly shows that nuclear arms control is not nuclear disarmament.

Mikhail Gorbachev's rise to Soviet power in 1985 set the central stage for changing not only the Soviet Union itself and the Soviet bloc, but also for changing the bipolar world system and its dangerous and regressive political and military rules upon which the East-West political, ideological and threatened nuclear confrontation had been based and conducted since the start of the Cold War and the beginning of the superpowers' nuclear arms race. Gorbachev managed to begin U.S.–Soviet nuclear disarmament by signing the INF and the START I and II Treaties. In addition, Gorbachev, by his 1986 proposal for the year 2000 global nuclear disarmament, showed his determination to create a nuclear weapons-free world by the end of the 20th century.

In addition to the contributions of the INF and START Treaties to the elimination of U.S.–Soviet nuclear weapons, these treaties have created a dynamic new international law of nuclear disarmament, which shows that a U.S.–Russian nuclear disarmament is both feasible and legally effective. The legal adoption of intrusive verification measures and procedures involving advanced and sophisticated available NTM, and especially on-site inspections, has created a legally-based international verification system which ensures the effective implementation of nuclear disarmament treaties between the nuclear superpowers.

The dissolution of the Soviet Union and the end of Soviet communism by the end of December 1991 bequeathed to the newly formed Commonwealth of Independent States a vast nuclear arsenal of approximately 27,000 strategic and tactical nuclear warheads. The disintegration of the former Soviet Union as a nuclear superpower has raised significant questions as to the safety and control of the former Soviet nuclear weapons, and about the potential danger of the unauthorized possession and use of such weapons, including their illegitimate transfer to third states trying to acquire nuclear weapons. The disintegration of the Soviet Union has also raised crucial questions about the illegitimate and clandestine transfer of former Soviet nuclear weapons–grade materials and technologies and the potential immigration of former Soviet nuclear scientists to would-be nuclear weapon states.

These problems of international concern, seem to have been so far responsibly handled by the Commonwealth of Independent States. The fact that Russia has become the sole nuclear heir of the former Soviet Union, and the fact that the Republics of Belarus, Ukraine and Kazakhstan have acceded to the NPT and have agreed to transfer all nuclear weapons deployed in their respective territories to Russia shows that Russia as the sole successor to the former Soviet nuclear arsenal has become a new nuclear superpower. Russian President Boris Yeltsin, with his January 1992 unilateral nuclear disarmament initiatives and proposals, demonstrated his determination to continue Gorbachev's legacy of U.S.–Russian nuclear disarmament.

Both the January 1992 Yeltsin-Bush unilateral initiatives and measures for further reducing their nuclear arsenals, and the Bush-Yeltsin Camp David meeting in February 1992 by which the two leaders established a new political partnership and alliance between the superpowers show the political willingness of the two nations to take meaningful steps in disarmament in the emerging new post–Cold War nuclear era. In conclusion, this evolving unique and dynamic Russo-American political relationship provides the required strategic legal environment for the elimination of all U.S.–Russian nuclear weapons through the rule of international law.

Above all, the two START treaties show that the nuclear superpowers have entered a new era of denuclearization. Indeed, the fact that both Russia and the United States by virtue of the two treaties would be obliged to reduce their strategic nuclear weapon arsenals to no more than 3,500 warheads by the year 2003 leaves no doubt that the nuclear superpowers are legally committed to nuclear disarmament under the rule of international law.

In general legal terms the INF Treaty of 1987 (whose effective implementation has already eliminated all of the U.S.–Soviet INF nuclear weapons on a global basis), the recent Soviet-American unilateral initiatives and measures for making deep reductions in their tactical nuclear arsenals, and the signature of the START I Treaty and the START II Treaty lead to the conclusion that treaty agreements between the superpowers have created a dynamic body of international disarmament law. In particular, the fact that both nuclear superpowers have undertaken the legal obligation under the START I and START II Treaties to reduce their current total of approximately 20,000 strategic nuclear warheads to no more than a total of 3,500 for each side by the year 2003, and the fact that pursuant to the START II Treaty both Russian and the United States are legally obliged to eliminate all of their land-based (silo-based) MIRVed multiple warhead strategic nuclear missiles by the year 2003, clearly show that these treaty arrangements constitute dynamic legal measures of enormous positive effect in the superpower denuclearization process in the post–Cold War era.

The evolving Russo-American nuclear relationship, political alliance and partnership has created a new strategic and legal environment between the nuclear superpowers in relation to their nuclear postures. The superpowers' constant threat of nuclear confrontation during the Cold War years no longer exists, and the legal process for their nuclear de-escalation and disengagement, including their nuclear building down, has already begun. To this extent, it is important that Russia, under the leadership of President Yeltsin, has officially declared that the United States, and generally the Western military and nuclear establishment, are no longer considered enemies by Russia. One must recognize the legal impact of the START treaties and other U.S.–Russian nuclear disarmament measures on the disarmament process between the superpowers, as well as their general enhancement of world peace and security, in spite of sufficient weapons remaining in the superpower nuclear arsenals to destroy civilization.

Although a direct and intentional nuclear war between Russia and the United States is unlikely in the post–Cold War era, regional and global developments might bring future crises and conflicts leading to new nuclear confrontations and possible nuclear war. The continued existence of nuclear weapons will always raise the possibility of their use. Therefore, until the last nuclear weapon has been effectively eliminated, and until a fully nuclear weapon disarmed world has been achieved through international law, the possibility of nuclear war will continue.

In view of the end of the Cold War, the evolving U.S.–Russian political relationship, partnership and alliance, and generally in view of the emerging global détente and economic integration, there exists a unique strategic environment and the most fundamental legal dynamics for an effective and comprehensive settlement of nuclear weapons disarmament not only between the nuclear superpowers, but on a global basis. In addition to valid political, military and economic arguments both for a U.S.–Russian and for a total and global nuclear disarmament, the new international law of nuclear disarmament, which has been developed by bilateral and multilateral treaties, ensures that such nuclear disarmament is both feasible and effective. The new international legal system of verification procedures can ensure effective nuclear disarmament.

Before proceeding with a legal analysis and exploration of the existing dynamics and future prospects for a total and comprehensive Russo-American nuclear disarmament, it is of particular importance to analyze the new strategic and military nuclear planning of both Russia and the United States. Based on the present military nuclear formulation and planning of the two nuclear superpowers, and in view of their nuclear arms reductions that may be effected by the START I Treaty, the START II Treaty, and their unilateral nuclear disarmament measures in their tactical nuclear forces, one can conclude that the nuclear superpowers have entered a new era of nuclear weapon reductions. The United States and Russia have moved from their old offensive strategic nuclear postures toward each other to a new strategic posture of defensive strategy against the eruption of nuclear war.

The United States is presently formulating and planning its new nuclear strategy. The new American nuclear strategy and posture will be characterized by the new nuclear doctrine of minimum nuclear deterrence capability.[481] Thus, the United States, in view of the disintegration of the former Soviet Union, and in view of its evolving political partnership and alliance with Russia, will adopt this new doctrine in place of its Cold War nuclear doctrine of strategic superiority and overkill capabilities against the former Soviet Union.

The Bush administration and, in particular, the former Secretary of Defense, Richard Cheney, who was the main architect of the doctrine of minimum nuclear deterrence capability for the 1990s and the 21st century, pointed out that America's minimum nuclear deterrence capability for the post–Cold War era would be absolutely irreducible because it is required to defend the United States.[482] However, the Bush administration avoided stating the approximate number of the required strategic nuclear forces to serve the objectives of the new deterrence doctrine.

In determining the approximate number of strategic nuclear forces required to meet the objectives of minimum nuclear deterrence and after having taken into account the reductions in U.S. nuclear forces required by the START I and START II Treaties by the year 2003, it has been estimated that by the year 2010 the current approximately 20,000 nuclear warheads in the U.S. arsenal will be reduced to about 2,000. The Bush administration in February 1991, projecting about an 85 percent reduction in the current U.S. nuclear arsenal by 2010, instructed the Department of Energy to substantially shrink America's nuclear bomb-building complex to a capability of providing fissile material for 3,000 nuclear warheads.[483] An overview of President Clinton's nuclear strategy appears to be consistent with that of Bush.[484]

Russia is formulating its own new strategic nuclear doctrine and posture. This new doctrine will be based on that of minimum nuclear sufficiency. To satisfy this doctrine, the Yeltsin administration is prepared to retain approximately 2,000 strategic nuclear warheads, and some tactical nuclear weapons. President Yeltsin has assured the Russian military complex and apparatus that Russia's doctrine of minimum nuclear sufficiency will not undermine the security of Russia and the CIS in general.[485]

Based on the preceding analysis of the new American and Russian strategic nuclear military planning for the 1990s and the 21st century, both the United States and Russia, even after the prospective final implementation of the START II Treaty, and unless they have agreed to deeper reductions in their nuclear forces in the interim, will each possess approximately 2,000 strategic nuclear warheads. Despite the sharp reductions in their current nuclear arsenals, it seems likely that for the foreseeable future Russia and the United States will continue to maintain their status as nuclear superpowers.

Based on the new strategic doctrines of minimum nuclear deterrence or minimum nuclear sufficiency presently formulated by the United States and Russia, it appears that both nations are determined to retain significant numbers of nuclear weapons. Thus, it seems highly unlikely that they would accept a total and comprehensive elimination of their nuclear weapons. Neither country has even mentioned the likelihood of its total denuclearization, unlike the former Soviet President, Mikhail Gorbachev, who had proposed a global nuclear disarmament by the year 2000.

The military-industrial complex of the United States also remains a powerful force that maintained a Cold War military planning and budget for at least the 1990s. Indeed, the U.S. military spending for the 1990s will clearly reflect a Cold War military planning designed to maintain large nuclear and conventional military forces for at least that decade. President Clinton requested more than $268 billion for the 1999-2000 Pentagon budget. American military spending by the end of this century will still reflect a regressive Cold War military structure unless pronounced political changes and military building down and restructuring are undertaken.

Although the United States has no strategic enemy in the post–Cold War era, the American industrial and military complex for its own narrow economic interests has already begun a campaign to foist new scare tactics and fears on the American public. To this end, the American military-industrial complex argues that, although the potential danger of a global thermonuclear war with Russia has been essentially eliminated, a particular future threat to the United States' national security interests will be posed by the horizontal proliferation of nuclear weapons and ballistic missiles of third world countries, leading to possible regional conflicts. The United States, in addition to its determination to remain the sole military superpower in the world in the 21st century, is also determined to prevent the emergence of even regional powers in any part of the globe.[486]

This new strategic planning of the United States may cause a new post–Cold War phenomenon. Any effort of the United States to impose on the members of the world community a new global Pax Americana will disrupt any future effort for world economic integration, and will also hurt world peace and security. In any case, any attempt of the United States to rule the post–Cold War world by its nuclear military might and arrogance will not be productive and will cause the chain reaction of a multidimensional and multilevel rivalry with other emerging global powers, such as Germany, Japan and China, and of course, Russia.

On the other hand, and by necessary implication, Russia cannot possibly accept its own unilateral nuclear disarmament if the United States will not follow suit. Although Russia has every economic interest in the reduction of its nuclear forces and in the drastic building down of its conventional military forces, it will be, nevertheless, difficult to envision Russia accepting any legal arrangement on its denuclearization while the United States remains a nuclear superpower. Already the Russian military establishment has pointed out that Russia as a great power cannot afford not to have strategic nuclear weapons, and that Russia cannot accept its unilateral nuclear disarmament if the United States does not reciprocate.[487]

Despite the fact that the end of the Cold War, the emerging global détente and the new international law of nuclear disarmament provide both the required strategic political environment and the legal dynamics not only for a total U.S.–Russian nuclear disarmament, but also for such disarmament on a global and comprehensive scale, neither the United States nor Russia has introduced an effective plan to this end.

A further analysis of the emerging political and legal debate over a total and comprehensive Russo-American nuclear disarmament reveals diametrically opposite views and approaches to this issue. Opponents of such disarmament, although favoring deep reductions in the U.S.–Russian nuclear stockpiles, argue that the retention of some 500 to 1,000 nuclear warheads by each side will serve the military objectives of the new U.S.–Russian strategic doctrines of minimum nuclear deterrence and sufficiency, which are designed to prevent a nuclear or even a conventional war on a large scale.[488]

Proponents of the permanent retention of such nuclear forces accept this new doctrine as an appropriate lesser evil. They also seem to accept the notion that the world could live with nuclear weapons in the future. The opponents of a U.S.–Russian total nuclear disarmament support the permanent retention by the two nuclear superpowers of very low levels of nuclear forces, and maintain that a legal goal of complete U.S.–Russian nuclear disarmament would not enhance strategic stability and would not prevent any potential threat to global peace and security.[489]

On the other hand, the proponents of a U.S.–Russian and a global and comprehensive nuclear disarmament maintain that the permanent retention of minimum nuclear forces by Russia and the United States cannot guarantee that these forces would not be used either intentionally, because of future military crises and conflicts, or accidentally, or even due to their unauthorized use. The permanent retention of approximately 500 to 1,000 nuclear warheads by both Russia and the United States for minimum nuclear deterrence will maintain forever the possibility of the use of such weapons. Since the most fundamental legal objective for the present era should not only be the prevention of a nuclear war, but also the literal elimination of the threat of such war, it must, therefore, be accepted that for apparent and self-evident reasons the permanent retention of even low level nuclear forces by Russia and the United States cannot achieve these legal ends.

In spite of the view that the doctrine of nuclear deterrence might have prevented a nuclear war between the superpowers during the Cold War, this same doctrine has kept both nations and the entire world under the perpetual menace and terror of a global thermonuclear holocaust and annihilation. The doctrine of nuclear deterrence not only fueled the vertical expansion of the nuclear weapon arsenals of the superpowers and their overkill capabilities by producing more powerful and sophisticated nuclear weapon systems, but also obstructed the international legal process for a total superpower nuclear disarmament, which would be the most effective way to eliminate the threat of nuclear war once and for all.

Valid and persuasive political, military and economic arguments, in view of the end of the Cold War, clearly support the case for the abolition of the doctrine of nuclear deterrence of any form or version and for a total and comprehensive Russo-American nuclear disarmament. Additionally, under international law the permanent retention, even if at a very low level, of U.S.–Russian nuclear armaments will be contrary to the legal objectives of the NPT. According to Article VI of the NPT, both nuclear superpowers, as nuclear weapons states, have assumed the legal obligation to pursue through negotiations in good faith the aim to cease the nuclear arms race as soon as possible, and also to pursue nuclear disarmament as part of the ultimate legal objective of general and complete disarmament.

To achieve complete U.S.–Russian nuclear disarmament, the adoption of a new strategic legal plan by both nations is required. Based on this proposed strategic legal plan, both must expedite the implementation of the START Treaties. Both should begin active negotiations on the conclusion of a START III Treaty by which the parties will agree to reduce the total number of their nuclear weapons to a level of no more than 500 nuclear warheads for each side.[490] It would be of particular legal importance not only to the promotion of the legal process for a U.S.–Russian total denuclearization, but also for the beginning of the multilateral international legal process for a global and comprehensive nuclear disarmament if the United States and Russia concluded a START III Treaty, which seems to be feasible. Russia has already expressed its interest in the negotiation and conclusion of a START III Treaty.[491]

In addition to beginning active negotiations for a START III Treaty, the United States and Russia, to strengthen their mutual trust and their national security concerns in relation to their denuclearization should agree on the legal adoption of the following measures and actions: (1) They must sign a pact of peace and nonaggression; (2) they must agree on banning the use of nuclear weapons against each other either in a first strike, or in any other context, including self defense; (3) the United States must begin building down and not expanding eastward the NATO alliance whose military presence in Western Europe no longer serves any legitimate and valid purpose, since the dissolution of the Warsaw Pact and the disintegration of the Soviet Union leave NATO with no strategic enemy in sight;[492] (4) Russia and the United States must agree on banning the development of any new nuclear weapon systems based on any future technological and physical principles, and must generally prohibit any future nuclear arms race between themselves; (5) both states must ban the production of any nuclear materials used for the construction of nuclear weapons and explosives; (6) both states must agree to dispose of their nuclear warheads by effective procedures and not to reuse them for military applications; and (7) both Russia and the United States must sign the required agreements with the IAEA and thus place all of their nuclear facilities under the control and the full scope nuclear safeguards of the IAEA, which can ensure that neither country is involved in the production of nuclear weapons materials or in the construction of nuclear weapons or nuclear explosive devices.

The preceding strategic legal plan and the other proposed legal measures and actions regarding the reduction and elimination of the U.S.–Russian nuclear weapons to approximately three to five percent of their current numbers should be undertaken by the nuclear superpowers in view of the 1995 NPT Review Conference which extended the NPT indefinitely, and in conformity with Article VI of the NPT.

If the above legal plan and actions were undertaken by both Russia and the United States it would undoubtedly provide the most dynamic political and legal environment in the history of nuclear arms control and disarmament for a comprehensive and multilateral legal, complete, and global elimination of nuclear weapons. The reduction of the current American and Russian nuclear weapons stockpiles to a level of 1,000 and 600 nuclear warheads on the basis of this proposed legal plan would provide all the required positive elements for the conclusion of a multilateral treaty which, in accordance with Article VI of the NPT, would impose a new international legal regime of effective measures and controls requiring the complete elimination of all nuclear weapons possessed by the de jure and de facto nuclear weapon states on a global basis, further safeguarding against the proliferation of such weapons.

Notwithstanding the legal complexities posed by the total elimination of nuclear weapons from the planet, in view of the evolving post–Cold War legal order, and in view of the dynamics presented by the new international law of nuclear disarmament, there exists the required legal basis to argue that a global and comprehensive nuclear disarmament can by achieved. Considering the emerging post–Cold War era, the entire world has a unique strategic environment and a unique legal opportunity for a comprehensive settlement of the nuclear weapons issue not only regarding the United States and Russia, but also on a global basis. The United States and Russia will certainly never agree to eliminate their nuclear arsenals without applying the same requirement to China, France, the United Kingdom, Israel, Pakistan and India.

Chapter 9

The End of the Cold War, the United Nations and Global Nuclear Disarmament (1986–1997)

The UN and Global Nuclear Disarmament 1986–1997

Disarmament Initiatives (1986–1997)

Before 1985, the United Nations had persistently retained the issue of global and comprehensive nuclear disarmament as an integral part of its permanent agenda of such disarmament regarding both nuclear and conventional weapons. Even though since the mid–1970s the United Nations has placed particular significance on nuclear disarmament, it has failed to reach a comprehensive legal solution to this question. Although the United Nations has played a positive role in the evolution of the new international legal regulation of issues related to nuclear disarmament, it has not dealt effectively through international law with the problem of nuclear proliferation and disarmament.

This failure must be primarily attributed to the world bipolarization, to the Cold War, and to the superpowers' uncontrolled and relentless nuclear arms race. Although nuclear disarmament constitutes a multilateral problem of imperative global concern, since the early 1960s both nuclear superpowers have taken the issue of their nuclear arms control and disarmament outside the UN forum and have treated it as a bilateral issue. In addition, both the United States and the Soviet Union opposed any UN multilateral legal effort and proposed measures in nuclear disarmament whenever such UN initiatives were contrary to U.S. and Soviet strategic interests. As a result, the United Nations has been improperly undermined and weakened in its legal role and organizational ability to solve the question of global nuclear disarmament through effective international processes and measures.

Notwithstanding its past failures, since 1985 the United Nations through its competent institutional organs has been actively involved in the solution of this question. While by 1985 the proliferation of nuclear weapons had led to a dangerous nuclear predicament involving the development of approximately

55,000 strategic and tactical nuclear weapons, Mikhail Gorbachev's rise to the leadership of the Soviet Union in March 1985 marked the beginning of a new era in global peace and security. Gorbachev's new strategic thinking for world peace, his peace offensive to the West and generally to the world, and his leadership to end the Cold War and to begin the U.S.–Soviet nuclear disarmament legal process created a new political and legal environment for the pursuit of a global and comprehensive nuclear disarmament. In essence, Mikhail Gorbachev's leadership set the legal and political foundations for such disarmament.

In view of these positive international developments, the United Nations since 1985 has begun to assume a more active role in global nuclear disarmament and other related issues. Since 1985 the United Nations has continued to retain its permanent agenda on general and complete world disarmament. The United Nations in general and its disarmament organs and institutions in particular have placed primary emphasis on the legal need to achieve global and comprehensive nuclear disarmament. To this end, the UN multilateral disarmament forums have been actively involved in the implementation of the UN agenda on four nuclear issues: the cessation of the nuclear arms race both in vertical and horizontal terms; nuclear disarmament; a comprehensive test ban; and the prevention of nuclear war. The UN agenda on nuclear disarmament has been occupied by the need to outlaw the use of nuclear weapons and to adopt effective and innovative nuclear disarmament verification procedures and measures.[493]

Since 1985 the UN General Assembly, the UN Disarmament Commission, and the UN Conference on Disarmament have intensified their efforts and initiatives to eliminate legally all nuclear weapons on a global and comprehensive basis under effective international procedures. The General Assembly has adopted a significant number of resolutions which have consistently called upon both nuclear superpowers and the other members of the Nuclear Club to expedite the international legal process for their ultimate denuclearization. The General Assembly has also emphasized the legal need to prevent the horizontal proliferation of nuclear weapons by urging the universalization and the strengthening of the NPT legal regime and its verification system. In addition, the General Assembly by its resolutions has condemned the acquisition of nuclear weapon capabilities by de facto nuclear weapon states, such as India, Israel, South Africa and Pakistan, and has called for their denuclearization and their accession to the NPT.[494]

As a positive response to the calls and resolutions of the General Assembly and of the other appropriate UN disarmament organs and forums, as has been already explained, in January 1986 Mikhail Gorbachev proposed a concrete timetable for the complete elimination of all nuclear weapons by the year 2000. The Western nuclear establishment, and particularly the United States, unjustifiably and inappropriately rejected the Gorbachev plan. Because of the Gorbachev proposal however, the legal objective of the creation of a nuclear weapons-free world has been firmly placed on the UN multilateral agenda of peace negotiations.

India, a non-party to the NPT, and a de facto nuclear weapon state, in June 1988 submitted to the Third UN Special Session on Disarmament its *Action Plan for Ushering in a Nuclear Weapon-Free and Non-Violent World Order*. In accordance with this plan, India proposed that in 1995, when the future extension of the NPT would be decided, international negotiations should begin on a new treaty to replace the NPT that would commit all nuclear weapon states to eliminate all of their nuclear weapons by the year 2010, and all non-nuclear weapon states not to cross the nuclear weapon threshold.[495] Although the Soviet Union, China and France have positively reacted to the Indian plan for global nuclear disarmament by the year 2010, and although these three nuclear weapon states are generally committed to the legal goal of global and comprehensive denuclearization, the United States and the United Kingdom have essentially rejected the Indian proposal.[496]

In addition to its multilateral legal initiatives and proposals in nuclear disarmament, the United Nations since 1985 has also concentrated its efforts on the cessation of the nuclear arms race. To this end, in December 1989 the General Assembly adopted its Resolution 44/117 D, which called upon the nuclear weapon states to agree, through a joint declaration, to a comprehensive nuclear-arms freeze. Furthermore, in December 1989 the General Assembly adopted Resolution 44/116 H, calling upon the UN member states concerned to agree on banning the production of fissionable materials for weapons. By the above resolution the General Assembly also requested the UN Conference on Disarmament to consider the question of adequately verified cessation and prohibition of the production of fissionable materials for nuclear weapons and other nuclear explosive devices.[497]

In 1989 through Resolution 44/118 Q, the General Assembly, while reviewing the role and activism of the United Nations in disarmament, emphasized that the United Nations in accordance with its charter had assumed a central role and primary responsibility in disarmament in general. With this resolution the General Assembly also stressed the need for the United Nations to play a stronger and more active role in both conventional and nuclear disarmament. Resolution 44/116 Q requested the UN Disarmament Commission and the Conference on Disarmament to intensify their role in disarmament.[498]

While the United Nations has defined and specified its agenda on the legal goal of a global and comprehensive nuclear disarmament for the 1990s, in December 1989 the General Assembly adopted Resolution 44/119 H, which declared the 1990s as the Third Disarmament Decade. By the above resolution the General Assembly reaffirmed the central legal responsibility of the United Nations in the attainment of both nuclear and conventional disarmament in the 1990s, and also expressed a desire for maintaining the current momentum in the nuclear disarmament process, and the conviction that the Third Disarmament Decade would accelerate the multilateral disarmament process. With Resolution 44/119 H, the UN Secretary-General was requested to render all necessary assistance to the Disarmament Commission in implementing this resolution. In 1989 by its Resolution 44/117 A the General Assembly decided to pursue the UN World Disarmament Campaign. This resolution emphasized that it is essential that not only governments, but also the peoples of the world, recognize and understand the dangers relating to all aspects of the arms race and war, and especially nuclear war. To this end, the General Assembly pointed out the need for mobilizing world public opinion on behalf of disarmament, and requested the Secretary-General to play an active role in this effort.[499]

With respect to preventing a nuclear war and the use of nuclear weapons, the United Nations has been significantly active. The 1978 UN *Final Document*, which was reaffirmed in 1982 by the General Assembly, has pointed out the catastrophic consequences of a nuclear war globally and has stressed the necessity to prevent such a war by outlawing the use of nuclear weapons. In 1989 the General Assembly, following the 1988 UN *Study on the Climatic and Other Global Effects of Nuclear War*, proposed specific legal measures for the prevention of nuclear war and for banning the use of nuclear weapons. The General Assembly in 1989 adopted Resolution 44/119 B, by which it reaffirmed the world recognition that the prevention of nuclear war has been and still remains the utmost priority and concern of the entire world, and also stressed the need that specific efforts, bilateral, regional or multilateral, must be vigorously pursued, and that measures should be strengthened to reduce and ultimately eliminate the risk of nuclear war. To this end, Resolution 44/119 B pointed out the legal need for a global and comprehensive nuclear disarmament, and proposed the establishment of a multilateral nuclear alert center to reduce the risk of fatal misinterpretation of unintentional and accidental nuclear launchings, and the conclusion of a multilateral convention on the prohibition of the first use of nuclear weapons.[500]

Particularly with respect to the legal necessity to prevent a direct and intentional nuclear war, in 1989 the General Assembly adopted Resolution 44/117 C, which repeated its conviction that the existence and use of nuclear weapons pose the greatest threat to the survival of humanity. In addition to its conviction that the only ultimate guarantee against the use of nuclear weapons is their total elimination, the General Assembly proposed the conclusion of a multilateral convention prohibiting the use or threat of use of nuclear weapons. In accordance with the preamble of the proposal by the General Assembly draft convention, which has been annexed to Resolution 44/117 C, any use of nuclear weapons constitutes a violation of the UN Charter and a crime against humanity. Article 1 of the above draft convention would impose the legal obligation upon its signatories not to use or threaten to use nuclear weapons under any circumstances.[501]

Although the legal adoption of this draft convention would ban the first use of nuclear weapons and would also be a positive legal measure and step toward the complete elimination of nuclear weapons under strict and effective international control, the Western nuclear establishment, namely, the United States, the

United Kingdom and France, has opposed the conclusion of such a convention.[502] Both the Soviet Union and China have categorically supported it. Regarding the Russian and Chinese legal policies on the first use of nuclear weapons, both Russia and China have by their legally binding unilateral declarations renounced their resort to such first use. In October 1991 Mikhail Gorbachev proposed that all nuclear weapon states make a joint statement on no first use of nuclear weapons. The Western nuclear establishment and particularly the United States failed to react positively to this proposal.[503]

At the beginning of 1990, the United Nations through its Disarmament Commission included on its nuclear disarmament agenda for the 1990s a number of items and priorities. The agenda would focus mainly on: (1) the arms race and nuclear disarmament; (2) the naval arms race and disarmament; (3) the Third Disarmament Decade; (4) regional nuclear disarmament; and (5) the process of nuclear disarmament in the framework of international peace and security. The United Nations by the beginning of the 1990s was determined to place particular importance on the preparation and success of the 1995 NPT review conference and on the conclusion of a CTBT.[504]

In 1990, intensive negotiations began between the United States and Russia, and with the involvement of the United Nations, with the aim to conclude a treaty on "open skies." Although the idea for "open skies" was first proposed by President Eisenhower in 1955, in 1989 Canada suggested to President Bush the need for the legal establishment of open skies as a positive measure for nuclear disarmament and verification purposes. Finally, on March 24, 1992, the Treaty on Open Skies was signed in Helsinki. A critical evaluation of the treaty clearly shows its legal importance in the confidence building measures among the states and their mutual openness to aerial inspection. This development constitutes a positive legal measure for the effective verification and implementation of nuclear disarmament agreements.[505]

In addition to the indefinite extension of the NPT in 1995, and the conclusion of the CTBT in 1996, which are significant legal breakthroughs in the quest for nuclear disarmament and which will be separately discussed later in this chapter, a number of nuclear disarmament proposals were introduced in the 1990s. The Group of 21 presented in August 1996 a "Program of Action for the Elimination of Nuclear Weapons" to the Conference on Disarmament. This program has three phases. The first phase, from 1996–2000, called for measures to reduce the nuclear threat and ending the qualitative improvement and advancement of nuclear weapons, and measures of nuclear disarmament, such as ratification of the START II Treaty and removal of nuclear weapon systems from operational readiness.[506]

The second phase of this proposal, which covers the years 2000–2010, requires the conclusion and entry into force of a treaty to eliminate nuclear weapons and reduce ballistic missiles for the delivery of nuclear weapons. In the third phase, from 2010–2020, the proposal requires the elimination of all nuclear weapons and the application of verification safeguards and measures to all nuclear facilities. Similarly, in 1996, Sweden, New Zealand, Australia and Japan called on the United Nations and its member states to undertake international efforts to sharply reduce nuclear weapons on a global basis with the aim of achieving a world without such weapons. Nevertheless, the nuclear weapon states have failed to support a global nuclear disarmament arrangement in the post–Cold War era.[507]

In view of the preceding analysis, the United Nations, as the most appropriate and legitimate world organization to legally manage and resolve the elimination of nuclear weapons on a global basis, has failed to make any significant legal breakthrough to that end. Although the indefinite extension of the NPT in 1995, and the conclusion of the CTBT in 1996 admittedly constitute significant legal developments in nuclear disarmament, they do not eliminate even one nuclear weapon from the world's arsenals. However, during the above period the international legal process for the reduction and gradual elimination of the U.S. and former Soviet nuclear weapons began. This constituted a significant level of development in global nuclear disarmament, since both the U.S. and former Soviet nuclear weapons stockpiles represent more than 90 percent of the existing nuclear weapons. Nevertheless, the United Nations has not been able to assume a leading and decisive legal role in global nuclear disarmament.

The New Nuclear Age and Expansion of Horizontal Proliferation (1986–1997): An Overview

With the vertical increase in production and deployment of nuclear weapons by the nuclear weapon states and particularly by the United States and the Soviet Union, by 1985 India,[508] Israel[509] and South Africa[510] had become de facto nuclear weapon states. These three states have not only developed nuclear weapons, but have acquired ballistic missiles to deliver such weapons.[511] Furthermore, by 1985 a number of nations in various regions of the globe were classified as threshold nuclear weapon states and as problem nuclear weapon states on the basis of how close their nuclear weapon programs had come to fruition. Argentina, Brazil and North Korea were reported to be near the point of developing nuclear weapons. Taiwan, Libya, Iran and Iraq were also reported to have launched significant efforts to acquire nuclear weapons. By 1985 it was obvious that not only a new nuclear age had begun, but also that this new age for the nuclearization of non-nuclear weapon states was expanding despite the NPT legal regime.[512]

An overview of horizontal nuclear proliferation on a global basis since 1985 shows the expansion of this new nuclear age. In addition to India, Israel and South Africa, which had already established themselves as de facto nuclear weapon states, by 1986 Pakistan had become the newest member of this group by acquiring nuclear weapons.[513] Brazil and Argentina are also widely considered to possess the technological capabilities to produce nuclear weapons within a short notice,[514] and North Korea, which has signed the NPT, was reported to be very close to the point of developing such weapons.[515]

Israel, not a party to the NPT, has reportedly developed and possesses 100–200 nuclear warheads, some with thermonuclear fusion. India, not a party to the NPT, has developed about 20–50 first-generation nuclear fission bombs. Pakistan, also not a party to NPT, has developed nearly a dozen first-generation nuclear fission bombs. Israel, India and Pakistan possess ballistic missiles capable of delivering their nuclear weapons.[516] South Africa in 1993 acceded to the NPT immediately after it publicly admitted that it had developed and possessed a number of nuclear weapons. South Africa has further stated that it has destroyed all the nuclear weapons which it had developed. The IAEA, which conducted thorough and comprehensive on-site inspection in South Africa, did not discover any nuclear weapons.[517]

The new age of horizontal proliferation of nuclear weapons, which began in the mid–1970s, has been expanded despite the NPT legal regime that prohibits the proliferation of nuclear weapons among non-nuclear weapon states. Indeed, it can be maintained that any non-nuclear weapon state that was determined to acquire nuclear weapons could obtain the required materials and technologies to develop and construct them. This situation clearly shows the failure of the United Nations and the NPT regime to effectively enforce and implement the nonproliferation of nuclear weapons.

With the exception of Iraq, whose nuclear weapon program has been effectively dismantled by the United Nations, there are, as previously noted, several threshold nuclear states. Due to the involvement of more states in the acquisition of nuclear technologies and materials for peaceful applications, the dual use of these technologies and materials for peaceful purposes and military applications means that in the post–Cold War era more states will be in a position to possess the means to develop nuclear weapons. It has been estimated that by the year 2000 approximately 30–40 countries will possess nuclear programs, which will enable them to develop nuclear weapons.[518]

The disintegration of the former Soviet Union has created the very real danger of illicit trafficking in nuclear weapon grade materials and nuclear weapon technologies from former Soviet republics to countries eager to obtain them and to advance their nuclear weapon programs. Due to the poor living conditions of nuclear weapon scientists and engineers in the former Soviet Union, there is the problem of their immigration to countries willing to hire them and to use their skills and knowledge to develop their own nuclear weapon programs. Additionally, current reports involving black market trade in nuclear weapon grade materials signal the high risks that such materials can be obtained by terrorist group and rogue states.[519]

In addition to the potential spread of nuclear technologies and materials in the post–Cold War era, more states will also be able to process ballistic missile systems capable of delivering nuclear warheads.[520] In view of the existing nuclear arsenals of the nuclear weapon states, and the projected proliferation of nuclear weapons to more non-nuclear weapon states in the future, it is imperative that the United Nations act effectively to prevent nuclear proliferation and achieve global nuclear disarmament.

The NPT Extension and the Legal Dynamics for Global Nuclear Disarmament in the Post-Cold War Era

THE 1995 NPT REVIEW CONFERENCE AND THE EXTENSION OF THE NPT

Article X (2) of the NPT required that:

> Twenty-five years after the entry into force of the Treaty, a conference shall be convened to decide whether the Treaty shall continue to force indefinitely, or shall be extended for an additional fixed period or periods. This decision shall be taken by a majority of the Parties of the Treaty.

Pursuant to this provision of the NPT in 1995, when 25 years had passed since the NPT had entered into force in 1970, a review conference of the NPT was held. After intensive negotiations, in May 1995 the NPT was extended indefinitely. It was also decided that the next NPT review conference would be held in the year 2000.

The indefinite extension of the force of the NPT constitutes a significant development in the legal efforts of the international community to deal with and resolve the proliferation of nuclear weapons, and generally to resolve the problem of global nuclear disarmament. The NPT has presently been signed by 188 states.[521] The NPT is a widely accepted international legal instrument, and the first multinational treaty concerning nuclear disarmament. The indefinite extension of the NPT indicates that the world is prepared through the rule of law to face and resolve the issue of global nuclear disarmament.

Despite its indefinite extension, the NPT arbitrarily divides the world into two classes of states, those with nuclear weapons and those without them. In essence, this legal division between nuclear and non-nuclear weapon states constitutes a structurally discriminatory element of the NPT, which has adversely affected the universal and dynamic effect of the NPT's role in nuclear disarmament. In particular, the NPT's discriminatory division between nuclear weapon and non-nuclear weapon states suggests that the NPT legal regime provided with legal cover the structure and distribution of world power for the post–World War II era.

The United States, the former Soviet Union, Britain, France and China, which had acquired nuclear weapon capabilities by 1968, formed the Nuclear Club. States which by 1968 had not acquired nuclear weapons undertook the explicit legal obligation by acceding to the NPT to denounce the acquisition of nuclear weapons and not to acquire them.[522]

The fundamental legal objective of the NPT has been, since 1968, to prevent the horizontal proliferation of nuclear weapons among non-nuclear weapon states and to achieve the nuclear disarmament of the nuclear weapon states. Additionally, the NPT legal regime was designed to provide the non-nuclear weapon states with the required nuclear technologies and materials to develop their peaceful nuclear energy programs under international control. To this end, the nuclear weapon states and the nuclear power supplier states were required under the NPT to assist non-nuclear weapon states in the peaceful application and use of the atom.

A critical review of the NPT shows that it has fundamentally failed to achieve its legal objectives and aims in global nuclear disarmament. Despite its signature in 1968, the NPT was not even an obstacle to the continued nuclear arms race between the Soviet Union and the United States. Notwithstanding their legal obligation under Article VI of the NPT to negotiate in good faith on effective measures relating to nuclear disarmament and to the cessation of their nuclear arms race, both nuclear superpowers went ahead to develop and deploy thousands of additional nuclear weapons. Even in the post–Cold War era, and the new strategic relationship of peaceful coexistence and partnership between the United States and Russia, both nations retain large nuclear arsenals. It is presently estimated that the United States has about 10,500 nuclear warheads, and Russia nearly 15,000.[523] Even after the successful implementation of their START I and START II treaties, both the United States and Russia at the beginning of the 21st century will be nuclear superpowers, with each of them possessing approximately 3,500 strategic nuclear weapons. It has also been reported that both Russia and the United States are presently producing more advanced nuclear weapons for the 21st century.[524]

Britain, which acceded to the NPT in 1968, continued to expand its nuclear weapon program contrary to its obligation under Article VI of the NPT. On the other hand, France and China refused to sign the NPT and continued to expand their nuclear arsenals. Finally, in 1992 both China and France acceded to the NPT. Britain now possesses nearly 200 nuclear warheads, France about 524, and China approximately 450.[525] China has reportedly been actively expanding its strategic nuclear arsenal and the advancement of its strategic nuclear missile capabilities for the 21st century.[526] Moreover, Japan,[527] Germany and Canada, which are parties to the NPT, have the technological capability and enough nuclear material to produce nuclear weapons within a short time.

The NPT has failed to include an explicit security guarantee that the nuclear weapon states will be completely prohibited from using or threatening to use nuclear weapons against non-nuclear weapon states. Thus, the non-nuclear weapon states by accepting the NPT legal regime have placed themselves at a military disadvantage. As a result of this legal shortcoming of the NPT, non-nuclear weapon states can become victims of nuclear blackmail by the Nuclear Club members.

The NPT poses a basic bargain: While the nuclear weapon states would retain their nuclear weapons, in return for forgoing the acquisition of nuclear weapons the non-nuclear weapon states extracted from the nuclear states the legal commitment to provide them with nuclear technology and materials suitable to the development of their peaceful nuclear energy programs. Nonetheless, there have been many instances where non-nuclear weapon states have been in a discriminatory manner denied by the nuclear weapon states and other nuclear power supplier states the acquisition of such technology and materials. On the other hand, the de facto nuclear weapon states have managed to obtain easier access to nuclear technologies and materials for the development and expansion of their nuclear bomb-building programs.

Notwithstanding the NPT's inherent discriminatory division between nuclear and non-nuclear weapon states and the negative implications of such a division, the United Nations has also failed to adopt a positive international legal regime of nuclear security guarantees against the threatened or actual use of nuclear weapons by the nuclear weapon states against non-nuclear states. In addition, in view of the horizontal proliferation of nuclear weapons in various volatile regions of the world, there exists the danger that enemy states in such regions might use military means to prevent other states in the same region from acquiring nuclear weapons by destroying the nuclear facilities and programs of such states. Accordingly, the United Nations should adopt an international legal regime by which individual states will be prohibited from any military action or aggressive act designed to destroy the nuclear facilities and programs of another state, and thus prevent such a state from acquiring nuclear weapons. Such a legal task and responsibility must be carried out in an effective manner by the appropriate organs of the United Nations.

During the 1995 NPT review conference all problems and failures of the NPT regime were actively discussed and negotiated. Although the NPT was indefinitely extended at this conference, the parties of the NPT did not resolve its problems and shortcomings, and thus failed to strengthen the NPT for the 21st century. The 1995 NPT review conference failed to address the NPT discriminatory division between nuclear and non-nuclear weapon states, particularly regarding their unequal obligations and status under the NPT. In essence, the indefinitely extended NPT has failed to impose upon the nuclear weapon states, as required by Article VI, a concrete timetable within which to actively negotiate and conclude the required treaty arrangements for their nuclear disarmament in the 21st century.

The review negotiations failed to produce an agreement outlawing the first use and generally the use of nuclear weapons under any circumstances by de jure and de facto nuclear weapon states. The NPT review conference also failed to strengthen the role of the IAEA in the effective implementation of the NPT. The indefinitely extended NPT is a repetition and perpetuation of the old and failed NPT regime. The 1995 NPT review conference was a lost historic opportunity to establish a new and dynamic NPT legal regime to solve the failures of the old regime and to achieve through the rule of international law global nuclear disarmament by the beginning of the 21st century.

The Future of the NPT and the Legal Dynamics for Global Nuclear Disarmament

Nuclear weapons nonproliferation and global nuclear disarmament is a complex world problem, which primarily concerns complicated questions of national security, national prestige involving military might and power, and global peace and security. Although the old NPT has played some positive role in restricting the proliferation of nuclear weapons, the perpetuation of the old and ineffective NPT regime for the solution of the nuclear disarmament problem in the 21st century is not the proper legal means even to approach an issue of such global importance. The approval of the continuation of the old NPT regime by the 1995 NPT review conference shows that the entire agenda of nuclear weapons and nuclear disarmament is today totally controlled by the club of nuclear weapon states, which appear to be determined to possess nuclear weapons in the 21st century.

Nevertheless, the end of the Cold War, and particularly the end of the nuclear arms race between the United States and the former Soviet Union, provides a unique political, military and strategic legal environment for a comprehensive and global elimination of nuclear weapons. The emerging and steadily evolving new Russo-American strategic partnership and cooperation create the fundamental basis for a post–Cold War détente, which, in turn, provides the required legal dynamics and prospects for a global denuclearization.

The collapse of communism, the disintegration of the former Soviet Union, and the expanding new era of strategic relations between Russia and the United States deprive both nuclear superpowers of any rational and valid argument for maintaining their Cold War strategies and approaches to the nuclear weapons problem in the post–Cold War era. The nuclear disengagement between the United States and Russia as a result of the end of the Cold War, and their bilateral legal engagement in their gradual denuclearization show that both nuclear superpowers have substituted their model of Cold War nuclear arms control with a new model of nuclear arms reductions.

The effective implementation of the INF Treaty, the presently ongoing implementation of the START I Treaty, and the conclusion of the START II Treaty support the legal argument forwarded by this study that a complete U.S.–Russian nuclear disarmament is both feasible and effective. Additionally, the current U.S.–Russian bilateral treaty arrangements for their gradual denuclearization are important legal developments in the expansion of the new international law of nuclear disarmament, and show that the two nuclear superpowers have already begun to carry out their legal obligations under Article VI of the NPT. Although neither the United States nor Russia has currently made a U.S.–Russian and global total nuclear disarmament proposal, the current superpower nuclear disarmament process under the rule of international law is a significant breakthrough.

The accession of both France and China to the NPT in 1992 is a new development that opens up the prospects for a multilateral approach to the nonproliferation of nuclear weapons and nuclear disarmament. The indefinite extension of the NPT in 1995, and the conclusion of the CTBT in 1996 have set the legal basis and dynamics for a new environment to address the global question of nuclear weapons. Prospects for global and comprehensive nuclear disarmament not only seem feasible and realistic, but also verifiably effective. The new law and techniques developed by the superpower nuclear disarmament process and their effectiveness in the implementation of their relevant agreements show that effective verification is no longer a problem in achieving nuclear disarmament agreements. In particular, the role of the United Nations in the effective elimination and destruction of the Iraqi nuclear weapons program by the application of intrusive and advanced verification measures and techniques shows that the IAEA can play a central role in the effective implementation of nuclear weapon disarmament agreements on a broader basis.

The existing large numbers of nuclear weapon arsenals possessed by the club of the nuclear weapon states, the proliferation of nuclear weapons by Israel, Pakistan and India, and generally the beginnings of a new nuclear age in the proliferation of nuclear weapons show the legal need for a global nuclear disarmament in the 21st century. In view of the end of the Cold War and the evolving and expanding global détente, no military theory or rationale can justify the retention of large numbers of nuclear weapons well into the 21st century. The permanent retention of even very low levels of nuclear weapons in the new century cannot be accepted as an appropriate lesser evil by the world community.

For the past approximately 50 years that community has been under the constant threat of nuclear holocaust. In view of the end of the Cold War, it is a great mistake to assume that the international community would willingly continue to live with nuclear weapons perpetuating the danger of a nuclear holocaust. The permanent retention of nuclear weapons in the 21st century would also be contrary to the legal objectives of Article VI of the NPT. In conclusion, the most effective way to prevent a nuclear holocaust in the 21st century is to eliminate the world's nuclear weapon arsenals through the legal process of nuclear disarmament, which is both feasible and effective.

To properly address the issue of global and comprehensive nuclear disarmament, the old legal approaches to and models of nuclear arms control and nonproliferation should be abandoned because they have failed to produce adequate results. Thus, there is an imperative need to consider the adoption of the legal strategic plan proposed below for a global and comprehensive nuclear disarmament. This plan should be legally adopted by the world community in the year 2000 when the next NPT review conference will take place.

A Proposal for Global and Comprehensive Nuclear Disarmament

(1) Russia should ratify the START II Treaty. Russia and the United States should expedite the implementation of both START I and START II treaties. Both nuclear superpowers should cease the modernization of their nuclear weapon arsenals and their delivery systems, and the production of new nuclear weapons and delivery systems. Both should cease the production of nuclear weapon making material, and open all of their nuclear weapon facilities and nuclear weapon making production material to the inspections and safeguards of the IAEA. The United States and Russia must conclude a START III Treaty before the year 2000 requiring them to reduce their nuclear weapons to no more than 500 for each side.

(2) Britain, France and China, as the lesser members of the club of nuclear weapons powers, should assume their responsibility in global nuclear disarmament.[528] These three nuclear powers should abandon their present plans for the modernization of their nuclear weapons for the 21st century. In particular, China, which is presently involved in the effort to expand its nuclear weapons arsenal and its ballistic missile capability, must abandon its plans to become a nuclear superpower in the 21st century. These three states must stop the production of new nuclear weapons and the production of nuclear weapon making materials. They should place all of their nuclear weapon facilities and nuclear weapon making material production facilities under the safeguards system of the IAEA. Immediately after the proposed conclusion of the START III Treaty between the United States and Russia before the year 2000, the United States, Russia, France, China and Britain, should sign a treaty which will require China, France and Britain to agree on the total elimination of their nuclear weapons within a certain time and thus to become nuclear weapon free countries on the condition that in the year 2000 Russia and the United States agree on the total elimination of their nuclear weapons.

(3) The de facto nuclear weapon states, namely, Israel, India and Pakistan, should immediately accede to the NPT and legally accept the elimination and destruction of their nuclear weapons. They should place all of their nuclear weapon facilities under the safeguards of the IAEA. If they refuse to cooperate to this end, the United Nations should apply pressure and strong sanctions on these states to force them to give up their nuclear weapons. The legal precedent set by the elimination and destruction of the Iraqi nuclear weapons program and facilities by the United Nations provides an appropriate model for achieving the denuclearization of these three de facto nuclear weapon states, and the international community should apply the same standard to them.

(4) In view of the horizontal proliferation of nuclear weapons and facilities which began by the mid–1970s, after an agreement has been concluded for the denuclearization of Israel, India and Pakistan, all near-nuclear weapon states, all nuclear weapon problem states, and all states with peaceful nuclear programs

should open all of their nuclear programs and facilities to the inspections and safeguards of the IAEA.

(5) The NPT's discriminatory structure and unequal treatment of nuclear and non-nuclear weapon states should be abolished. Article VI of the NPT should be amended to legally and explicitly require the nuclear weapon states to proceed immediately with their total nuclear disarmament. Additionally, the NPT regime should prohibit the unequal and discriminatory practices of the nuclear supplier powers against the countries developing their peaceful nuclear programs. To this end, it would be appropriate to create an international organization to supervise and control the provision and transfer of nuclear technologies and materials by the nuclear supplier states to the states pursuing the development of their peaceful nuclear programs.

(6) All nuclear weapon states, including the de facto nuclear weapon states, should immediately, categorically and unconditionally agree to renounce the resort to the first use of nuclear weapons against each other, and against the non-nuclear weapon states. Immediately after reaching such an agreement, an international agreement should be concluded which would explicitly prohibit the use or threat of use of nuclear weapons under any circumstances and even in the case of self defense by nuclear weapon states against each other or against non-nuclear weapon states.

(7) The IAEA, as the central international organ for the effective implementation of the NPT and global nuclear disarmament, in view of its past failures and present inadequacies, should be provided with the required resources and advanced technological means to carry out its duty regarding the effective implementation of a global nuclear disarmament regime. Since the permissibility of the peaceful application of the atom constitutes a legal path and cover to the development of nuclear weapons, the IAEA must be empowered with a dynamic and intrusive verification system of advanced technical means, of on-site inspections at random at all nuclear facilities and programs of all states, and with the legal power to destroy the nuclear program of a proliferant state. In view of the current incidents of illicit and black market transfer of nuclear technologies and nuclear weapon grade materials, the IAEA should also have an intelligence system to assist it to ensure the effective prevention of the proliferation of nuclear weapons by states and other entities.

(8) To increase the confidence of the nations and peoples of the world in the ability of the United Nations to preserve peace and security in the post–Cold War era, and thus to facilitate the international legal process of global nuclear disarmament, the UN should be empowered with the required means not only to carry out peacekeeping operations, but also to the eruption of military conflicts, to make peace and even to enforce peace. To this end, and in conformity with Chapter VII of its charter, the United Nations must create its own military machine equipped with all advanced and sophisticated weapons and systems enabling it to deal effectively with peacemaking and peacekeeping operations

on a worldwide scale. The discriminatory organizational formation and structure of the Security Council and the veto powers of its five permanent powers, namely, the United States, Russia, Britain, France and China, should be abolished. The domination of the Security Council and thus of the entire United Nations by these five states has not only been anachronistic and counterproductive in global nuclear disarmament, but this elite of powers with their veto rights has essentially dominated the world arena and agenda, in many instances to the detriment of the entire world. The proposed new Security Council should comprise a rotating number of member states serving for a limited time and adopting its decisions and resolutions based on the majority rule. The composition of the new Security Council must represent the global nature of the United Nations.

(9) The previously suggested measures and their legal adoption will set the basis and prepare the ground for achieving the conclusion of a multinational treaty for a global and comprehensive nuclear disarmament, and for the final settlement of the question of nuclear disarmament in the year 2000 when the NPT review conference occurs. Moreover, in the year 2000 all countries of the world must conclude a global disarmament treaty, which should require the verified elimination and destruction of all nuclear weapons of the world no later than the year 2010, including their ballistic missile systems. The proposed conclusion of a nuclear disarmament treaty in the year 2000 should also impose the obligation upon all states to dismantle and destroy their nuclear weapon making facilities and to open all of their nuclear facilities to the IAEA. Furthermore, the above proposed disarmament treaty should incorporate the individual suggestions and measures previously proposed.

(10) Even the most effective and sophisticated systems of the implementation of the proposed nuclear disarmament treaty early in the 21st century cannot be foolproof safeguards ensuring the continued existence of a world free of nuclear weapons. There is always the possibility that one or more states will illegally attempt to obtain or even illegally possess nuclear weapons. Such states, armed with nuclear weapons, in any given conflict, could be in a powerful position to blackmail the entire world with the threat to use their nuclear weapons. To counter this situation, only the United Nations should have in its possession a very limited number of nuclear weapons. The United Nations would be able in a collective way to deal effectively with such situations, and to have also the means to ensure the denuclearization of any nuclearized states in the 21st century.

Based on the preceding analysis and the proposed new strategic legal plan for a global and comprehensive nuclear disarmament through the rule of international law, it should be agreed that there is currently the appropriate legal environment and legal dynamics for achieving nuclear disarmament. The preceding discussion shows that, regarding the new international law of nuclear disarmament, such a settlement can be both feasible and effective. The adoption of the proposed new strategic legal plan and the conclusion of a global nuclear disarmament treaty in the year 2000 in the context of the NPT review conference seems to be realistic. The proposed elimination and destruction of all nuclear weapons no later than the year 2010 also seems to be feasible.

The fact that the United States, Russia and the other nuclear weapon states have not put forward a global nuclear disarmament plan for the 21st century and have not at least stated their political willingness to establish a nuclear weapons free world should not discourage the nations of the world and particularly the peoples of the world from applying continued pressure upon the two nuclear superpowers and the other members of the Nuclear Club to finally agree on their nuclear disarmament. In December 1996 approximately 70 former generals from all over the world, including American and Russian former generals who were in charge of launching nuclear weapons in wartime, began their disarmament campaign by calling upon Russia and the United States and the other nuclear weapon states to begin nuclear disarmament with the ultimate objective of establishing a nuclear weapons free world in the 21st century. Additionally, the conclusion of the CTBT in September 1996, which comprehensively prohibits nuclear weapon testing, is a significant legal breakthrough which greatly facilitates the legal process for a global nuclear disarmament in the 21st century.

For more than half a century the entire world has lived under the constant fear of nuclear holocaust. During the past 50 years the world has lost several historic opportunities for the final settlement of the question of nuclear weapons and their elimination. In the year 2000, the world is called to make its most important choice in the history of its modern civilization: Either achieve through the rule of international law the elimination of all nuclear weapons, and thus establish at the beginning of the 21st century a nuclear weapons free world, or begin the century with the continued existence and threat of nuclear weapons.

The Comprehensive Nuclear Test Ban Treaty (September 1996) and Its Impact on Global Nuclear Disarmament

CTBT Content and Objectives

Almost since the first nuclear explosion in 1945, the international community has been involved in the quest to establish an international legal regime on the global prohibition of nuclear weapon testing. Since 1945, such testing has been a significant means for the qualitative advancement of nuclear weapons, in both vertical and horizontal proliferation. Nuclear weapon testing has significantly contributed to the development of advanced new types of weapons with far more destructive power.

Although the United States and former Soviet Union were involved since 1945 in nuclear weapon testing due to their arms race, the other lesser nuclear weapon states, Britain, France and China, were also conducting their own such testing. Both China and France carried out nuclear weapon testing in 1996, and not too long before the conclusion of the Comprehensive Nuclear Test Ban Treaty. An estimate of the known nuclear weapon tests conducted on a worldwide scale from 1945 to 1996 in the atmosphere and underground shows a total of about 2,045 such tests. This high number of tests in the past half century demonstrates the fundamental importance of nuclear weapon testing in developing nuclear armaments on a global basis.[529]

Despite intensive negotiations and significant proposals for the legal prohibition of nuclear testing, the world had failed before 1996 to make any legal progress or breakthroughs toward a global ban. Nevertheless, a more favorable world environment now exists for such a ban in the 21st century. On September 11, 1996, the UN General Assembly by a large majority of member states adopted the Comprehensive Nuclear Test Ban Treaty (CTBT), and thus the treaty, concluded in 1995 after extensive negotiations, was formally opened to the signature of individual countries.[530]

After the production of approximately 100,000 nuclear weapons on a global basis, the conclusion of the CTBT has ended a vicious cycle of 50 years of nuclear weapon testing. The conclusion of the CTBT constitutes a great legal development and breakthrough in the effort to achieve an effective global nuclear disarmament in the 21st century.

The preamble to the CTBT stresses the need for continued systematic and progressive efforts to reduce the number of nuclear weapons on a global basis, with the ultimate goal of eliminating all such weapons and achieving complete nuclear disarmament under effective verification means and international control. Additionally, the treaty emphasizes that its most fundamental legal objective, the cessation of all nuclear weapon test explosions and all other nuclear explosions, will not only contribute in the prevention of the development and qualitative improvement of nuclear weapons, and the development of more advanced new nuclear weapons, but also constitute an effective measure of nuclear disarmament and nonproliferation. The preamble of the treaty recognizes that the ending of all nuclear weapon explosions will be a significant step toward a systematic nuclear disarmament.

In the treaty, Article I in paragraph 1 states, "Each state party undertakes not to carry out any nuclear weapon test explosion or any other nuclear explosion, and to prohibit and prevent any such nuclear explosion at any place under its jurisdiction." Paragraph 2 of Article I states further, "Each state party undertakes, furthermore, to refrain from causing, encouraging, or in any way participating in the carrying out of any nuclear weapon test explosion or any other nuclear explosion." The treaty legally provides and imposes a total and comprehensive end to all nuclear weapon explosions and all other nuclear explosions.

The adoption of the CTBT brings to an end through the rule of international law an entire era of continuous development of more destructive nuclear weapons through their testing. The legal prohibition of all nuclear weapon explosions and all other nuclear explosions is a significant legal breakthrough in constraining the development and qualitative improvement of more lethal nuclear weapons.

The legal impact of the CTBT on achieving nuclear disarmament is of fundamental significance. The ending of nuclear weapon testing by the treaty will greatly assist in the international legal effort to realize a nuclear weapons free world. Specifically, the older types of existing nuclear weapons and the aging nuclear weapons stockpiles throughout the world will be finally eliminated and destroyed due to the prohibition of their testing to ensure their proper function. This will substantially reduce the nuclear weapons of the nuclear weapon states; this reduction will, in turn, promote the legal goal of global nuclear disarmament. The ending of all nuclear test explosions by the CTBT will also prevent the proliferation of nuclear weapons by non-nuclear weapon states in the new century.

Although the CTBT outlaws all nuclear weapon tests and all other nuclear explosions, the treaty fails to explicitly and specifically prohibit computer simulations or tests of nuclear weapons involving what are known as "sub-critical" blasts with no radioactive yield. All nuclear weapon states and other technologically developed countries possess sophisticated laboratories and computer systems, not prohibited by the treaty, which allow them to conduct computer simulated tests of nuclear weapons. This shortcoming of the treaty may be exploited by the nuclear weapon states and other technologically advanced countries to pursue a new kind of nuclear arms race by using their sophisticated laboratories and computer systems to carry out unverifiable illegal simulated tests of their nuclear weapons. On the other hand, states which have no such technological capabilities will be prohibited by the treaty from carrying out nuclear weapon tests and explosions.[531]

This will create a new inequality and division among states party to the CTBT, and will further provide countries with advanced laboratories and computers a great advantage over most countries of the world which do not have them in nuclear weapon testing and development. This flaw in the treaty will hamper the universal acceptance of the treaty, and it may jeopardize its objective to outlaw nuclear weapon testing on a global basis. Accordingly, the need exists to adopt an amendment of the CTBT, which will prohibit laboratory and computer simulated tests and explosions of nuclear weapons. Such an addition to the CTBT will greatly facilitate the universal acceptance of the treaty and the end of nuclear weapon testing.

Paragraph 1 of Article XIV of the treaty provides that it will enter into force 180 days after the date of deposit of the instruments of ratification by all states listed in Annex 2 of the treaty, but in no case earlier than two years after its opening for signature. According to Annex 2, there are 44 states which have nuclear power reactors and research reactors; all must sign and ratify the treaty before it enters into force. Since its opening for signing in September 1996, the CTBT has been signed by 158 states. All nuclear weapon states have signed the treaty. Israel, a de facto nuclear weapon state, has signed it, as have other states with nuclear power and research reactors listed in Annex 2. However, both India and Pakistan, de facto nuclear weapon states, have announced that they will not sign the treaty. India has officially announced that it will not sign. India justifies its refusal to sign the treaty by arguing that it is unequal, and that the nuclear weapon states have not legally committed themselves to a certain deadline for the total elimination of their nuclear weapons.[532]

If India does not sign the CTBT, then it will not enter into force, and it will not develop the legal effect of an international treaty. If the treaty has not entered into force three years after the date of the anniversary of its opening for signature, then according to paragraph 2 of Article XIV of the treaty, a conference of states that have already deposited their instruments of ratification must convene to decide what measures may be undertaken to accelerate and facilitate the early entry into force of the treaty. The CTBT is of unlimited duration. Even if it does not enter into force, it still can develop legal effect if it becomes a customary rule of international law. India and Pakistan carried out several underground nuclear weapon tests in 1999. Also, in October 1999, the U.S. Senate voted against the ratification of the CTBT. These developments constitute major setbacks to the CTBT.

CTBT Implementation and Verification

To ensure its effective implementation, the CTBT has created an organizational structure and a verification system featuring innovative legal approaches. Article II of the treaty establishes a treaty organization consisting of all states party to the treaty. The fundamental objective of the organization is to achieve the object and purpose of the treaty, to ensure the implementation of its provisions, including those for international verification of compliance with it, and to provide a forum for consultation and cooperation among the states party to the treaty. The organization has been empowered with the responsibility of verification activities provided by the treaty, to ensure its effective implementation. The organization enjoys under the treaty all privileges and immunities necessary to exercise its functions.

The conference of states established by the CTBT constitutes a principal organ of the organization. It consists of all states party to the treaty. According to Article II, Section B, the conference has the power to consider any questions and issues within the scope of the treaty. Additionally, it can make recommendations and decisions on issues pertaining to the scope of the treaty. The conference has the obligation under the treaty to oversee the implementation of the treaty, to review effective compliance, and to act in a manner that promotes the objectives of the treaty.

The Executive Council consists of 51 states party to the treaty. Although all such states have the right to serve on the Executive Council, state representation to this organ of the treaty must be based on an equitable geographical distribution. This organ has the responsibility to promote the effective implementation of the treaty and to ensure compliance. To this end the Executive Council has been provided with a wide range of powers and responsibilities. Of particular importance are its powers to receive, consider, and take actions on requests for on-site inspections, and the reports of such inspections in accordance with Article IV of the treaty. It also has the power to approve and oversee the operation of agreements or arrangements relating to the implementation of verification activities with treaty signatories and with other states. Moreover, the Executive Council has the power to consider any concern raised by a state party to the treaty regarding possible noncompliance and abuse of the rights provided by the treaty. It is further the responsibility of this organ to take appropriate measures to redress the situation.

The Technical Secretariat consists of all states party to the treaty. This organ is designed by the treaty to help the conference and the Executive Council perform their functions under the treaty. The Technical Secretariat is a significant treaty organ with a wide range of powers and responsibilities to carry out the difficult task of achieving the effective implementation of the treaty. Its responsibilities regarding verification of compliance with the treaty, pursuant to Article IV and the protocol, include such functions as: (a) the responsibility for supervising and coordinating the operation of the International Monitoring System; (b) the operation of the International Data Center; (c) the routine receiving, processing, analyzing and reporting of International Monitoring System data; (d) the provision of technical assistance and support for the installation and operation of monitoring stations; and (e) the receiving of requests for on-site inspections and their processing, and also the carrying out of preparations for on-site inspections.

The treaty has established an innovative and elaborate system to verify its implementation. Article III of the treaty provides a system of national measures designed to implement the obligations of states party to the treaty. It imposes upon these states an obligation to prohibit natural and legal persons anywhere on their territories or in any other place under their jurisdiction from undertaking any activities prohibited by the treaty. Article III also requires states party to the CTBT to form a National Authority to serve as the national focal point for liaison with the organization and with other signatories.

Most importantly, the CTBT has created a significant international system to verify compliance with the treaty and carry out its implementation in an effective manner. Article IV of the treaty creates a verification regime consisting of the following elements: (a) an International Monitoring System; (b) consultation and clarification; (c) on-site inspections; and (d) confidence-building measures. The verification activities of the CTBT are to be carried out on the basis of full respect for the sovereignty of states party to the treaty, and in the least intrusive manner possible consistent with the effective and timely accomplishment of their objectives. The treaty also requires signatories to refrain from any abuse of the right of verification.

According to the treaty, each signatory undertakes the obligation to cooperate with the organization and the other states to facilitate the verification of compliance with the treaty. The treaty requires member states to perform the following: (a) establish the necessary facilities to participate in the verification measures; (b) provide data obtained from national stations that are part of the International Monitoring System; (c) permit the conduct of on-site inspections, and (d) participate in confidence-building measures.

The CTBT clearly provides that all member states, regardless of their technical and financial capabilities, must enjoy an equal right of verification and assume an equal obligation to accept verification. The provision of equal rights and obligations regarding the verification of the treaty by on-site inspections in particular creates a new international legal system and regime of intrusive verification, which is capable of ensuring the effective implementation of the treaty. The legal adoption of on-site inspections on the international level by the CTBT creates further a new international law of verification measures, which can be of imperative importance in ensuring the effective implementation of international nuclear disarmament agreements.

Although consultation and clarification and confidence-building measures can play a positive role as verification measures for ensuring the effective compliance with the treaty, the International Monitoring System and the system of on-site inspections are the most effective and dynamic means of verifying the implementation of the treaty. The International Monitoring System includes means and facilities for seismological monitoring, radio-nuclide monitoring, certified laboratories, hydroacoustic monitoring, infrasound monitoring and respective means of communication. The technological advancement and sophistication of seismological means of monitoring can play an especially significant role in the verification of compliance with the treaty.[533]

The sole purpose of on-site inspections is to clarify whether a nuclear weapon test explosion or any other nuclear explosion was carried out in violation of Article I of the CTBT. To this end, the treaty provides each state party to the treaty with the right to request such inspections. Thus, if a state requests on-site inspections, and after several procedural requirements have been met, the Executive Council can approve the conduct of on-site inspections on the territory of the state to be inspected. An inspection team must be sent to conduct the approved on-site inspection. The state to be inspected is required by the treaty to permit the inspection and to enable the inspection team to fulfill its mandate. In particular, the state subject to on-site inspection is required by the treaty not to impede the inspection team from moving within the inspection area to carry out its inspection activities. The inspection team must conduct on-site inspections in the least intrusive manner possible, and collect only information to ensure compliance with the treaty. Thus, the Executive Council has the power not to approve frivolous or abusive on-site inspections and may terminate such inspections.

If there is sufficient information that a state has violated the treaty, the Executive Council should take the necessary measures to redress and remedy the situation to ensure compliance. The treaty provides a system for peaceful resolution of the issues and disputes involved, including resort to the International Court of Justice in accordance with the Statute of the Court. If the Executive Council fails to resolve issues involving compliance, then the conference may decide to restrict or suspend the violator state from the exercise of its rights and privileges under the treaty until the conference decides otherwise.

The preceding analysis shows that the CTBT has adopted a verification system of significant and innovative means to effectively achieve the purpose of the treaty. In particular, the international verification system of on-site inspections adopted by the treaty constitutes a substantial legal step for the effective implementation of the CTBT, and the new international law of verification through on-site inspections can facilitate effective nuclear disarmament.

Nevertheless, the CTBT did not adopt random on-site inspections. Contrary to on-site inspections that can be carried out only by request and approval, procedures of the treaty which are fairly expedited, random on-site inspections would more effectively ensure compliance with the treaty, because inspection teams would be empowered with the right to go to any territory of any state party to the treaty to conduct on-site inspection without advance notice. Such on-site inspections would not give the inspected parties the required time to destroy and conceal evidence that would show violations of the treaty.

The legal need for the adoption of a system of random on-site inspections becomes important in view of the fact that small nuclear-weapon testing explosions of up to a few kilotons are possible in a large underground cavity. This kind of small nuclear weapon explosion could escape the International Monitoring System because the energy released by the seismic signal would lie below the level required by the technical capability of the International Monitoring System to detect it. The International Monitoring System can monitor all seismic events down to a seismic magnitude of 4.25 and can locate these events within an area of a thousand square kilometers.[534]

Random on-site inspections, combined with the establishment by the CTBT of an international intelligence system designed to collect information and data relating to the adherence to the treaty, would have created a more effective and dynamic verification system.

In view of the legal precedent set by the direct involvement of the United Nations in the successful dismantling and destruction of the Iraqi nuclear weapons program on the basis of the agreements concluded in the aftermath of the Persian Gulf War, the CTBT, in addition to the proposed adoption of random on-site inspections, should have also empowered its inspection teams with the right to physically destroy, or to seize, or to remove from any inspected territory and facility any nuclear material and other means which could be used for nuclear weapon explosions and testing in violation of the treaty. Moreover, the CTBT, in view of the precedent set by the severe international sanctions imposed upon Iraq, should have provided the imposition of international sanctions of severe form upon the states party to the treaty and any other states not party to the treaty which are involved in nuclear testing.

NWFZs and the Future of Regional Nuclear Disarmament in the Post–Cold War Era

The Korean Peninsula NWFZ (December 1991)

After several years of negotiations, North and South Korea signed a denuclearization agreement in December 1991 establishing a nuclear weapon-free zone in the Korean peninsula. In their Joint Declaration for a Non-Nuclear Korean Peninsula, both nations undertook not to test, produce, receive, possess, store, deploy or use nuclear weapons. However, any progress toward implementation of the denuclearization agreement and the final establishment of a nuclear weapon-free Korean peninsula has moved slowly, and suffered a major setback when North Korea withdrew from the NPT in 1993.[535]

China, a significant nuclear weapon state with the ambition to become a nuclear superpower in the 21st century, has continuously supported the establishment of a nuclear weapon-free Korean peninsula and the peaceful reunification of both Koreas. Russia has also supported a nuclear weapon-free Korean peninsula, and has withdrawn its technical support for the North Korean nuclear facilities and program. The United States has likewise supported a Korean NWFZ, and since 1991 has removed all of its nuclear weapons from South Korea. Additionally, Japan has been in support of the establishment of a nuclear weapon-free Korean peninsula.[536]

The decision of North Korea to withdraw from the NPT in 1993, and not allow the IAEA to conduct on-site inspections of its nuclear facilities, has negatively affected the legal effort for the denuclearization of the Korean peninsula. Although North Korea suspended in the same year its withdrawal from the NPT, reports that it had created an advanced nuclear weapon program and that it had the technological capability to develop nuclear weapons caused more friction between the two Koreas, and had a negative political impact on the region. Nevertheless, after intensive negotiations between North Korea and the United States, both parties agreed in 1994 that North Korea would freeze its nuclear activities and that it would allow IAEA inspectors to verify the freeze.[537]

Further negotiations between the United States and North Korea led to a new agreement, in the fall of 1995, in which North Korea agreed to dismantle its existing nuclear facilities in exchange for receiving light water reactors and interim energy supplies. South Korea in 1995 also ratified the NPT. Furthermore, the United States agreed that it would not use or threaten to use nuclear weapons against North Korea. These developments have deflated the tension in the Korean peninsula and may further facilitate the process for a nuclear weapon-free Korean peninsula by implementing the relevant denuclearization agreement. Moreover, the denuclearization of the Korean peninsula will greatly facilitate the process for achieving and maintaining a Northeast Asian NWFZ.[538]

The failure to finally establish a Korean peninsula NWFZ will have unfortunate consequences for the region. If North Korea acquires nuclear weapons, then Japan will be within the range of North Korea's ballistic missiles capable of delivering them. Such a development would provide the required justification to the Japanese government to proceed immediately with the development of its own nuclear weapons. Japan, an NPT member state, supported that treaty's indefinite extension in 1995. However, Japanese government officials in 1993 expressed their desire to acquire the nuclear bomb as an option. Japan has already the technological capabilities and the required materials to develop nuclear weapons. It has accumulated more than ten tons of plutonium, sufficient for a large number of nuclear weapons.[539]

The denuclearization of the Korean peninsula would facilitate the process for a Northeast Asian nuclear weapon-free area. Most importantly, it would prevent a nuclear arms race in the region in the 21st century, which would involve the acquisition of nuclear weapons by Japan in violation of its obligations under the NPT. Indeed, Japan, a global economic superpower, will not accept remaining nuclear weapon-free if North Korea finally develops nuclear weapons enabling it to threaten Japan with nuclear war and nuclear blackmail.

The Southeast Asian NWFZ (December 1995)

On December 15, 1995, the leaders of all ten Southeast Asian nations signed this treaty, which established the Southeast Asian NWFZ. This NWFZ comprises Myanmar (formerly Burma), Laos, Cambodia, and the ASEAN countries of Brunei, Indonesia, Malaysia, the Philippines, Singapore, Thailand and Vietnam.[540] The fundamental objective of this NWFZ is, pursuant to its Article 3, to prohibit its signatories from developing, manufacturing or otherwise acquiring or having control over nuclear weapons anywhere inside or outside this zone; and from stationing or transporting nuclear weapons by any means, or from testing nuclear weapons. Additionally, Article 3 of the treaty obliges the states party to the treaty not to allow in their respective territories any other state to carry out the above activities. The treaty prohibits the dumping of nuclear materials and radioactive wastes in the region.[541]

The treaty further has provided an organizational system to implement its purposes and objectives. The principal organs of the treaty are the Commission and the Executive Committee. Although the Commission has the power to supervise the implementation of the treaty, the Executive Committee has, as its primary function, the duty to ensure the proper operation of verification measures in accordance with the provisions of the control system of the treaty, which provisions are stipulated in its Article 10. This control system, which is designed to ensure the verified compliance with the treaty, provides as verification means the application of the IAEA safeguards system, report and exchange of information, request for clarification, and request and procedures for a fact-finding mission.[542]

Although neither China nor the United States supports the Southeast Asian NWFZ,[543] an overall evaluation of the objectives of this agreement shows the legal commitment of its signatories to create a nuclear weapon-free zone in their region. The establishment of this zone promotes peace and security in the region and safeguards against the proliferation of nuclear weapons. Thus, this NWFZ is a significant legal measure against regional nuclear weapons proliferation, and a substantial step in the quest for a global nuclear disarmament.

The African NWFZ (April 1996)

The Organization of African Unity began in 1964, under the aegis of the United Nations, negotiations for the conclusion of a treaty establishing an African NWFZ. Notwithstanding negotiations to that end in the past, it was in 1990 when the hopes for the establishment of the zone were heightened when South Africa announced that it would sign the NPT. South Africa, which had become a de facto nuclear weapon state, signed the NPT in 1991. In 1993, South Africa stated publicly that it had developed nuclear weapons, but it had destroyed all of them.[544]

The accession of South Africa to the NPT and its verified denuclearization by the IAEA paved the road for the conclusion of the African NWFZ, which was signed in Cairo on April 11, 1996.[545] The treaty is a significant legal development in regional nuclear disarmament. It is the first international legal instrument in nuclear weapons nonproliferation and disarmament which requires the denuclearization of an entire continent.

The African NWFZ covers 53 states. So far 45 states have signed the treaty. South Africa has signed the treaty. Ghana and Zaire, which have nuclear research reactors, have also signed, as has Nigeria, which threatened in the past to acquire nuclear weapons. The North African states of Egypt, Libya and Algeria, which have been involved in nuclear activities, have all signed.[546]

The fundamental legal objective of the treaty is to denuclearize and maintain the entire African continent free of nuclear weapons. The treaty prohibits its signatories from stationing or testing nuclear explosive devices. The treaty further provides for the declaration, destruction, dismantling or conversion of nuclear explosive devices and the facilities for their manufacture. The treaty prohibits the dumping of radioactive wastes, and it is the first multinational legal instrument that provides for the physical protection of nuclear materials and facilities and prohibits explicitly the armed attack on nuclear installations.[547]

To ensure the peaceful application and use of nuclear energy, the treaty has created a mechanism of compliance placed under the African Commission on Nuclear Energy, formed by the treaty. The treaty further provides a system of verification for ensuring the effective implementation of its purposes. The treaty requires the involvement of the IAEA in the verification of compliance by applying its nuclear safeguards. It also provides a system for annual reporting and exchanges of information regarding its implementation. The treaty, which is of unlimited duration and indefinite force, provides, as means of the settlement of disputes over treaty issues, negotiations and arbitration.[548]

An overall evaluation of the establishment of the African NWFZ shows that it is a significant legal achievement in regional nuclear weapons nonproliferation. Indeed, it is the first time in the history of nuclear disarmament that an entire continent has been declared and established as an NWFZ. This legal development could be used as a model for the denuclearization of other continents. China, France, Britain and the United States have signed both Protocols I and II to the treaty concerning the legal relationship of the nuclear weapon states and of those states controlling territories in Africa. (Russia has not signed.) Protocol I requires the nuclear weapon states not to use or threaten to use a nuclear explosive device against the parties to the treaty. Protocol II requires the nuclear weapon states not to test any nuclear explosive devices within the zone. Protocol III, already signed by France and Spain, requires both countries to cooperate with the treaty, since these two countries are internationally responsible for territories within the African NWFZ.[549]

The Prospects for New NWFZs in the Post–Cold War Era

Since the late 1950s, when the concept of the NWFZ was introduced as an international legal measure for the prevention of the proliferation of nuclear weapons, a number of NWFZs and even Peace Zones have been proposed. Nevertheless, so far only the Latin American, the South Pacific, the Korean Peninsula, the Southeast Asian, and African NWFZs have been established. There exist the old, but still open, proposals for the establishment of the following NWFZs and Peace Zones: (1) a Central European NWFZ; (2) a Balkan NWFZ; (3) a Nordic NWFZ; (4) a Mediterranean NWFZ; (5) a Middle East NWFZ; (6) a South Asian NWFZ; (7) an Indian Ocean Zone of Peace, and (8) an Arctic NWFZ.[550]

The legal establishment of the proposed NWFZs and Peace Zones, which cover vast regions of the world, would be an important measure for regional nuclear weapons nonproliferation and generally for regional denuclearization and nuclear disarmament. The adoption of these proposed NWFZs will have legal benefits for global and comprehensive nuclear disarmament. In essence, the legal adoption of any proposed NWFZ in any region of the world will make a significant contribution to the cause of nuclear disarmament.

Although the prospects for the establishment of each of the proposed NWFZs demand their own analysis, the following discussion will concentrate on the prospects and legal need for the creation of NWFZs in the Middle East and the South Asian regions. The introduction of nuclear weapons in these two regions, the existence of historic conflicts and the volatile situations in these regions demand the denuclearization of both. The existence of nuclear weapons in these regions, and the potential for their use in a war could not only cause a regional nuclear holocaust, but could also pose a grave danger to global peace and security, perhaps even triggering a global nuclear war.

The proposal for the creation of a Middle East NWFZ, which would comprise the Arab states, Israel and Iran, was set forth in 1974 by Iran because of the rapid diffusion of nuclear technology and materials in the region. Despite UN resolutions and regional efforts for the legal adoption of a Middle East NWFZ, it has not been established.[551] The historic conflict and confrontations between Israel and the Arab states, and, above all, the regional nuclear weapons monopoly by Israel, are great obstacles to the establishment of a Middle East NWFZ.

The nuclear weapons monopoly of Israel, which has refused to accede to the NPT and to accept the nuclear safeguards of the IAEA, and the cool Israeli reaction to the proposed creation of a Middle East NWFZ[552] have decreased the legal prospects for this NWFZ. On the other hand, a number of militarily significant Arab states have expressed support for a Middle East NWFZ. The destruction and dismantling of Iraq's nuclear weapons program during the Persian Gulf War in 1991 and afterwards by the United Nations inspection teams[553] should increase the legal prospects for a Middle East NWFZ. In fact, the dismantling of Iraq's nuclear weapons program should prevent any Israeli argument against a Middle East NWFZ; the danger of the building of nuclear weapons by Iraq to be primarily used against Israel no longer exists.

Although none of the Arab states in the Middle East now possesses nuclear weapons, and although it is unlikely that any Arab state will be able to acquire nuclear weapons in the near future, Israel's nuclear weapons monopoly in the region diminishes the prospects of a denuclearized Middle East, and increases the possibility of the acquisition of nuclear weapons by the Arab states in the future to counter Israel's nuclear monopoly. This, in turn, would pose a constant threat of nuclear war in the Middle East, particularly due to the historic Arab-Israeli tensions. Iran, which does not possess nuclear weapons, has launched a major effort to build a nuclear weapons program. If Iran attains nuclear capability, it will further increase the threat of a nuclear war in the Middle East. Nonetheless, the Iranian government has recently expressed its support for a Middle East NWFZ.[554]

In addition to Israel's nuclear weapons monopoly and its determination to retain its nuclear weapons, which have become major obstacles to any legal breakthrough in the creation of a denuclearized Middle East, the United States has also obstructed the effort to establish a Middle East NWFZ. Although the United States has supported the creation of a Middle East NWFZ, and despite the fact that almost immediately after the end of the Persian Gulf War President Bush proposed that Middle Eastern states halt the production of enriched uranium and processed plutonium, the United States has failed to be a catalyst in ending

Israel's nuclear monopoly and in establishing a Middle Eastern NWFZ. The Bush proposal for halting the proliferation of nuclear bomb-building materials in the Middle East was rejected by Egypt and other Arab states, because the legal adoption of this proposal would have permitted Israel to retain its nuclear weapons.[555]

The United States has applied an unacceptable double standard of policy on proliferation of nuclear weapons in the Middle East. It has vigorously opposed any Arab state in its effort to acquire nuclear weapons. The United States was quick during the Persian Gulf War in 1991 and afterwards to destroy the Iraqi nuclear program and facilities, and then prevent it from building nuclear weapons. On the other hand, the United States has deliberately failed not only to pressure Israel to forgo its nuclear weapons, but also, and most importantly, the United States has not even acknowledged that Israel has nuclear weapons.

Although it will be a difficult legal task to create a nuclear weapons-free Middle East due to the historic conflict and animosity between Israel and the Arab states, the end of the Cold War, which had involved the superpowers in the Middle East, and the presently evolving Arab-Israeli peace negotiations and agreements provide a legal environment and improved prospects for the final adoption of a Middle East NWFZ. To achieve this legal objective, Israel should abandon its argument that its nuclear weapons are a deterrent against Arab aggression and against a possible Arab nuclear threat.[556] Moreover, Israel should accede to the NPT, to open up and place all of its nuclear facilities and material under the control of the IAEA and to verifiably destroy all of its nuclear weapons.

Israel and the Arab states have a great security interest in ensuring that their region remains free from nuclear weapons in the future. Because no Arab state has acquired nuclear weapons, it would be easier to create a Middle East NWFZ. Israel also has an enormous security interest in forgoing its nuclear weapons with the objective of establishing a Middle East NWFZ before the Arab states acquire nuclear weapons and end Israel's nuclear monopoly. If Israel insists on retaining its nuclear weapons, then some militarily significant Middle Eastern states will be pushed to acquire nuclear weapons to end that monopoly. In view of the existing proliferation of nuclear technologies and materials, some Arab states will be able to build nuclear weapons in the future. An Arab-Israeli nuclear arms race in the Middle East would pose a grave threat of nuclear war in the region, with an immediate threat to world peace and security. Despite the existing difficulties which lower the prospects of a Middle East NWFZ in the foreseeable future, the legal need for the establishment of such a zone is clear.

Pakistan proposed a South Asian NWFZ in 1974 when India tested a nuclear explosive device. Since 1976, the United Nations General Assembly has passed a string of resolutions calling for the establishment of an NWFZ in South Asia. Since the late 1970s, Pakistan has proposed to India their joint signing of the NPT, and joint agreement to full-scope safeguards, or bilateral inspection. However, India has rejected these Pakistani proposals. In 1987 and in 1990 Pakistan also offered a joint declaration of South Asia as an NWFZ.[557]

In December 1985, India and Pakistan agreed not to attack each other's nuclear facilities and to resume negotiations on a nonaggression pact or friendship treaty. The first agreement was signed on December 31, 1988, and ratified by Pakistan on August 10, 1989. The two sides exchanged instruments of ratification on January 27, 1991, at which point the treaty entered into force. Pakistan made its latest effort to create an NWFZ in South Asia in June 1991, when Pakistan offered five-power nuclear disarmament talks with the Soviet Union, China and the United States mediating between India and Pakistan. Although such a meeting was initially scheduled to be held in 1992 in Washington, D.C., this meeting has not taken place.[558]

Despite the repeated efforts for the establishment of a South Asian NWFZ, these efforts have not produced any positive legal results. Above all, the reported acquisition of nuclear weapons by Pakistan by the end of the 1980s had a great negative impact on the legal prospects for the creation of this NWFZ. Although the five de jure nuclear weapon states support the creation of such an NWFZ, its establishment faces enormous difficulties.[559]

Although India opposes the legal adoption of a South Asian NWFZ because it has abandoned attempts at regional disarmament in favor of a global nuclear disarmament, the fundamental reasons for the failure to denuclearize this region can be found in the difficult historical relationships between India and Pakistan, and India and China. India, which fears nuclear-armed China with whom it has warred in the past, cannot agree with Pakistan alone on the creation of a South Asian NWFZ. India will not forgo its nuclear weapons by agreeing on a South Asian NWFZ if China remains a nuclear power. Furthermore, since India is determined because of the Chinese factor to retain its nuclear capabilities, Pakistan, because of its conflict with India over Kashmir, will not forgo its nuclear weapons by accepting an NWFZ in the region if India retains its nuclear capabilities.[560]

Thus it seems that the legal prospects for the establishment of a South Asian NWFZ are substantially decreased. In essence, the troubled histories between India and China, and India and Pakistan are major obstacles which prevent both Pakistan and India from forgoing their nuclear weapons by the legal adoption of a South Asian NWFZ. In particular, the conflict between India and Pakistan over Kashmir might fuel a nuclear arms race between these two states. Such a development would increase the threat of a nuclear war between the two nations in the event of a major conflict. The establishment of the proposed South Asian NWFZ covering Pakistan and India and the other states in the region would put an end to the threat of a nuclear war between Pakistan and India. To dispel the fears of a Chinese nuclear attack against India and thus assist in the participation of India in the South Asian NWFZ, China should provide a nuclear security guarantee to India.[561]

The end of the Cold War, the greatly diminished threat of nuclear war between the superpowers, and the beginning of a post–Cold War global détente have become vital political and legal factors in the international efforts for both regional and global nuclear disarmament, and substantially improve the legal dynamics and prospects for regional nuclear disarmament by establishing new NWFZs.

During the Cold War, the European continent was considered the most likely main battlefield of a U.S.–Soviet nuclear war. However, the dissolution of the Warsaw Pact, the disintegration of the Soviet Union, and the withdrawal of the former Soviet nuclear forces from Eastern Europe leave the United States and generally the NATO powers in Western Europe with no strategic enemy in sight. Similarly, the deflation of superpower nuclear tensions in the Asian continent and their nuclear disarmament from the various regions of this continent constitute significant developments in the regional legal efforts for nuclear disarmament.[562]

The end of the Cold War and the beginning of the post–Cold War era provide the required legal dynamics and improved prospects for regional nuclear disarmament throughout the world through the establishment of NWFZs. The pursuit of NWFZs and the expansion of the regional nuclear disarmament and anti-nuclear war movement will enhance the legal prospects for regional denuclearization. The creation of NWFZs will be a significant legal measure for the prevention of the regional proliferation of nuclear weapons. The legal promotion of regional nuclear disarmament will greatly facilitate the international legal process for a global and comprehensive nuclear disarmament.

On the Legality of the Use, Development, Possession and Deployment of Nuclear Weapons

Legality According to the International Court of Justice

The UN General Assembly requested the International Court of Justice (ICJ) in 1994 to render an advisory opinion on the following question: "Is the threat or use of nuclear weapons in any circumstance permitted under international law?" The ICJ, on July 8, 1996, handed down its advisory opinion on the question. Although it deserves its own analysis and critical evaluation, the following discussion will focus on a brief and concise analysis of the main legal conclusions reached by the ICJ on this question of paramount legal significance and of ultimate practical concern to humanity.

The ICJ unanimously concluded that there is in neither customary nor conventional international law any specific authorization of the threat or use of nuclear weapons. The ICJ also by an 11–3 vote stated that there is in neither customary nor conventional international law any comprehensive and universal prohibition of the threat or use of nuclear weapons as such. The ICJ further unanimously concluded that a threat or use of force by means of nuclear weapons that is contrary to Article 2, paragraph 4, of the United Nations Charter and that fails to meet all the requirements of Article 51, is unlawful.

The ICJ unanimously stated that a threat or use of nuclear weapons should also be compatible with the requirements of the international law applicable in armed conflict, particularly regarding the principles and rules of international humanitarian law, as well as with specific obligations under treaties and other undertakings which expressly deal with nuclear weapons. To this end, the ICJ, in a 7–7 vote, argued that the threat or use of nuclear weapons would generally be contrary to the rules of international law applicable in armed conflict, and in particular the principles and rules of humanitarian law. The ICJ concluded that in view, however, of the current state of international law, and of the elements of fact at its disposal, the court cannot conclude definitively whether the threat or use of nuclear weapons would be lawful or unlawful in an extreme circumstance of self defense, in which the very survival of a state would be at stake.

Nevertheless, the court appears to agree that generally in the normal context of self-defense, and generally in situations which do not involve an extreme circumstance placing at stake the very survival of a state, the threat or use of nuclear weapons in such situations of self-defense would be prohibited under international law. The court lost a historic opportunity by failing to declare that the threat or use of nuclear weapons is illegal in any circumstances whatsoever. Such an opinion would have found support in international law. Simply, since the court accepts that the threat or use of nuclear weapons is unlawful under the principles and rules of international humanitarian law, in the same legal rationale it should have concluded that even if the threat or use of such weapons occurred in an extreme circumstance of self-defense involving the very survival of a state, still the international humanitarian law would prohibit the use or threat of nuclear weapons.

In essence, the court concluded that the threat or use of nuclear weapons to wage an aggressive nuclear war generally violates international law. Thus, one can argue that the threat or use of nuclear weapons as means of an aggressive war is prohibited by international law. This conclusion reached by the ICJ constitutes a significant legal development and contribution generally in nuclear war and nuclear disarmament.

The court's conclusion that there exists a legal obligation to pursue in good faith and to conclude negotiations leading to nuclear disarmament in all its aspects under strict and effective international legal controls is also legally significant. Indeed, the court recognizes that there is a legal obligation under international law that requires general nuclear disarmament. This conclusion has a positive legal impact on the requirement for global and comprehensive nuclear disarmament as an international legal obligation, which imposes upon all nuclear weapon states a requirement to achieve such disarmament. This conclusion also provides significant support to this study's argument that nuclear disarmament is required by international law.

Legality According to the UN Charter

The question of the legality of the use of nuclear weapons by a nuclear weapon state against an enemy state for aggressive purposes has been posed with ever-increasing frequency and intensity since 1945.[563]

Regarding the legality of the aggressive use[564] of nuclear weapons by one state against another under the UN Charter, one cannot look for any specific regulatory language because the charter was adopted before the atomic bomb was developed. Nevertheless, Article 2 (4) of the charter provides that "All Members shall refrain in their international relations from the threat or use of force against the territorial integrity or political independence of any state, or in any other manner inconsistent with the purposes of the United Nations."

Based on the rule of law created by Article 2 (4), the threat or use of force for waging an aggressive war is absolutely prohibited. The prohibition of the threat or use of force is not only a positive rule of international law, but has also been established as a customary and compelling rule of international law. Accordingly, since any threat or use of force for waging an aggressive war involves the threat or use of weapons, it can be further suggested that by virtue of Article 2 (4) of the UN Charter and by necessary legal implications the threat or use of nuclear weapons is prohibited.[565]

Concerning the legality of the first use of nuclear weapons for waging an aggressive war, China, by its legally binding declaration, has undertaken not to be the first to use nuclear weapons at any time or under any circumstances. China has also undertaken not to use or threaten to use nuclear weapons against non-nuclear weapon states or nuclear weapon-free zones at any time or under any circumstances. On the other hand, the United States, Russia, France and Britain, by their respective and legally binding declarations, have stated that they will not use nuclear weapons against non-nuclear weapon states parties to the NPT, except in the case of an invasion or other attack on their territories, their armed forces, their allies, or states with which they have security commitments, carried out or sustained by a non-nuclear weapon state, in association or alliance with a nuclear weapon state.[566]

However, under Article 2 (4) of the UN Charter, all nuclear weapon states, either de jure or de facto, are prohibited from resorting to the first use of their nuclear weapons, including the threat of using them against any state to wage aggressive war or to make first use of nuclear weapons.[567] This legal conclusion is further supported by the UN General Assembly 1653 (XVI), adopted in 1961, which stated that the use of nuclear and thermonuclear weapons is a direct violation of the organization's charter.[568] The International Court of Justice has reached the same conclusion on this question in its advisory opinion.

Although the threat or use of nuclear weapons in a first-use scenario or for the purposes of waging an aggressive nuclear war is implicitly prohibited by Article 2 (4) of the UN Charter, Article 51 of the charter, which embodies the doctrine of self-defense, permits a state to use armed force in self-defense if an armed attack occurs against it. But since Article 51 permits the use of armed force, the question arises whether nuclear weapons could be used in self-defense and under what circumstances and criteria.

The use of force in self-defense under Article 51 constitutes an exception to the rule adopted by Article 2 (4) of the charter, which outlaws war and the threat or use of force for the waging of aggressive wars. Therefore, the use of force in exercising the inherent right of a state in self-defense against an armed attack must be exceptionally applied and it must conform to the legal doctrine of self-defense. However, since war has been outlawed by virtue of Article 2 (4) of the UN Charter, then it should be agreed that the charter has established a new legal order of a warless world community. Accordingly, in view of the law of peace established by the UN Charter, the use of armed force according to the doctrine of self-defense must conform to the law of peace and must not defeat the objectives of this body of law.

Although the juridical concept of the right to use armed force in self-defense constitutes a traditional concept of international law, the advent of nuclear weapons and particularly the unprecedented mass destructive capabilities of such weapons necessitates the philosophical and legal rethinking of the doctrine of self-defense and its validity in the nuclear age. The concept of self-defense has always been predicated on the notion that an attacked country will be able to respond to the attack. But with the development of nuclear weapons, this assumption seems to be no longer valid.[569] Indeed, the massive potential for wholesale destruction associated with the use of either strategic or tactical nuclear weapons,[570] even in a scenario involving self-defense, clearly would not only exceed the limits imposed by the doctrine of self-defense, but also would defeat the very objective of this doctrine.

The legal analysis of this question can revolve principally upon three scenarios. The first would occur when a nation has been attacked by conventional weapons. In this scenario, the proportionality principle mandates that the force used, even in a defensive posture, must be proportional to the force used by the aggressor. Because of the vast disparity in magnitude between any nuclear weapons and any conventional weapons of warfare, it is difficult to conceive of a proportionate nuclear defense to a conventional attack.[571] Therefore, the use of nuclear weapons by a state to defend itself against a conventional armed attack would violate Article 51 of the UN Charter.

The second scenario involves a nuclear response to a nuclear attack. Although this situation could present the stronger case for permitting a nuclear strike in some capacity, it is, however, still difficult to ascertain what degree of response is appropriate. The doctrine of self-defense applies only to prevent further damage to citizens and territories of the state under armed attack. Moreover, the right to self-defense does not include the right to an armed attack for retaliatory purposes. Thus, any nuclear attack on the civilian population would be unlawful, since it would not further a defensive objective. Defending against the threat of additional nuclear attack could only be achieved by a counterforce strike against the aggressor's available nuclear weapons.[572]

Either military strategy would violate international law: A full-scale assault on all of the aggressor's nuclear forces would undoubtedly result in incalculable destruction and would therefore be disproportionate to all but an all-out assault; a more limited counterforce strike would not achieve the objective of self-defense to eliminate the aggressor's nuclear forces and, hence, to prevent the aggressor from inflicting additional damage. Therein lies the flaw with nuclear responses in self-defense against a nuclear attack: The degree of force needed to effectively defend against future attacks is inherently disproportionate to the destruction that it would necessarily cause, particularly given the fact that there is no guarantee that the aggressor would launch additional weapons.[573]

Therefore, the use of nuclear weapons by a state defending itself against a nuclear attack cannot be permitted under Article 51 of the UN Charter, even though that document embodies the legal doctrine of self-defense. Furthermore, it must be emphasized that a nuclear response to a nuclear attack would result in the annihilation of the parties involved in such a conflict. Therefore, the nuclear holocaust of the parties involved would not only exceed the purposes of the doctrine of self-defense, but also, and most importantly, would defeat its legal objectives.[574]

The third scenario contemplates anticipatory self-defense or the use of nuclear weapons to prevent an imminent attack. Although Article 51 of the UN Charter restricts the use of force in self-defense to reactions against armed attack, several commentators have proffered reasons for which Article 51 should be interpreted to sanction anticipatory self-defense. It is argued that the definition of an armed attack must be altered to take account of the advent of nuclear weapons. Because of the enormous potential for destruction caused by the use of nuclear weapons, it is imperative that such an attack be prevented if it is, in fact, imminent. Moreover, it is argued that the traditional assumptions underlying the right of self-defense are no longer valid with the development of nuclear weapons. Thus, it is proposed that for self-defense to retain its effectiveness, Article 51 of the UN Charter must be interpreted to allow a proportionate armed strike in anticipatory self-defense.[575]

Nevertheless, the proposed permissibility of the use of nuclear weapons under the doctrine of anticipatory self-defense cannot find any legal basis in Article 51. Because of the unprecedented destruction caused by the use of nuclear weapons, any doctrine that purports to broaden a state's right to resort to the use of nuclear weapons cannot be legally justified and accepted. Additionally, based on the legal argument forwarded by this thesis that even the defensive use of nuclear weapons is not permitted by the doctrine of self-defense under Article 51, then by the same legal rationale the use of nuclear weapons on the basis of the doctrine of anticipatory self-defense is not permissible under international law.

The military use of nuclear weapons has been defended by invoking the legal defense of the doctrine of military necessity under the principle of proportionality. More specifically, the doctrine of military necessity has been defined as the necessity of those measures which are indispensable for securing the ends of war, and which are lawful according to modern law and usages of law. A more useful concept of evaluating the lawfulness of wartime conduct under the military necessity doctrine is the principle of proportionality. Proportionality is the fundamental concept that balances the legitimacy of military ends against the means used to achieve them. Under the test of proportionality, the relevant inquiry is not whether a particular weapon violates international law, but whether the destruction caused by a weapon is proportionate to a legitimate military objective.[576]

Of course, the doctrine of military necessity is by no means unlimited. It is universally recognized that international law places constraints on military necessity. In essence, the mere presence of a military objective does not in itself permit unlimited destruction. Destruction as an end in itself is also a violation of international law.[577] Even if the doctrine of military necessity is evaluated and specified by the test of the principle of proportionality, with the development of nuclear weapons and their unprecedented destructive capabilities the doctrine of military necessity under the test of proportionality cannot be accepted as a valid legal ground and defense for justifying the use of such weapons.

Although the doctrine of military necessity under the test of proportionality can be applied when conventional weapons are employed, this doctrine cannot be invoked as an appropriate legal defense for permitting the use of nuclear weapons. The doctrine of military necessity under the test of the principle of proportionality can be an equally effective tool to condemn any use of nuclear weapons. Necessarily, an attack on a single target by a nuclear weapon would cause a proportionally greater degree of destruction to people, property and the environment than would its conventional counterpart. Additionally, the element of radioactive fallout gives these weapons an inhumane quality that contravenes several principles of international law. The cumulative effect of these destructive properties leads to the conclusion that no degree of military necessity would justify using nuclear weaponry.[578] In the final analysis, nuclear weapons are an inherently disproportionate means of warfare. The International Court of Justice has concluded in its advisory opinion that the principle of proportionality may not in itself exclude the use of nuclear weapons in self-defense in all circumstances, but the proportionate use of force in self-defense to be lawful must be in compliance with the rules and principles of international humanitarian law.

In view of the above analysis, one can argue that the threat or use of nuclear weapons even in self-defense is prohibited by international law. Regarding the legality of threat or use of nuclear weapons by a state to defend itself if its survival is at stake, remember that the International Court of Justice was unable in its advisory opinion to resolve this question. It left the question unanswered and said nothing.

Nuclear weapons are incapable of distinguishing between civilians and military personnel and could kill many thousands if not millions of civilians. Their use would cause superfluous injury and unnecessary suffering to survivors, affect future generations, damage hospitals, and contaminate the natural environment, food, and drinking water with radioactivity. Thus, nuclear war survivors would be deprived of the means of survival in violation of the Geneva Conventions of 1949 and the 1977 Additional Protocol I.[579]

The use of nuclear weapons by a state even in an extreme circumstance placing its survival at risk is prohibited by international law. Even if a state declared that the use of nuclear weapons to defend its very survival was lawful, the use of such weapons would still be prohibited under the principles and rules of international humanitarian law.

Legality According to the Laws of War

Nuclear Weapons and Unnecessary Suffering. The laws and principles of humanity require combatants to minimize the degree of suffering and destruction caused to opposing forces. To this end, the Declaration of St. Petersburg of 1868[580] emphasizes in its preamble that the only legitimate object which a state should endeavor to accomplish during war is to weaken the military forces of the enemy. For this purpose it is sufficient to disable the greatest possible number of men. But this objective would be exceeded by the employment of arms which uselessly aggravate the suffering of disabled men or render their deaths inevitable. Additionally, the preamble to the Declaration of St. Petersburg points out that the employment of such arms would be contrary to the laws of humanity.[581]

This convention was the first legal document to recognize a limitation on the means available to accomplish military objectives. The legal principles enunciated in the Declaration of St. Petersburg were reiterated and expanded upon in the regulations annexed to the Fourth Hague Convention of 1907. Thus, Article 32(b) prohibits the treacherous killing or wounding of enemy soldiers, while Article 23(e) forbids the employment of arms, projectiles or material which is calculated to cause unnecessary suffering.[582] A more recent international agreement prohibiting the use of weapons that cause unnecessary suffering is Protocol I of the 1977 Additional to the Geneva Conventions of 1949 and Relating to the Protection of Victims in International Armed Conflicts.[583] The prohibition of the use of weapons capable of causing unnecessary suffering to enemy forces is not only established as a positive rule of international law, but has become a customary rule of international law of universal applicability and binding legal force.

Even the smallest of nuclear weapons would be inherently incapable of avoiding destruction and suffering unnecessary to the military goal. The long-lasting effect of radioactive fallout caused by the use of nuclear weapons on the immediate victims and their offspring are certainly unnecessary to any military objective. In a nuclear attack, victims would occupy an area heavily contaminated by nuclear radiation. Adequate medical care and treatment would be impossible, causing additional suffering.[584] The military use of nuclear weapons would violate the established rule of international law prohibiting the causing of unnecessary suffering to enemy forces; nuclear weapons inherently cause unnecessary and excessive human suffering. This legal conclusion is further supported by the judgment of the Tokyo District Court in the Shimoda Case, which concerned the legality of the atomic bombings of Hiroshima and Nagasaki.[585] The International Court of Justice, in its previously discussed advisory opinion, reached the same conclusion.

Nuclear Weapons and the Prohibition of the Use of Poison and Gas Weapons. The legal principles embodied in the Declaration of St. Petersburg regarding the prohibition of weapons causing unnecessary and excessive suffering are also the basis for the prohibition against the use of poison or poisoned weapons found in Article 23(a) of the regulations annexed to the Hague Convention of 1907.[586] The Geneva Gas Protocol of 1925, which establishes a set of principles of humanity, accepts the universal recognition that the use in war of poisonous or other gases and all other related substances are illegal under international law. Additionally, the prohibition of the military use of poison and gas weapons has become a customary rule of international law. Thus, the prohibition of the military use of poison and gas weapons is universally binding.[587]

The question which arises is whether nuclear weapons would be legally described as poison and gas weapons, with their military use thus prohibited under the Hague Convention and the Geneva Gas Protocol. Regarding whether nuclear weapons are legally poison weapons, the military use of these weapons would release radiation or radioactive fallout, which, taken into the human body, would produce symptoms similar to, and in some respects more serious than, those induced by poison. Uranium, a central element in a nuclear weapon, is highly toxic. A nuclear explosion also releases a variety of other toxic chemicals and substances, including some whose toxicity endures for thousands of years.[588]

The release of such substances by nuclear weapons explosions in their military use thus renders them poison weapons. In particular, since nuclear weapons cause radioactive fallout, which contaminates and poisons people, property and the environment, the effect of such contamination seems sufficiently analogous to the effect of a poison or poisoned weapon. Therefore, there is sufficient legal ground to argue that, at least by legal analogy, the military use of nuclear weapons as poison weapons is prohibited by Article 23(a) of the regulations annexed to the Hague Convention.[589]

One can also argue that human exposure to radiation or radioactive fallout released by the explosion of nuclear weapons produces symptoms and effects similar to, and in some respects more serious than, those of poison, including delayed disease and genetic distortion. In any case, the poisonous effects of nuclear radioactive contamination renders the use of nuclear weapons illegal regardless of whether nuclear radiation is treated as a gas, liquid or solid. Therefore, nuclear weapons are poisonous and gas weapons, and generally weapons capable of releasing substances whose military use is prohibited under the Geneva Gas Protocol.[590] However, the International Court of Justice in its advisory opinion stated that nuclear weapons seem not to be gas, poison or asphyxiating weapons, and thus their use is not prohibited by the aforementioned rules of international law.

Nuclear Weapons and the Protection of Civilians During War. Another fundamental legal principle of humanity and international law that would be endangered by the use of nuclear weapons is the distinction between combatants and civilians. It is a well established precept of international law that noncombatants are immune from enemy attack.[591] That the legal protection of civilians is at the very heart of the laws of war was also evident in the Declaration of St. Petersburg of 1868, which stipulated that the only legitimate object which states should endeavor to accomplish during war is to weaken the military forces of the enemy. Thus, as long as civilian population does not participate actively in combat, it is shielded form direct attacks.[592]

The legal protection of and respect for the civilian population was the major premise of the 1923 Hague Draft Rules on Aerial Warfare. In accordance with Article 24 (3) of these rules, only military targets could be bombed, and only if this could be done without indiscriminate bombardment of civilians. The 1923 Hague Draft Rules sought to prohibit aerial bombardment of a civilian population undertaken with the clear objective of terrorizing it to win the war. Although these Hague Draft Rules were never translated into an international treaty, they provide sufficient evidence that customary international law recognizes that attacks upon military targets which cause indiscriminate killing and suffering to a civilian population should be prohibited.[593]

The legal protection of and respect for the civilian population during war is further incorporated in Protocol I of the 1977 Additional to the Geneva Conventions of 1949. Article 48 of Protocol I provides that:

> in order to ensure respect for and protection of the civilian population and civilian objects, the Parties to the conflict shall at all times distinguish between the civilian population and combatants and between civilian and military objectives and accordingly shall direct their operations only against military objectives.

Article 51 of Protocol I also provides that the civilian population as such, as well as individual civilians, must not be the object of attack, that acts and threats of violence whose primary purpose is to spread terror among the civilian population are prohibited, and that discriminate attacks are also prohibited.[594]

Based on that legal analysis, it can safely be concluded that both customary and positive rules of international law provide for the protection of civilian populations against indiscriminate attacks and killing, as well as their protection against attacks designed to spread terror among them during war. Thus, the use of nuclear weapons in an international military conflict is prohibited under the rules of war because nuclear weapons, either strategic or tactical, are inherently capable of resulting in the indiscriminate destruction and terror of civilian populations. Since the stated threat and potential objective of the use of nuclear weapons is the assured destruction of the enemy state on the premise of nuclear deterrence, then the terrorization of civilian populations would be an inevitable result of nuclear weapon use. A partial annihilation or extermination of civilian populations would occur if nuclear weapons were used. In conclusion, any effort to legitimize the use of nuclear weapons would result in the elimination of the international legal rules of war, since the use of nuclear weapons would destroy the very objects intended to be protected by these rules of law.[595] The International Court of Justice arrived at the same legal conclusion on this matter in its advisory opinion.

The Use of Nuclear Weapons and the Inviolability of Neutrals

There should be no doubt that the military use of nuclear weapons in war would intrude upon the territory of nonparticipating states, which have assumed a status of neutrality. Since the radioactive fallout released by the explosion of nuclear weapons can be carried by wind hundreds of miles in an unpredictable direction, the region of nuclear warfare cannot be confined with any precision to the belligerent territories, or to their airspace and waters. Thus, with the uncontrollable, unpredictable and indiscriminate effects of nuclear bombardment, the theater of a nuclear war, with its vast area of damaging effects, could spread to any part of the globe, affecting neutral states and permanently neutralized territories.[596]

But international law has long recognized two related principles: first, that belligerent states cannot be allowed to extend the field of combat onto the territory of a neutral party; and, second, that neutral states have a right to exclude belligerents who enter their territory. The prohibition against violating a neutral state's territory is absolute, and it cannot be excused by invoking any of the traditional defenses of international law. In this respect, it should be noted that the Hague Convention states that the territory of neutral powers is inviolable.[597]

Based on the international legal principles of neutrality and the inviolability of the territoriality of neutral states, the wartime use of nuclear weapons, with the attendant uncontrollable radiation and radioactive fallout, certainly would have a direct impact upon neutral states. Thus, the military use of nuclear weapons would intrude upon the territory of neutral states, in violation of the international law of neutrality and of the basic intent of the laws of war and the dictates of humanity. Because the uncontrollable harmful effects of nuclear radiation and radioactive fallout caused by the use of nuclear weapons cannot guarantee the nuclear neutrality of nonparticipating states in a nuclear war, the use of nuclear weapons would violate the international law that protects the inviolability of the territoriality of neutral states.[598] The International Court of Justice reached the same conclusion on this question in its advisory opinion.

The Use of Nuclear Weapons, the Crime of Genocide and the Crime Against Humanity

The development of the atomic bomb and its use on Hiroshima and Nagasaki has irrevocably changed the nature and objective of war. Since 1945, humanity has lived on the edge of its nuclear holocaust, with human history and civilization hanging in the balance. The existence of more than 50,000 nuclear weapons has the distinct potential for annihilating a substantial portion of the Earth's population, devastating and contaminating vast areas of the Earth's surface and producing unpredictable and uncontrollable biological and environmental consequences.[599]

In view of the destructive capabilities of nuclear weapons, the following legal analysis will explore whether their military use would constitute a crime of genocide and a crime against humanity. In 1948 the UN Convention on the Prevention and Punishment of the Crime of Genocide was adopted. By specifically criminalizing genocide, the international community has spoken as forcefully as it can about its commitment to the protection of the rights of individual civilians and groups to be free from and protected against an enemy's wanton depredations on a people based on their national, ethnic, racial or religious characteristics. Furthermore, the prohibition of genocide is not only a positive norm of international law, but has become a compelling rule of international law with universal applicability and binding legal force.[600]

Based on the preceding discussion, a nuclear holocaust would represent either an individual commission of genocide or the incrementally greater crime of universal genocide. In essence, to target an enemy state with nuclear weapons is tantamount to planning the mass extinction of that state. To engage in a nuclear war which would inevitably destroy all or nearly all higher forms of life in the enemy state under attack would constitute a crime of national genocide. A massive nuclear attack in a large or a global nuclear war, which would inevitably destroy all or almost all higher forms of life on this planet, would constitute mega-genocide.[601]

Therefore, the use of any nuclear weapons under any circumstances against an enemy state or in the context of a total nuclear war would directly violate the Genocide Convention and would constitute a punishable crime of genocide. Furthermore, because the Genocide Convention, in addition to its prohibition and criminal punishment of genocide, prohibits and punishes conspiracy to commit genocide, incitement to commit genocide, attempt to commit genocide and complicity in genocide, policy makers who establish contingency plans for nuclear war can be guilty of the crime of conspiracy to commit genocide. Since the Genocide Convention imposes individual criminal liability on those who commit genocide, or incite or attempt to commit such a crime, or are in complicity in genocide, national rulers, public officials and even private individuals who commit genocide through nuclear weapons are criminally liable for genocide on an individual basis.[602]

Whether the military use of nuclear weapons would constitute a crime against humanity, by virtue of Article 6 of the Charter of the International Military Tribunal of 1945, the commission of murder, extermination and other inhumane acts committed against any civilian population before or during a war constitute crimes against humanity. The UN General Assembly Resolution 1653 (XVI), adopted by an overwhelming majority, provides that the use of nuclear and thermonuclear weapons would exceed even the scope of war and cause indiscriminate suffering and destruction to humanity and civilization and, as such, is contrary to the rules of international law and to the laws of humanity. The above resolution also states that the use of nuclear and thermonuclear weapons would represent a war directed not against an enemy or enemies, but against humanity in general, since peoples of the world not involved in such a war would be subjected to all the evils generated by the use of nuclear weapons. UN General Assembly Resolution 36/100, also adopted by an overwhelming majority, holds that states and statesmen resorting to the first use of nuclear weapons would be committing the gravest crime against humanity.[603]

Since a limited nuclear war would result in the mass extermination of civilian populations, and since a global thermonuclear war would threaten the very existence of humanity, it can be argued that under existing rules of international law the use of nuclear weapons would constitute a crime against humanity.[604] If the Nazi war criminals were indicted and tried by the International Military Tribunal in 1945 for committing crimes against humanity, then by the same legal rationale there should be no doubt that the use of any nuclear weapons under any circumstances would be a crime against humanity.

The use of nuclear weapons under any circumstances, then, would indeed constitute a punishable crime of genocide and a crime against humanity. The use of nuclear weapons would not only constitute a war crime,[605] but also a crime against peace,[606] since use of nuclear weapons under any circumstances would be in direct violation of the international rules of law and the laws of humanity. The new order created by the end of World War II, and which evolved thereafter, has established a new warless legal order and a new international law of peace and humanity. The use of nuclear weapons, which by virtue of their destructive capabilities and characteristics is inherently evil, would destroy humanity and end the rule of international law aimed at the protection of humanity. But the International Court of Justice in its advisory opinion concluded that the use of nuclear weapons would constitute genocide if nuclear weapons were intentionally used against a specific group as such.

The Use of Nuclear Weapons and the International Legal Protection of the Environment

The UN Convention on the Prohibition of Military or Any Other Hostile Use of Environment Modification Techniques of 1977 has as a fundamental legal objective to prevent and prohibit the use of any environmental or geographical modification activity as a weapon of war. To this end, Article I (1) of the convention sets forth the legal obligation that: "Each State Party to this Convention undertakes not to engage in military or any other hostile use of environmental modification techniques having widespread, long-lasting or severe effects as the means of destruction, damage or injury to any other State Party." Although this convention constitutes a positive legal measure declaring the peaceful uses of the environment and its geophysical structure, it fails to explicitly prohibit and outlaw the military use of nuclear weapons.[607]

Nevertheless, by legal implication, it can be suggested that the use of nuclear weapons in either a limited or a global nuclear war would result in catastrophic environmental and ecological disasters. In turn, the environmental holocaust caused by the use of nuclear weapons would set in motion forces of environmental and geophysical modification which would become destructive to the world's population. The use of nuclear weapons would release harmful nuclear radiation and radioactive fallout which would cause catastrophic climatic changes, rendering the environment a hostile place and a weapon of war against humankind.[608]

Additionally, Protocol I of the 1977 Additional to the Geneva Conventions of 1949 by virtue of its Article 35 (3) prohibits methods or means of warfare which are intended, or may be expected, to cause widespread, long-term and severe damage to the natural environment. Although under this provision there are definitional problems to be faced, as well as the status of the rule with regard to states not party to this protocol,[609] this positive rule of international law clearly prohibits the use of nuclear weapons because of their catastrophic effects on the natural environment. The evolving new international environmental law, and various international agreements and conferences which have addressed significant environmental and ecological issues, are unanimous in their condemnation of nuclear weapons.[610] Nevertheless, the International Court of Justice in its advisory opinion expressed the belief that the existing international law relating to the protection of the environment does not specifically prohibit the use of nuclear weapons.

More Thoughts on Legality

Since no international treaty specifically and explicitly prohibits the development, possession and deployment of nuclear weapons, the following analysis will attempt to explore whether such activity is prohibited in the context of existing applicable rules of international law. The issue of the development, possession and deployment of nuclear weapons constitutes a strictly interrelated problem. Any legal argument that would support the illegality of either such development, possession or deployment would eventually determine the illegality of nuclear weapons in these areas in a comprehensive manner. For methodological reasons, the ensuing legal discussion will first concentrate on the legality of deployment, and then on the possession and development of nuclear weapons.

Despite the nonexistence of a positive rule of international law prohibiting the deployment of nuclear weapons on a global basis, a variety of international treaties clearly prohibit their deployment in several regions. Under pertinent international treaties, the deployment of nuclear weapons in Antarctica, Latin America, the South Pacific, on the seabed beyond the 12-mile limit of national territorial waters, in outer space and on celestial bodies is clearly prohibited.[611] The deployment of nuclear weapons in these regions would violate positive rules of international law. Since there is no legal prohibition of nuclear weapons on a global basis, it would seem, at first glance, that the deployment of nuclear weapons in places other than the aforesaid regions would not be prohibited.

Nevertheless, the deployment of nuclear weapons is an extremely serious threat to the inherent right to life, the supreme right which is protected and guaranteed by both customary and positive international law and which is not subject to derogation even in time of public emergency threatening the life of a nation. To this end, the UN Human Rights Committee has declared that states have the supreme duty to prevent wars, and that every effort made to avert the danger of war, especially thermonuclear war, constitutes the most important condition and guarantee for the protection of the right to life. The committee has declared that the designing, testing, manufacture, possession and deployment of nuclear weapons are among the greatest threats to the right of life which confront humanity. Based on this legal rationale and philosophy, it has concluded that these activities should be prohibited and recognized as crimes against humanity.[612]

Instead of averting the danger of a nuclear holocaust, the deployment of nuclear weapons makes nuclear war more likely and therefore undermines the right to life. Furthermore, the deployment of nuclear weapons would violate Article 6(a) of the Charter of the International Military Tribunal of 1945, which represents customary international law, and which provides that crimes against peace include the planning or preparation of a war of aggression or a war in violation of international treaties, assurances or agreements. Since a nuclear war would violate international law under any circumstances, then the deployment of nuclear weapons would constitute a crime against peace, because such deployment would be a planning or a preparatory act for a nuclear war.[613]

The deployment of nuclear weapons would also constitute a conspiracy to commit genocide, which is prohibited and punishable under the 1948 Genocide Convention.[614] By necessary legal implication the deployment of nuclear weapons should be prohibited under the international legal norms prohibiting crimes against humanity, since the deployment of nuclear weapons would constitute an immediate step in the commission of such crimes. Since nuclear weapons are inherently evil due to their destructiveness, and since their use is illegal under international law and the laws of humanity, then it can be argued that the deployment of such weapons is also illegal under international law and the laws of humanity.[615]

In the context of the preceding legal rationale one can further argue that the mere possession and the development of nuclear weapons are illegal under international law. In the same legal rationale, nuclear testing to develop nuclear weapons or for determining the reliability of existing nuclear weapons is illegal under international law.

Despite the lack of international law explicitly prohibiting the development and possession of nuclear weapons on a global basis, the peace treaties signed by the Allies with Bulgaria, Finland, Hungary, Italy and Romania on February 10, 1947, explicitly prohibit the possession, construction and testing of nuclear weapons by the latter states. Similarly, the Austrian State Treaty of May 15, 1955, prohibits Austria from becoming a nuclear weapons power.[616] Additionally, the new international law of regional nuclear disarmament and denuclearization, inaugurated by the creation of nuclear weapon-free zones, clearly forbids the development, possession and deployment of nuclear weapons in the covered regions in absolute terms.

Most importantly, the NPT of 1968, which has been accepted by approximately 188 states[617] and which has the legal potential of evolving into a customary rule of international law, absolutely prohibits the development, possession and testing of nuclear weapons of any kind by the non-nuclear weapon states. Although the NPT allows the club of nuclear powers, for reasons which are inherently and structurally discriminatory, to develop and possess nuclear weapons, Article VI of the NPT imposes the legal obligation upon states party to that treaty to pursue negotiations in good faith on effective measures relating to cessation of the nuclear arms race and to nuclear disarmament. Therefore, Article VI of the NPT recognizes the inherent illegality of nuclear weapons and requires their elimination. Nevertheless, the International Court of Justice in its advisory opinion seems to conclude that there is no general prohibition of development, deployment, acquisition and possession of nuclear weapons under international law.

Although the pre-atomic rules of international law prohibit the use of nuclear weapons,[618] the new international law of peace which was founded by the end of World War II, and particularly the new international law of nuclear disarmament, render nuclear weapons absolutely unlawful in all of their aspects and under any circumstances. In this regard, this legal conclusion can be further supported by the declaration made by the Nuclear Warfare Tribunal convened in London in January 1985 to consider the legal, moral and scientific implications of nuclear weapons. This tribunal held that current and planned nuclear weapons developments, strategies and deployments violate the basic rules and principles of international law, both customary and conventional. The procurement and use of such weapons involve infringements of the UN Charter and the Laws of War. The tribunal held that the Nuremberg Principles and the Genocide Convention are being violated in the most extreme fashion by ongoing preparation to wage nuclear war, especially to the extent that plans include indiscriminate, poisonous and massive destruction of civilian populations, amounting to a conspiracy to wage aggressive war.[619]

Any effort to argue the legality of the use, deployment, development and possession of nuclear weapons would defy human rationale and reason. In essence, to argue the legality of nuclear weapons, which are capable of threatening the very existence of humanity and civilization, would be preposterous and contrary to the fundamental norms and principles of humanity that are embodied in the new international law of peace and nuclear disarmament.[620]

Based on the preceding legal analysis, not only the use, deployment, possession and development of nuclear weapons is illegal, but the new international law of nuclear disarmament also requires the elimination of nuclear weapons in comprehensive terms and on a global basis.

Chapter 10

Concluding Remarks and an Analysis of Future Prospects

Since the development of nuclear weapons, the entire world has witnessed that nuclear weapons are not just more weapons, but weapons of unprecedented destructive power which could destroy the physical integrity of our planet and the very existence of civilization. The use of atomic weapons by the United States against Hiroshima and Nagasaki in 1945 showed the entire world that nuclear weapons are weapons of mass destruction posing a novel and immediate threat to humanity.

The adoption of the United Nations Charter provided the fundamental constitutional basis for a new international legal order for the post–World War II era under the rule of international law. The United Nations has assumed the ultimate legal task to preserve succeeding generations from the scourge of war and to reaffirm faith in the dignity and worth of the human person, and generally to preserve international peace and security. But, most importantly, the UN Charter has created a new international law of peace, which has outlawed war as an instrument of national policy. In essence, the new international law of peace created by the UN Charter has provided the juridical and constitutional foundation for a new warless international legal order, and for peaceful coexistence and political cooperation under the rule of world law and through the organizational power of the United Nations.

The development of nuclear weapons and their first military use posed an ultimate legal challenge to the UN Charter and its legal principles and norms of peace and humanism. Therefore, it was a great and juridically justified legal expectation of the entire world that the United Nations, through the instrumental value of the rule of international law, would eliminate nuclear weapons on a global basis and in comprehensive terms by creating a global and effective nuclear disarmament legal regime.

The United Nations failed to establish this regime at the very beginning of the new postwar international legal order. Despite the submission of the Baruch and the Gromyko Plans to the United Nations in 1946 aimed at the creation of such a regime, the United Nations failed to adopt such a legal regime particularly due to the growing tension and conflict between the United States and the

Soviet Union. The growing ideological and military conflict and confrontation almost immediately after the end of World War II between the United States and the Soviet Union and generally between East and West severely undermined the United Nations in playing a dynamic and central role in nuclear disarmament.

The failure of the United Nations to bring about global nuclear disarmament through the power of international law at the very beginning of nuclear armaments showed that the United Nations was not an independent international organization capable of effectively resolving such world problems. It became clear that the United Nations was but another international organization, which could be effective to the extent its member states agreed to provide it with the required legal powers and means. Above all, the lack of organizational dynamism of the United Nations and its inability to create and impose an effective and timely international legal regime of global nuclear disarmament resulted in the predicament of nuclear armaments in the postwar era. This predicament apparently rendered the new postwar international legal order a new international legal disorder regarding nuclear weapons.

The eruption of the Cold War between the Soviet Union and the United States and generally between East and West became the most negative factor in the paralysis of the new international postwar legal order, and in the failure to establish a global nuclear disarmament legal regime. The relentless ideological conflict between the communist and capitalist political systems and ideologies became the focal point of the East-West nuclear arms race, antagonism and constant threat of nuclear confrontation during the Cold War.

The American-Soviet nuclear arms race resulted in the development and construction of more destructive and sophisticated nuclear weapons. By the end of the Cold War, both possessed a combined total of approximately 50,000 strategic and tactical nuclear weapons.

During the Cold War years, the entire world community suffered the constant nightmare and terror of a nuclear holocaust springing from a superpower confrontation. During the Cold War the nuclear superpowers sometimes came close to a nuclear war; the Cuban missile crisis of 1962 constitutes the most pivotal episode in the nuclear age which brought them to the brink of a global nuclear war.

Despite the recognition that the Cold War had become the ultimate factor in the superpowers' nuclear arms race and in the failure of a global nuclear disarmament through the power of international law, perhaps the Cold War was inevitable. As has been emphasized throughout this study, there should be no doubt that the Cold War contravened the legal norms and political principles of the UN Charter, which provided the foundation for building a peaceful and legal world order in the postwar years.

Due to the failure of global nuclear disarmament, and in addition to the superpowers' nuclear arms race, the proliferation of nuclear weapons began to take place. Thus, the so-called great powers, namely, Britain, France and China, acquired nuclear weapons by the early 1960s. As a result, nuclear disarmament became a more difficult and complicated problem. In spite of the adoption of the NPT in 1968, since the early 1970s a new nuclear age has begun with the horizontal proliferation of nuclear weapons. Thus, India, Israel, South Africa and Pakistan acquired nuclear weapon capabilities and became de facto nuclear powers. Consequently, achieving global nuclear disarmament became an even more elusive goal.

Although during the Cold War the legal quest for global and comprehensive nuclear disarmament was not likely to prove successful, the United Nations, despite its organizational limitations, played a positive role in the creation and development of the new international law of nuclear disarmament. As has been specifically analyzed throughout this study, the United Nations during the Cold War adopted the legal model of nuclear arms control and on a step-by-step legal basis pursued its strategy. The United Nations by resorting to the instrumental value and the power of the rule of international law formulated legal norms and principles designed to manage nuclear weapons and nuclear war during the Cold War.

During the Cold War, and especially after the near-nuclear war created by the Cuban Missile Crisis of 1962, a new era of détente emerged between the superpowers regarding their nuclear behavior and their bilateral relations. During the superpower détente era, the United States and the Soviet Union attempted to convert their ideological conflict and their relentless nuclear arms race and constant threat of nuclear confrontation into a new era of peaceful coexistence, cooperation and controlled nuclear behavior. During superpower détente, a significant number of nuclear arms control agreements were adopted between the superpowers. As a result, this superpower law of détente promoted and expanded even further the new international law of nuclear arms control and disarmament.

During the Cold War the legal model of and approach to nuclear arms control, which was adopted both by the United Nations and the superpowers, was inherently incapable of achieving global nuclear disarmament because nuclear arms control is not nuclear disarmament. Nevertheless, the superpowers and generally the international community recognized the instrumental value and power of the rule of international law in controlling the nuclear arms race and in preventing a global thermonuclear war. In general, during the Cold War the foundations of the norms and principles of the international law of nuclear disarmament were created, despite the failure to achieve global and comprehensive nuclear disarmament during that era.

There should be no doubt that the Cold War not only caused the nuclear predicament in the postwar era, but also, and most importantly, posed strategic political and legal obstacles to global and comprehensive nuclear disarmament. However, the end of the Cold War marked the beginning of a new world era which provides a new dynamic and strategic political and legal environment for the effective global elimination of nuclear weapons. With the end of the Cold War, all causes of the nuclear arms race and all obstacles that resulted in the nuclear predicament during the Cold War and in the failure of nuclear disarmament during that era have been largely removed. There can no longer be valid reasons, arguments and justifications for continuing the nuclear predicament into the 21st century.

Although the end of the Cold War has created a new political relationship between the nuclear superpowers, their evolving relationship is at a very critical stage of transition. In particular, to ensure that a new version of a Cold War will not reoccur, the Western world and generally the entire international community must play a positive role in assisting Russia and the other states of the Commonwealth of Independent States in their efforts for political and economic democratization and reforms. To this end, the United States and the Western capitalist establishment must provide particularly Russia, as well as the other states of the CIS, with all possible economic and technical assistance to succeed in their efforts for democratic reforms on the basis of their own pertinent plans and terms.

If, however, the United States and the Western capitalist and nuclear establishment attempt to exploit the economic predicament of Russia, and thus to undermine its power in the post–Cold War era, this would be a great mistake. Moreover, any effort of the United States to undercut Russian power and to impose a Pax Americana in the emerging new era would be entirely counterproductive and capable of reigniting a Cold War with Russia. Russia, despite its enormous economic problems, is a military nuclear superpower capable of destroying the entire planet with its nuclear weapons. If the democratic reforms in Russia fail, if Russia is encircled by the Western capitalist and nuclear establishment and by the eastward NATO expansion, and if the normal transition to a democratic and free post–Soviet world is not secured, such failures could cause a new confrontation between Russia and the West, including ignition of a new Cold War in the 21st century.

The transition from the Cold War to a new post–Cold War international legal order is at a critical stage. Although the end of the Cold War has removed a threat to global peace and security, it has also released forces of ethnic war resulting in the dissolution of traditional nation-states, including the potential of major regional conflicts which were suppressed during the Cold War. The evolution of world affairs and the preservation of regional and international peace and security are uncertain and dangerous in many respects. The new post–Cold War era has begun with the existence of thousands of nuclear weapons in the nuclear arsenals of the United States, the former Soviet Union and the other members of the club of nuclear powers. Additionally, a dangerous new nuclear age has been established and is presently expanding through the horizontal proliferation of nuclear weapons.

Any effort to manage and resolve global and regional problems of international and regional peace and security by resorting to approaches and solutions applied during the Cold War would be a great mistake. To ensure a safe transition to a functional new world era, new dynamic approaches are required for the world's institutional and organizational shape and foundation. To this end, as has been already suggested by this study, the United Nations, restructured and empowered as specifically proposed here, could ensure the proper function of the new post–Cold War era under the value and the power of the rule of world law.

To effectively meet the challenges and the dangers that will be posed to regional and global peace and security in the post–Cold War era, the United Nations must cease to be a bureaucratic and powerless world forum used by the so-called great powers to serve their unilateral interests. The United Nations must be the center of world power under the rule of international law. Moreover, the United Nations, as has been proposed by this study, must be empowered with the required legal powers and means to carry out peacekeeping operations in an effective manner. Additionally, the United Nations must be a global institution with powers of policy making and lawmaking, and with the powers and means to enforce the rule of international law.

The beginning of the new post–Cold War era not only provides a unique historic opportunity for the restoration of the international legal order established by the end of World War II, but also provides a new strategic environment and dynamic legal prospects for achieving global and comprehensive nuclear disarmament. Indeed, with the end of the Cold War, there exists a realistic historic opportunity to effectively eliminate all nuclear weapons through the rule of international law, and thus to restore the international legitimacy which has been violated by the existence of such unlawful weapons of mass destruction. The feasibility and effectiveness of a global nuclear disarmament in the post–Cold War era is clearly shown by the recent nuclear disarmament legal arrangements between the nuclear superpowers and the stated willingness of the other nuclear powers to participate in a multilateral international legal process for nuclear disarmament.

Based on the thesis established by this study, global and comprehensive nuclear disarmament is both feasible and verifiably effective, and is also required by the new international law of nuclear disarmament. This legal thesis provides the juridical rationale for a global and comprehensive nuclear disarmament in the 21st century. It has shown that, under the new international law of peace and nuclear disarmament, the development, deployment and use of nuclear weapons, including the testing of such weapons, are illegal. It has also shown that any legalistic argument proposing the permanent retention of nuclear armaments under the doctrine of nuclear deterrence and the use of such arms would violate the applicable rules of international law. This thesis has emphasized that until the last nuclear weapons have been effectively eliminated, the eventual use of nuclear weapons is inevitable.

The NPT Review Conference in the year 2000 can become a global forum where a multilateral legal arrangement on global and comprehensive nuclear disarmament can be reached. By the end of the year 2010 all nuclear weapons can be effectively eliminated, and thus a nuclear weapons-free world can be achieved. To this end, the United Nations, the International Atomic Energy Agency and generally other appropriate organs of the international community can play central roles in the effective denuclearization of the planet and in safeguarding against the acquisition of nuclear weapons in a new nuclear disarmament era.

The international community must continue to reinvigorate and expand its movement and pressure for achieving global nuclear disarmament. The world community of peoples and their governments must continue to treat nuclear war and the need for nuclear disarmament with top priority status on the world agenda. Nuclear war has been, still is and will be in the future a real threat as long as nuclear weapons exist. Until the last nuclear weapons are effectively eliminated and destroyed, no assurance can be given to the international community that the intentional military use, the unauthorized or accidental use, or the use of nuclear weapons by terrorist groups will be avoided.

The international community has only one way to avoid an eventual nuclear holocaust, and that is to achieve a global and comprehensive nuclear disarmament through the instrumental value of international law. To this end, this study has suggested the legal basis and rationale for such disarmament. It has further suggested that a global and comprehensive nuclear disarmament is both feasible and effective under the new international law of nuclear disarmament, and has also proposed a strategic plan for achieving such disarmament in the context of the NPT review conference in the year 2000, and to create a new nuclear weapons free world in the year 2010. Today's global political environment encourages vigorous pursuit of comprehensive nuclear disarmament. Humanity cannot afford to lose present historic opportunities in the quest to establish a nuclear weapons-free world.

Notes

Chapter 1

1. Quoted in Drell, S.D., *Facing the Threat of Nuclear Weapons,* pp. 5–6 (1989).

2. Powaski, R.E., *March to Armageddon: The United States and the Nuclear Arms Race, 1939 to Present,* 3 (1987). See also Smyth, H.D., *Atomic Energy for Military Purposes: The Official Report on the Development of the Atomic Bomb under the Auspices of the Unites States Government, 1940–1945,* 5 *et seq.* (1945).

3. Powaski, 3.

4. The foreboding news of the Hahn-Strassmann discovery was brought by Niels Bohr, a Danish physicist, to the American physicists at the conference of theoretical physicists, held in Washington, D.C., on January 26, 1939. Enrico Fermi and Leo Szilard had conducted similar experiments, showing that uranium, if present in sufficient quantity (called its "critical mass"), could generate enough neutrons to produce a chain reaction, without which nuclear fission could not be sustained. (Powaski, 4.) Fermi, Szilard and Einstein attempted to persuade the American government to launch its own program to build the atomic bomb first. See Grodzins, M., and E. Rabinowitz, *The Atomic Age: Scientists in National and World Affairs,* 1–2 (1963).

5. On December 2, 1942, Fermi engineered the first nuclear chain reaction at the University of Chicago. (Powaski, 6.) In the summer of 1941 the British Maud Committee, the agency that headed the British atomic research project, informed the American government that if an all-out effort were to begin, an atomic bomb could be developed within two years. See Gowing, M., *Britain and Atomic Energy: 1939–1945,* 389 *et seq.* (1964).

6. See generally: Smyth, 208 *et seq.*; Noel-Baker, P., *The Arms Race; A Programme for World Disarmament,* 95 *et seq.* (1958); and Gowing, M., "Britain, America and the Bomb" in *British Foreign Policy, 1945–56,* eds. Dockrill, M., and J.W. Young, 33 *et seq.* (1989).

7. The full text of this report can be found in Smyth, 918.

8. For a fuller description of the destructive capability of the atomic bomb see the views of Dr. J. Robert Oppenheimer quoted in Feis, H., *The Atomic Bomb and the End of World War II,* 55 (1966).

9. See also Dunn, F.S., "The Common Problem" in *The Absolute Weapon: Atomic Power and World Order,* ed. Brodie, B., 3 *et seq.* (1946).

10. See also Noel-Baker, 94 *et seq.*

11. The entire American nuclear project to develop the atomic bomb cost $2 billion. See Johnson, L.K., "Three Windows on Armageddon" in *Through the Straits of Armageddon: Arms Control Issues and Prospects,* eds. Diehl, P.F., and L.K. Johnson, 243 (1987).

12. See also Mandelbaum, M., *The Nuclear Revolution: International Politics Before and After Hiroshima,* 23 *et seq.* (1981).

13. For a discussion of the peaceful uses of atomic energy as envisaged by nuclear scientists in 1945 see Noel-Baker, 111 *et seq.*

14. The atomic bomb is four weapons in one: (1) Its blast is many thousands of times more powerful than the largest TNT bombs; (2) its heat-flash is a potent fireraiser; (3) its explosion is accompanied by highly penetrating and harmful, but invisible rays called "gamma radiation"; and (4) the substances remaining after a nuclear explosion, known as the "residual radioactivity," are radioactive for an extended period. (Noel-Baker 120–121.) See also Singh, N., and E. McWhinney, *Nuclear Weapons and Contemporary International Law,* 29 *et seq.* (2d ed. 1989).

15. See also Drell, *Facing the Threat,* 5–6.

16. The full text of the UN Charter can be found in Simma, B., ed., *The Charter of the United Nations: A Commentary,* XIX–XXXVIII (1995).

17. See also the analysis of Shaw, M.N., "Nuclear Weapons and International Law" in *Nuclear Weapons and International Law,* ed. Pogany, I., 6 (1987). Note, however, that war can be exceptionally waged in self-defense in accordance with Article 51 of the UN Charter. For a comprehensive legal analysis of this article see Singh and McWhinney, 86 *et seq.*

18. See also Kelsen, H., "The Old and the New League: The Covenant and the Dumbarton Oaks Proposals," 39 *American Journal of International Law,* 83 *et seq.* (1945); and Reitzel, W., et al., *United States Foreign Policy 1945–1955,* 237 *et seq.* (1956).

19. See Article 43, paragraph 1 of the UN Charter in Simma, XXVI–XXVII.

20. For a fuller discussion of these early proposals for the prevention of nuclear arms race in the postwar years see generally: Powaski, 7 *et seq.*; and Grodzins and Rabinowitz, 13 *et seq.*

21. Beyond the almost entire material destruction of both Hiroshima and Nagasaki, the atomic bombs killed approximately 100,000 people and wounded 90,000 in the two cities, whose total population before the atomic bombings was about 600,000 people. See Cassese, A., *Violence and Law in the Modern Age,* 9 *et seq.* (1988), and Boyle, F.A., *The Future of International Law and American Foreign Policy,* 331 *et seq.* (1989). For a revisionist view, which argues that the use of the atomic bomb by the United States was not required to achieve Japan's capitulation, and that it was used against Japan to intimidate the Soviets in respect to their expansion in Eastern Europe, see generally Alperovitz, G., *Atomic Diplomacy: Hiroshima and Potsdam; The Use of the Atomic Bomb and the American Confrontation with Soviet Power,* 226 *et seq.* (1965). For some persuasive views which argue the illegality of the use of the atomic bomb against Japan in light of the prenuclear age Laws of War applicable in 1945, see generally: Cassese, 14 *et seq.*; Falk, R., "The Shimoda Case: A Legal Appraisal of the Atomic Attacks Upon Hiroshima and Nagasaki," 59 *American Journal of International Law,* 759–793 (1965); and Boyle, 317 *et seq.*

Chapter 2

22. For a further discussion of American efforts to confront the expansion of communism since the end of World War II see Paterson, T.G., *Meeting the Communist Threat: Truman to Reagan* (1988).

23. For an interesting analysis of the strategic and political implications of the American atomic monopoly in American-Soviet relations in the early years of the Cold War see Herken, G., *The Winning Weapon: The Atomic Bomb in the Cold War, 1945–1950,* 195 *et seq.* (1980).

24. Powaski, 33.

25. See also Lundestad, G., *East, West, North, South: Major Developments in International Politics 1945–1986*, 147 (1986).

26. For an extensive analysis of the proposals made by H. Stimson and V. Bush see Powaski, 32 *et seq.*

27. Powaski, 32 *et seq.*

28. Powaski, 30.

29. See also Herken, 97 *et seq.*

30. The Agreed Declaration made by the United States, Britain and Canada proposed the establishment of a commission under the United Nations to prepare recommendations to be further submitted to the United Nations for the legal prohibition of the use of atomic energy for warfare. See Sethna, J.M.J., *International Legal Controls and Sanctions Concerning the Production and Use of Atomic Energy*, 3 (1966).

31. See *The United Nations and Disarmament: 1945–1985*, ed. United Nations (Department for Disarmament Affairs), 1 *et seq.* (1985). The UN Atomic Energy Commission was composed of those states permanently represented on the UN Security Council, including also Canada. See Schoenbaum, T.J., "A Historical Perspective on Arms Control Agreements" in Diehl and Johnson, 23.

32. In analyzing the Baruch Plan, I have relied on Sheehan, M., *Arms Control: Theory and Practice,* 3 (1988); Sethna, 3 *et seq.*; and Schoenbaum, 23. The Baruch Plan proposed the criminal punishment of the violators of international agreements imposing nuclear disarmament and the peaceful use of atomic energy. Sethna, 5–6.

33. Sheehan, 3.

34. Schoenbaum, 24.

35. For a concise and comprehensive discussion of the Gromyko Plan see Powaski, 44.

36. Schoenbaum, 24.

37. Sheehan, 3.

38. Schoenbaum, 24.

39. Schoenbaum, 24.

40. Schoenbaum, 25. For an early detailed legal analysis of the failure of the UN Atomic Energy Commission to lay down the legal framework for the peaceful uses of nuclear energy, and generally for the failure of the United Nations to legally control the atomic bomb and initiate nuclear disarmament see Shills, E., "The Failure of the United Nations Atomic Energy Commission: An Interpretation," 15 *University of Chicago Law Review,* 855–876 (1948); and Farmer, F., "The Atomic Bomb Can Be Controlled," 19 *Tennessee Law Review*, 40–43 (1945).

41. Shaw, 9–10.

42. For a fuller discussion of the Soviet efforts to build their own atomic bomb see Powaski, 53.

43. See Nogee, J.L., and R.H. Donaldson, *Soviet Foreign Policy Since World War II,* 81 (3d ed. 1988).

44. The Soviet Union had been deliberately excluded from the scientific secrets for the development of the atomic bomb which were shared by the United States and Britain. Nevertheless, the Soviets by their spying activities in both the United States and Canada acquired crucial scientific information and thus accelerated the scientific process for the development of their own atomic bomb. See Lundestad, 149; and Davies, T.H., "Soviet Atomic Espionage" in Grodzins and Rabinowitz, 361 *et seq.*

45. See also the views of Andrei D. Sakharov quoted in Drell, *Facing the Threat,* 64 *et seq.*

46. Powaski, 53.

Chapter 3

47. See Rourke, J.T., *Making Foreign Policy: United States, Soviet Union, China,* 22 (1990).

48. For an extensive discussion of West Germany's incorporation into NATO and its rearmament see generally Cioc, M., *Pax Atomica: The Nuclear Defense Debate in West Germany During the Adenauer Era,* 12 *et seq.* (1988).

49. For a general analysis of the creation of the Warsaw Pact and its military implications see Holden, G., *The Warsaw Pact, Soviet Security and Block Politics* (1989).

50. See McNamara, R.S., *Out of the Cold: New Thinking for American Foreign and Defense Policy in the 21st Century,* 46 (1989).

51. Indeed, on January 30, 1949, President Truman directed the United States Atomic Energy Commission to accelerate its scientific work on all forms of atomic energy weapons, including the hydrogen bomb. See *Disarmament: Negotiations and Treaties, 1946–1971,* ed. Keesing Publications, 4 (1972). Although the United States possessed more than enough atomic weapons to deter Soviet aggression in the event the Soviets developed a hydrogen bomb, the development of the H-bomb by the United States had already caught the imagination of both congressional and military people. See Powaski, 55.

52. For an analysis of the chemical reaction of the H-bomb see Johnson, 243 *et seq.*

53. Powaski, 59. For a further analysis of the nuclear effects of the H-bomb as a superbomb and as a thermonuclear weapon see Noel-Baker, 130 *et seq.*

54. See *Disarmament: Negotiations and Treaties, 1946–1971,* 5–6.

55. For a concise analysis of the development of the British and French nuclear bombs see Lundestad, 157–159.

56. Powaski, 63.

57. Rourke, 18. Furthermore, while Khrushchev had started the process of the de-Stalinization of the Soviet Union, the most serious unrest and anti-Soviet outbreak in Eastern Europe occurred in 1956, when the Hungarians openly rebelled, replaced their government and proclaimed their intention to withdraw from the Warsaw Pact. But the Soviets, in their effort to maintain their bloc control and cohesion in Eastern Europe, reacted violently by invading Hungary and bloodily suppressing the uprising.

58. Rourke, 18. See also Powaski, 65 *et seq.*; and Lundestad, 156.

59. For a fuller analysis of Khrushchev's shifting from conventional forces to the reliance on nuclear weaponry see Rourke, 19.

60. Powaski, 93. See also Boyle, 318.

61. For an extensive discussion of the 1961 Berlin crisis see McNamara, 61 *et seq.* See also Rourke, 22.

62. See also Pope, R.R., *Soviet Views on the Cuban Missile Crisis: Myth and Reality in Foreign Policy Analysis,* IX *et seq.* (1982); Rourke, 22; and Allison, G.T., "Conceptual Models and the Cuban Missile Crisis" in *International Relations: Contemporary Theory and Practice,* eds. Lopez, G.A. and M.S. Stohl, 107 *et seq.* (1989).

63. Rourke, 23.

64. *The United Nations and Disarmament: 1945–1985,* 2.

65. Schoenbaum, 25.

66. See Warburg, J.P., *Disarmament: The Challenge of the Nineteen Sixties,* 46 (1961).

67. Warburg, 54.

68. *The United Nations and Disarmament: 1945–1965,* ed. United Nations, 50.

69. Warburg, 54.

70. For the session of the 1955 Geneva summit conference on disarmament see *The United Nations and Disarmament: 1945–1965,* 57–58. Regarding the "Open Skies" pro-

posal, see Schoenbaum, 26–27. For a more detailed discussion of the "Open Skies" proposal see generally Rostow, W.W., *Open Skies: Eisenhower's Proposal of July 21, 1955* (1982).

71. See also Schoenbaum 26–27.

72. Warburg, 60. The UN General Assembly by its resolution 914 (X) on December 16, 1955, after having recognized that special technical difficulties had arisen in regard to the detection and control of nuclear weapons material, and that inspection and control of disarmament could best be achieved in an atmosphere free of fear and suspicion, urged the conclusion of an international agreement of such confidence building measures as the "Open Skies" plan and the Bulganin plan for establishing control posts at strategic centers. It further suggested the suspension of experimental explosions of nuclear weapons as had been proposed by India and recommended that further scientific research should be continued by states for the discovery of methods that would make possible effective inspection and control of nuclear weapons material, which could facilitate comprehensive nuclear disarmament. For the full text of this resolution see *The United Nations and Disarmament: 1945–1965,* 58–62.

73. Schoenbaum, 27.

74. See generally *The United Nations and Disarmament: 1945–1965,* 64 *et seq.*

75. Schoenbaum, 28.

76. For a comprehensive analysis of the Rapacki Plan see generally Ozinga, J.R., *The Rapacki Plan: The 1957 Proposal to Denuclearize Central Europe, and an Analysis of Its Rejection* (1989).

77. For an extensive discussion of the UN negotiations which led to the establishment of the IAEA and the adoption of its statute, see *Disarmament: Negotiations and Treaties, 1946–1971,* 58 *et seq.*

78. For an early and detailed legal analysis of the Agency's objectives and legal mechanisms for the promotion of the peaceful applications of nuclear energy and the prevention of the military applications of such energy, see Bechoefer, B.G., and E. Stein, "Atoms for Peace: The New International Atomic Energy Agency," 55 *Michigan Law Review,* 747–798 (1957). For an analysis of the legal need for international cooperation in the peaceful use of nuclear energy see generally Cavers, D.F., "International Cooperation in the Peaceful Uses of Atomic Energy," 12 *Vanderbilt Law Review,* 17–49 (1958-1959).

79. With respect to the agency's legal techniques of verification and safeguards to ensure the non-diversion of nuclear material and technology for peaceful purposes to military applications see generally McNight, A., *Atomic Safeguards: A Study in International Verification* (1971). See also *The Washington Post,* A17 (April 10, 1995).

80. Schoenbaum, 28–29. See further Warburg, 72 *et seq.*; and *The United Nations and Disarmament: 1945–1965,* 78.

81. See further *The United Nations and Disarmament: 1945–1965,* 78.

82. For the full text of this Soviet proposal on general and complete disarmament of September 18, 1959, see *The Soviet Stand on Disarmament,* ed. Crosscurrents Press, 9–24 (1962).

83. For a fuller analysis of the reasons for which the United States rejected the Soviet plan on general and complete disarmament see *The United Nations and Disarmament, 1945–1965,* 79.

84. For a comprehensive analysis of the negotiations which led to the conclusion of the Antarctic Treaty see generally Myhre, J.D., *The Antarctic Treaty System: Politics, Law and Diplomacy,* 23 *et seq.* (1986). For the full text of this treaty see *Arms Control: A Survey and Appraisal of Multilateral Agreements,* ed. Stockholm International Peace Research Institute, 72–75 (1978). See further Almond, H.H., Jr., "Demilitarization and

Arms Control: Antarctica," 17 *Case Western Reserve Journal of International Law,* 229–284 (1985). In addition, note that the treaty to ensure its effective compliance by its signatories in its Article VII provides that they have the right to carry out on-site inspections by their designated observer and inspection teams. In fact, these teams have the right of complete freedom of access at any time to any or all areas of Antarctica. Specifically, they have the right of on-site inspections of all stations, equipment, ships, aircraft, etc. To date Argentina, Australia, New Zealand, the United Kingdom and the United States have exercised their right of inspections. See Blechman, B.M., *Preventing Nuclear War: A Realistic Approach,* 32 (1985). The history of compliance to the treaty shows that it has been fully observed. Indeed, the already conducted inspections have not discovered any activities violating the treaty. Accordingly, the verification technique of on-site inspection as provided by the treaty has proved to be of imperative legal practicality and importance in the UN effort to maintain Antarctica as a non-nuclearized and generally as a non-militarized zone.

85. *The United Nations and Disarmament: 1945–1965,* 86–88.

86. The Eighteen-Nation Committee on Disarmament was established as a result of an agreement between the United States and the Soviet Union, which was endorsed by the UN General Assembly resolution 1722 (XVI) on December 31, 1961. See *The United Nations and Disarmament: 1945–1985,* 3.

87. *The United Nations and Disarmament: 1945–1970,* ed. United Nations, 91 (1970).

88. Ibid.

Chapter 4

89. See generally Moulton, H.B., *From Superiority to Parity: The United States and the Strategic Arms Race, 1961–1971* (1973).

90. For a discussion of the development of the Chinese atomic bomb see Moulton, 181–182.

91. For the full text of the Hot Line Agreement, which entered into force on the date of its signature, see 14 *US Treaties* and other international agreements. Note that the Hot Line Agreement had called for a direct and wholly private teletype link passing through Helsinki, Stockholm and London and it became operable even before the end of the summer of 1963. Additionally, this hot line communication between the White House and the Kremlin has been activated in several international crises since its establishment, as one side or the other has sought to prevent misunderstanding of some action it had taken or was about to take. See Seaborg, G.T., *Kennedy, Khrushchev and the Test Ban,* 206–207 (1981). See also Ury, W.L., *Beyond the Hotline: How Crisis Control Can Prevent Nuclear War,* 145 *et seq.* (1985).

92. For the full text of the LTBT (officially the "Treaty Banning Nuclear Weapon Tests in the Atmosphere, in Outer Space, and Under Water") which entered into force on October 10, 1963, see 14 *US Treaties* 1313.

93. Schoenbaum, 31. The French atmospheric nuclear tests in the South Pacific in 1973 and 1974 became the subject of judicial review by the International Court of Justice upon the action brought by both Australia and New Zealand against France. While the ICJ was asked by the applicant states to declare the illegality of the French tests and order their prohibition, the court in its final judgement declared the case moot, since the French government had stated its intention to cease its nuclear tests in the region. See generally: *Nuclear Tests (Australia v. France), Interim Protection Order of June 22, 1973*; ICJ *Reports 1973,* 99–135, and *Nuclear Tests (Australia v. France), Judgment of December*

1974, ICJ *Reports*, 1974. For a legal analysis of this case see Singh and McWhinney, 295 *et seq*.

94. For a comprehensive discussion of the superpower limited détente and negotiations which ultimately resulted in the conclusion of the LTBT see Seaborg, 235 *et seq*.; McBride, J.H., *The Test Ban Treaty: Military, Technological, and Political Implications* (1967); and Dean, A.H., *Test Ban and Disarmament: The Path of Negotiation* (1966).

95. See Article I of the LTBT, 14 *US Treaties*, 1316–1317.

96. See also Schoenbaum, 31. Nevertheless, even the underground nuclear explosions allowed by the LTBT often also release radioactive substances into the air. See *Agreements for Arms Control: A Critical Survey*, ed. SIPRI, 24 (1982).

97. The preamble of the LTBT emphasizes the contracting parties' determination to further seek to achieve the prohibition of all underground nuclear explosions and tests by concluding such an agreement. But since underground nuclear explosions and tests of nuclear weapons were not banned by the LTBT, both nuclear superpowers, the United Kingdom, and other powers which were about to acquire nuclear weapons could legally continue to carry out underground nuclear weapon tests. See the preamble and Article I 1(b) of the LTBT, 14 *US Treaties*, 1317.

98. *Agreements for Arms Control*, 25.

99. The Soviet Union had been accused by the US government of releasing nuclear debris into the atmosphere beyond the Soviet borders during its tests, a practice banned by the LTBT. See Menos, D., *The Superpowers and Nuclear Arms Control: Rhetoric and Reality*, 77 (1990).

100. Menos, *The Superpowers*, 25–26.

101. For the full text of the agreement see 22 *US Treaties*, 1598.

102. For an analysis of the agreement, I have heavily relied on Dahlitz, J., *Nuclear Arms Control with Effective International Agreements*, 29 (1983).

103. For the full text of this agreement see 23 *US Treaties*; for a brief analysis see Schoenbaum, 38.

104. See further Blacker, C.D., *Reluctant Warriors: The United States, the Soviet Union and Arms Control*, 110–111 (1987). See also the brief analysis by Dahlitz, 30.

105. Dahlitz, 30. On May 30, 1973, a US–USSR Protocol was signed. It entered into force on the same date, and provides the procedural rules for the functions of the SCC. Ibid.

106. For a brief analysis of this agreement see Schoenbaum, 37.

107. For the full text of the TTBT see *Arms Control and Disarmament Agreements*, ed. United States Arms Control and Disarmament Agency, 167–168 (1980). The TTBT specifies the test sites of the contracting parties and also deals with the verification of the treaty by the exchange of data. However, the question of the effective implementation of the TTBT led the US Senate to a prolonged debate over the ratification of this treaty. Although on September 25, 1990, the Senate ratified the treaty, its instrument of ratification is followed by a 107-page verification protocol. See Bailey, K., "This Is Not Arms Control" in *The Washington Post*, A11 (December 17, 1990).

108. See also generally the views of McWhinney, E., *The International Law of Détente* (1978); and Singh and McWhinney, 223 *et seq*.

109. For a comprehensive discussion of the negotiating record of the SALT I process which led to the conclusion of the ABM Treaty see Austin, B.J., T.J. Irvin, S.A. Kelly, and G.P. Kralik, "The History of Nuclear Arms Negotiations Between the United States and the Soviet Union," 15 *Journal of Legislation*, 210–217 (1989); and Newhouse, J., *Cold Down: The Story of SALT* (1989).

110. Dahlitz, 29. For the full text of the ABM Treaty see 23 *US Treaties*, 3435.

111. See further Blacker, 106 *et seq*.; Kintner, W.R., and R.L. Pfaltzgraff, Jr., *SALT:*

Implications for Arms Control in the 1970s (1973); and Payne, S.B., Jr., *The Soviet Union and SALT* (1980).

112. See also Blacker, 106.

113. See Article I (2) of the ABM Treaty 23 *US Treaties*, 3438. See also Singh and McWhinney, 263.

114. See Article III of the ABM Treaty. Note also that the exception of Article III, which permitted under certain terms each superpower to have two separate deployed ABM systems, was intended for protection against a surprise nuclear attack, thereby permitting a response to such an attack by using the ICBMs protected by the second ABM system.

115. Singh and McWhinney, 263.

116. See Article V (1) of the ABM Treaty and Common Understanding C. See also the legal analysis of Calvo-Goller, N.K. and M.A. Calvo, *The SALT Agreements: Content-Application-Verification,* 18–19 (1987).

117. Calvo-Goller and Calvo, 18–19.

118. The American SDI was born with President Reagan's "Star Wars" speech of March 1983. The SDI idea brings together four basic concepts identified as promising to the needs of a multilayered ABM defense: space-based lasers, ground-based lasers, space-based particle beams, and nuclear-directed energy weapons. See Menos, *The Superpowers*, 16.

119. Calvo-Goller and Calvo, 229.

120. Calvo-Goller and Calvo, 229.

121. See Sohn, L.B., "Verification Dilemmas" in Diehl and Johnson, 194. Additional NTM of verification include far-reaching listening devices that can monitor distant conversations, sensors able to detect large underground explosions, equipment for testing the atmosphere for traces of telltale radioactive elements, and underwater sonars for spotting submarines. Ibid.

122. Sohn, 194.

123. See Potter, W.C., *Verification and SALT: The Challenge of Strategic Deception* (1980).

124. For an extensive analysis of active and passive interference to prevent NTM from serving their objective of effective verification, see Cohen, S.A., "The Evolution of Soviet Views on SALT Verification: Implications for the Future" in Potter, 154 *et seq.*; and Sohn, 195.

125. See Article XII (2) and (3); and the preamble of the ABM Treaty, 23 *US Treaties,* 3443–3437.

126. For the full text of the interim agreement see *Arms Control and Disarmament Agreements*, 150–152. For a brief and concise analysis of the superpower negotiations which led to the interim agreement, See George, J.L., *The New Nuclear Rules: Strategy and Arms Control after INF and START*, 82 *et seq.* (1990).

127. See Article VIII (2) of the agreement, 23 *US Treaties*, 3467. See also Singh and McWhinney, 265.

128. See Articles VII and VIII (2) of the interim agreement. See also Calvo-Goller and Calvo, 31.

129. Schoenbaum, 36.

130. See further Blacker, 107. Note, however, that President Nixon believed that these issues could be resolved through negotiations with the Soviets, and that a superpower bilateral treaty imposing limitations on their offensive nuclear arms would be concluded before Nixon's presidential term was over.

131. Schoenbaum, 36.

132. See George, 83–84. The Soviets had in operation 62 strategic submarines while the United States had only 41. Ibid.

133. See also George, 84.

134. See also Calvo-Goller and Calvo, 30.

135. These limitations apply to both the "soft" and "hard" launchers. See Calvo-Goller and Calvo, 31.

136. Schoenbaum, 36. The Interim Agreement failed to legally describe the term "start of construction." But according to the Nixon administration construction was to begin only with construction of a silo or a launcher in the field or when the digging or drilling of an ICBM silo started. See Calvo-Goller and Calvo, 32. The Interim Agreement also failed to define "ICBM launchers." Its definition was later given by the Agreed Statement H, which defined that launchers for strategic ballistic missiles capable of ranges in excess of the shortest distance between the Northeastern border of the continental United States and the Northwestern continental Soviet Union were considered ICBM launchers. In fact, their range of distance was approximately 5,500 kilometers. Ibid.

137. Schoenbaum, 36.

138. Calvo-Goller and Calvo, 32. At the time of the signature of the Interim Agreement the Soviet Union had 91 land-based ICBM launchers under active construction whose completion was allowed. Ibid.

139. See Article IV of the interim agreement, 23 *US Treaties*, 3465. Note, however, that according to the Agreed Statement C, modernization and replacement of land-based ICBM silo launchers could not be increased more than 15 percent. See also Schoenbaum, 36.

140. See Schoenbaum, 36. The Interim Agreement concentrated on launchers rather than warheads or missiles, primarily because launchers could be easily and adequately verified by national technical means of verification. Ibid. Article IV of the agreement provided that the verification of the content and compliance with its requirements would be conducted through NTM of verification. See further Calvo-Goller and Calvo, 35–36.

141. For a further analysis of the interim agreement and its protocol see Singh and McWhinney, 265–268.

142. The Nixon-Brezhnev summit meeting in Washington in June 1973 resulted in the signature of the US-Soviet Accord on Principles of Negotiations on the Further Limitation of Strategic Offensive Arms of June 21, 1973. This accord provided that during the next two years both sides would undertake serious negotiating efforts to replace the Interim Agreement with a permanent agreement or more complete measures on the limitation of their strategic offensive arms. For the full text of this accord see Singh and McWhinney, 366–367.

143. For a comprehensive analysis of the causes which resulted in the deterioration of the superpower relations since 1973 see Blacker, 14 *et seq.*

144. See further Blacker, 114 *et seq.* See also Calvo-Goller and Calvo, 39.

145. Calvo-Goller and Calvo, 43. The full text of the Vladivostok Declaration can be found in Calvo-Goller and Calvo, 370.

146. Dahlitz, 31.

147. Calvo-Goller and Calvo, 44.

148. For a further analysis and critical assessment of the Vladivostok Declaration see Singh and McWhinney, 270–27.

Chapter 5

149. For a comprehensive discussion of the various UN proposals on general and complete disarmament, including also nuclear disarmament, see generally: *The United*

Nations and Disarmament, 1945–1965, 98 *et seq.*; *The United Nations and Disarmament: 1945–1985,* 25 *et seq.*; and *The United Nations and Disarmament, 1970–1975,* ed. United Nations, 1 *et seq.*

150. Dahlitz, 15.

151. Menos, *The Superpowers,* 53.

152. Menos, *The Superpowers,* 50.

153. See also Menos, *The Superpowers,* 50.

154. For an extensive discussion of the UN failed efforts to adopt a treaty absolutely banning the use of the nuclear weapons for war see Epstein, W., *The Prevention of Nuclear War: A United Nations Perspective,* 18 *et seq.* (1984).

155. Epstein, *Prevention of Nuclear War,* 24–25.

156. For a concise discussion of the UN negotiations on the conclusion of a CTB Treaty see Epstein, W., *The Last Chance: Nuclear Proliferation and Arms Control,* 185–187 (1976).

157. For an analysis of the violations of these treaties committed by both superpowers see Menos, *The Superpowers,* 77–78.

158. For the full text of this treaty see *Arms Control and Disarmament Agreements,* 51–55 (1980).

159. For a comprehensive legal analysis of the Outer Space Treaty see Singh and McWhinney, 234–237. For a detailed discussion of the principle of the peaceful uses of outer space as opposed to its military uses, see generally Goldman, N.C., *American Space Law, International and Domestic,* 73–74. (1988).

160. Goldman, 73–74.

161. For the full content of Article XI see the Outer Space Treaty. Article X of the treaty can play a legal role in ensuring the conformity of the contracting parties with the purposes of the treaty. It provides that contracting parties can request to be afforded an opportunity to observe the flight of space object launched by those contracting parties involved in space activities. But such an opportunity to observe the flight of space objects can be legally possible only on the basis of the conclusion of a separate agreement among the interested contracting parties. Nonetheless, mere observation of the flight of space objects is not a complete and effective inspection technique. In essence, contracting parties afforded the opportunity of mere observation of such flight without having the right to inspect the payload to be launched, cannot normally ascertain whether such payload contained nuclear weapons, mass destruction weapons or other military weapons, which the launching state is determined to place in outer space in violation of its treaty obligations.

162. See further Goldman, 73. The on-site inspection provided by Article XII does not extend to space objects in orbit or in free space. See also Menos, *The Superpowers,* 59–60, and George, 165–166.

163. For a discussion of these four rationales for the creation of NWFZs see Macdonald, R. St. J., "Nuclear Weapon-Free Zones and Principles of International Law" in *International Law and Its Sources,* ed. Heere, W.P., 48 (1988).

164. For an analysis of the efforts to create a Balkan NWFZ see generally Pamir, P., "The Quest for a Balkan Nuclear-Weapons-Free Zone" in *Nuclear-Free Zones,* eds. Pitt, D., and G. Thompson, 94–105 (1987).

165. See Pitt, D., "Nuclear-Free Zones: An Idea Whose Time Has Come," in Pitt and Thompson, 2. For a concise discussion of the evolution of the negotiations and the progress made on the proposed Nordic NWFZ since 1961 see Macdonald, 53–54.

166. For a more detailed analysis of the negotiating efforts and prospects for the establishment of an African NWFZ see generally Epstein, W., "A Nuclear-Weapon-Free Zone in Africa?" in Pitt and Thompson, 110–127.

167. For this modified version of the Rapacki Plan, which was introduced to the United Nations, see Coates, K., "For A Nuclear-Free Europe" in Pitt and Thompson, 82.

168. For a short discussion of the proposed Near East NWFZ see Coates, 84.

169. See Epstein, *The Prevention of Nuclear War*. For the full text of the Treaty of Tlatelolco see *Arms Control and Disarmament Agreements* (1980), 63–76. For a fuller analysis of the negotiations which led to the conclusion of this treaty see generally Robles, A.G., *The Denuclearization of Latin America* (1967).

170. Macdonald, 57.

171. See *The Arms Control Reporter*, Section 452.A, 1–3. (1996).

172. In particular, Brazil and Argentina are rapidly approaching the threshold of developing nuclear weapons. They also possess ballistic missiles. For a more detailed analysis of the involvement of both Brazil and Argentina in the development of nuclear weapons see *New Threats: Responding to the Proliferation of Nuclear, Chemical, and Delivery Capabilities in the Third World*, ed. The Aspen Strategy Group, 3–4, 107 (1990).

173. For a further analysis of the content of Article 1 see Robles, "The Treaty for the Prohibition of Nuclear Weapons in Latin America" in Pitt and Thompson, 16; and Macdonald, 57.

174. For a further concise discussion of the permission for the peaceful uses of nuclear energy and the carrying out of nuclear explosions for the same purpose see Robles, "The Treaty for the Prohibition," 17–18.

175. See *The Arms Control Reporter*, Section 706.A, 3, and Section 706.E, 1 (1996).

176. For a more detailed discussion of the composition of the Treaty Agency see Robles "The Treaty for the Prohibition," 15.

177. For a further analysis of the legal role of the agency's organs in the implementation of the treaty as specifically provided by Articles 9–11 see Robles, "The Treaty for the Prohibition," 15.

178. Robles, "The Treaty for the Prohibition," 15.

179. Robles, "The Treaty for the Prohibition," 15. See also Macdonald, 60.

180. For the full text of Additional Protocol I see *Arms Control and Disarmament Agreements*, 75 (1980).

181. See *The Arms Control Reporter*, Section 452.A, 4 (1996).

182. For the full text of Additional Protocol II see *Arms Control and Disarmament Agreements*, 76 (1980).

183. See *The Arms Control Reporter*, Section 452.A, 4 (1996).

184. See Singh and McWhinney, 247–248. For a general discussion of the negotiations which led to the conclusion of the treaty see *International Negotiations of the Seabed Arms Control Treaty* ed. United States Arms Control and Disarmament Agency (1973). For the full text of the treaty see *Arms Control and Disarmament Agreements*, 102–105 (1980).

185. See Singh and McWhinney, 249.

186. Singh and McWhinney, 249.

187. See Wilmhurst, M.J., "The Development of Current Non-Proliferation Policies" in *The International Nuclear Non-Proliferation System: Challenge and Choices*, eds. Simpson, J., and A.G. McGrew, 19 (1984).

188. See also Epstein, *Prevention of Nuclear War*, 48; and Singh and McWhinney, 238.

189. See *Arms Control and Disarmament Agreements*, 82 (1980).

190. Ibid.

191. Singh and McWhinney, 240.

192. Singh and McWhinney, 240–241. For the full text of the NPT see *Arms Control and Disarmament Agreements*, 90–94 (1980).

193. For a concise description of the technical concept of horizontal nuclear proliferation see Epstein, *Prevention of Nuclear War,* 48.

194. See Marks, A.W., *NPT: Paradoxes and Problems,* 4, (1975); and Singh and McWhinney, 241. For a more detailed analysis of the nuclear weapon states' security guarantees and assurances to the non-nuclear weapon states in view of the UN Security Council Resolution 255 see generally Lenefsky, D., "The United Nations Security Council Resolution on Security Assurances for Non-Nuclear Weapon States," 3 *New York University Journal of International Law and Politics,* 56–71 (1970).

195. Singh and McWhinney, 241.

196. Singh and McWhinney, 241.

197. See *The Arms Control Reporter,* Section 602.B, 310 (1996).

198. For a further specific analysis of the Israeli and Indian nuclear weapon capabilities and their ballistic missile systems see *New Threats,* 49–56.

199. See Shaker, M.I., "The Non-Proliferation Treaty Regime, A Reading Before 1995" in *Beyond 1995: The Future of the NPT Regime,* Pilat, J.F., and R.E. Pendley, 10 (1990).

200. See *The Arms Control Reporter,* Section 602.A, 5 (1990).

201. Ibid., 5–6.

202. Ibid.

203. Ibid.

204. Ibid.

Chapter 6

205. See Krepon, M., *Arms Control in the Reagan Administration,* 11 (1989).

206. See generally Calvo-Goller and Calvo, 46 *et seq.*; Menos, D., *World at Risk: The Debate Over Arms Control,* 15 *et seq.* (1986), and *Arms Control and Disarmament Agreements,* 171 (1980). For the full text of the PNET, its protocol and the agreed statement, see ibid., 173–189.

207. For a concise and comprehensive discussion of the ratification of the TTBT and PNET by the US Senate and the resolution of the Senate, which lists a number of safeguards in relation to the effective verification and implementation of both treaties, see *The Arms Control Reporter,* Section 605.B, 109–113 (1990).

208. For this justification provided by India see Halsted, T.A., "Nuclear Testing—No End In Sight?" in *The Arms Race in the Era of Star Wars,* eds. Carlton, D. and C. Schaerf, 215 (1988).

209. See also the similar views expressed in Halsted, 216–217. In fact, it must have been an extraordinary wrench for the Soviet Union to agree to allow adversary inspectors on Soviet soil, and to grant them at least some latitude in their activities at the site of a nuclear explosion. Ibid.

210. See George, 54–55. See also Risse-Kappen, T., *The Zero Option: INF, West Germany, and Arms Control,* 10 (1988).

211. For a general discussion of the superpower negotiations which led to the conclusion of SALT II see Wolfe, T.W., *The SALT Experience,* 219 *et seq.* (1979).

212. For the full text of the SALT II Agreement, its protocol and the agreed statements and common understandings, see *Arms Control and Disarmament Agreements,* 246–271 (1984).

213. This characterization of the SALT II made by President Carter is quoted in Menos, *The Superpowers,* 80.

214. For a general discussion of the US Senate's severe criticism and opposition to

the ratification of SALT II, I have heavily relied on Krepon, 1 *et seq.*; Menos, *The Superpowers*, 80–81; and Calvo-Goller and Calvo, 4 *et seq.*

215. See Meredith, P.M., "The Legality of a High-Technology Missile Defense System: The ABM and Outer Space Treaties," 78 *American Journal of International Law*, 418 (1984).

216. See Lopez, G.A., "Forward: The Reagan Legacy and the Strategic Defense Initiative," 15 *Journal of Legislation*, 77 (1989). For a discussion of the military, industrial, political, scientific and bureaucratic lobbying efforts on President Reagan to adopt and announce the SDI system see generally Grossman, J., "The Politics of 'Star Wars'" in ibid., 93–101. Reagan's SDI was born in an American popular culture dominated by space adventure movies like *Star Trek, Star Wars,* and *Close Encounters of the Third Kind.* Thus, in SDI, both fantasy and policy merged. Grossman, 96.

217. See Menos, *The Superpowers*, 16. For a further analysis of the technical description of the SDI system see generally: Dallmeyer, D.G., "Space Weapons: Arming Man's Last Frontier," in Diehl and Johnson, 91–117; Johnson, T.H., "Technologies of Ballistic Missile Defense" in *The ABM Treaty: To Defend or Not to Defend?* Eds. Stützle, W., *et al.*, 91–102 (1987); York, H.F., " 'Star Wars': Origins and Overview" in Carlton and Schaerf, 213–231; Lin, H. *New Weapon Technologies and the ABM Treaty* (1988); Gall, R., "Militarization of Space" in *Scientists, Peace and Disarmament* eds. Lemarchand, G.A., and A.R. Pedace, 326–333 (1988); and Westerkamp, J.F., "On the Strategic Defense Initiative and the Anti-ballistic Missile Treaty" in Lemarchand and Pedace, 334–352; and Bes, D., "The Vertical Meaning of the Strategic Defense Initiative" in Lemarchand and Pedace, 360–378.

218. Menos, *The Superpowers*, 16. See also Dallmeyer, 93 *et seq.*

219. For a more detailed discussion of the Phase I scheduled deployment of the SDI system into outer space in late 1993 and the technological development and continued tests and improvement of the Brilliant Pebbles see *The Arms Control Reporter*, Section 575.E, 2, 11, and Section 505.0, 5 *et seq.* (1990).

220. See generally the views of Sagdeyev, R.Z., Y.P. Velikhov, and A.A. Kokoshin, "Strategic and Political Aspects of the Strategic Defense Initiative: A Soviet Viewpoint," 15 *Journal of Legislation*, 179–198 (1989).

221. Abraham Sofaer, the former legal advisor to the State Department, was the inventor and supporter of the broader interpretation of the ABM Treaty to justify the compatibility of the Reagan-proposed space-based SDI program. See generally Sofaer, A.D., "The ABM Treaty and the Strategic Defense Initiative," 99 *Harvard Law Review*, 1972–1985 (1986). Sofaer in his legal efforts to justify the legality of the initial objective of the Reagan administration to develop and test its SDI program argued, on the basis of what he called "the treaty language" or a "restrictive interpretation" of the ABM Treaty, that in accordance with Agreed Statement D the contracting parties have the right to develop and test substitute devices for anti-ballistic missile systems or components based on other physical principles than those used in developing ABM missile defense systems at the time of the signature of the treaty. Thus, Sofaer suggests that Agreed Statement D is a qualification (or amplification) of Article V (1) of the treaty, which prohibits the deployment of space-based ABM systems or components. Accordingly, Sofaer concludes that since the SDI contemplates other physical principles than those that existed at the time of the signature of the treaty, the development, testing and the deployment of a space-based SDI system by the United States would be compatible with the ABM Treaty, and that any limitations on the SDI anti-ballistic missile defenses, as provided in Agreed Statement D, would be subject to further negotiation between the two parties under Article XIII of the treaty, and, if need be, to agreement for amendment of the treaty under Article XIV. See ibid. See also Singh and McWhinney, 333–334; and De Tar, R.A., "The Proposal

for Reinterpreting the ABM Agreement: Death of a Treaty," 3 *American University Journal of International Law and Policy*, 427 *et seq.* (1988). Although the US administration initially argued the legality of the development and testing of the proposed SDI system in view of the ABM Treaty, by the end of 1985, President Reagan's secretary of state, George Shultz, said that the Reagan administration had adopted a broader interpretation of the ABM Treaty, which was legally justified and which allowed the United States to proceed with the development, testing and deployment of the SDI program. Nonetheless, Shultz indicated that the issue of the SDI deployment as based on other physical principles would be the subject of US-Soviet negotiations. See Gross, D.G., "Negotiated Treaty Amendment: The Solution to the SDI-ABM Treaty Conflict," 28 *Harvard International Law Journal*, 46 *et seq.* (1987).

222. See further *The Washington Post*, A21 (July 15, 1993). See also *The 1996 Arms Control Reporter*, Section 576.A, 1. See further *The Defense Monitor*, 5 (June 1997).

Chapter 7

223. The Ad Hoc Committee on the World Disarmament Conference was established by the UN General Assembly in 1973. Its main task was to examine the possibility and the preparation of the ground for a world disarmament conference. For a further analysis see generally *The United Nations Disarmament Yearbook*, ed. United Nations, 53 *et seq.* (1979).

224. For the full text of the *Final Document* see *The United Nations Disarmament Yearbook*, 473–490 (1979). Indeed, for the first time in the history of disarmament negotiations, the international community unanimously agreed on a comprehensive strategy for disarmament. See *Everyone's United Nations*, ed. United Nations, 150 (1986).

225. See generally, *The United Nations Disarmament Yearbook*, 478–487 (1979).

226. Ibid., 476–477.

227. Ibid., 479.

228. Ibid., 477–478.

229. Ibid., 490.

230. See also *Everyone's United Nations*, 151.

231. The complete title of the 1980 report of the UN Secretary-General is: *General and Complete Disarmament: Comprehensive Study on Nuclear Weapons: Report of the Secretary-General.* For the full text of this report see *Nuclear Weapons: Report of the Secretary-General*, ed. United Nations (1980).

232. Ibid.; for a more detailed discussion see Appendix I in ibid., 193 *et seq.* Note also that in accordance with the report the largest nuclear weapon ever tested released an explosive power nearly 4,000 times greater than that of the atomic bomb that leveled Hiroshima. Ibid., 8.

233. Ibid., 89 *et seq.*

234. Ibid.

235. Ibid., 92 *et seq.*

236. Ibid.

237. Ibid., 188.

238. Ibid.

239. Ibid., 192. For a further consideration of the 1975 NPT Review Conference see generally *The United Nations and Disarmament: 1970–1975*, 82–92.

240. For a general discussion of the UN initiatives in relation to the question of global nuclear disarmament during 1975–1980 see generally: *The United Nations Disarmament Yearbook* (1979 and 1980). See also *Everyone's United Nations*, 164. These trilateral

negotiations on the formulation of a CTBT proved unable to overcome the legal and technical difficulties raised by the question of verification of such a treaty by seismic monitoring, on-site inspection and the participation of other parties in its implementation. Ibid.

241. For the full text of this convention see *Arms Control and Disarmament Agreements,* 193–198 (1980).

242. Ibid., 190.

243. For a further discussion of the 1975 NPT Review Conference see generally *The United Nations and Disarmament: 1970–1975,* 82–92 (1976).

244. See *The United Nations Disarmament Yearbook,* 199–200 (1981).

245. Ibid., 201–202.

246. Ibid., 228. See also *Everyone's United Nations,* 168–169.

247. See *The United Nations Disarmament Yearbook,* 208 (1981).

248. Ibid.

249. Ibid., 204–206.

250. For a general consideration and analysis of the 1980 NPT Review Conference see ibid., 126 *et seq.*

251. For a discussion of the trends in horizontal nuclear weapons proliferation by the near-nuclear weapon states and the nuclear problem states since the beginning of the 1980s see generally: *Limiting Nuclear Proliferation,* eds. Snyder, J.C. and S.F. Wells, Jr., 3 *et seq.* (1985); and *Nuclear Non-Proliferation: An Agenda for the 1990s,* ed. J. Simpson, 24 *et seq.* (1987). See further *The Arms Control Reporter,* Section 602.A, 1 *et seq.* (1996).

252. In relation to the prevention of the proliferation of ballistic missiles, in the late 1970s the Missile Technology Control Regime (MTCR) was to be formed with the objective of dealing with the export of ballistic missiles and technologies to produce such missiles for non-nuclear weapon states. Finally, the MTCR was formally created in April 1987 with the simultaneous announcement by the United States, Canada, France, West Germany, Italy, Japan and Britain of a new policy to restrict exports that could contribute to the acquisition of ballistic missiles capable of delivering nuclear warheads. However, the MTCR does not constitute a multilateral treaty and thus lacks any legal force. On the contrary, it constitutes a multilateral organ setting out the policies of its participant states for a joint regulation of the prevention of the proliferation of ballistic missiles to the non-nuclear weapon states. See further *New Threats,* 13–15. For a detailed list of countries presently possessing ballistic missile capabilities, see *The Arms Control Reporter,* Section 706.E, 1–2 (1996).

253. See *Everyone's United Nations,* 165.

254. Ibid., 156.

255. Ibid., 157.

256. Ibid., 157–158.

257. Ibid.

258. Ibid.

259. Ibid.

260. For a further detailed analysis of the popular movement for a nuclear arms freeze and nuclear disarmament, particularly in Western Europe and the United States in the 1980s, see Menos, *The Superpowers,* 61 *et seq.*

261. Ibid.

262. See *The United Nations Disarmament Yearbook,* 190–191 (1981).

263. See *The United Nations Disarmament Yearbook,* 277–278 (1982).

264. See *The Arms Control Reporter,* Section 455.A, 1 (1996).

265. See *The United Nations Disarmament Yearbook,* 277–278 (1982).

266. See *The Arms Control Reporter,* Section 453.A, 4 (1996). See also *The Washington Times,* A10 (April 8, 1996).

267. See *The United Nations Disarmament Yearbook,* 277–278 (1982).

268. See *Everyone's United Nations,* 168–169.

269. Ibid.

270. Ibid.

271. For a further analysis of the trends towards regional proliferation of nuclear weapons during the 1980s see generally: *Everyone's United Nations,* 58–60.

272. For a general discussion of the prospects for the nuclearization of the Middle East and its implications see generally Bhatia, S., *Nuclear Rivals in the Middle East* (1989).

273. As has been previously discussed, while by the mid–1970s Israel, a non-NPT state party, had acquired in a de facto manner nuclear weapons, by the beginning of the 1980s a number of Middle East states possessed significant nuclear programs. In fact, Iraq and Iran were considered nuclear weapon problem states. For a more detailed analysis of the proliferation of nuclear technologies and materials for the development of nuclear weapons in the Middle East see Bhatia, 34 *et seq.*

274. See *The Arms Control Reporter,* Sections 453.A, 1–2 and 453.B, 77 *et seq.* (1990). See also *Everyone's United Nations,* 172.

275. See *The Arms Control Reporter,* Section 454.A, 1 (1990). See also *Everyone's United Nations,* 172–173.

276. See *The Arms Control Reporter,* Section 454.A, 1 (1990).

277. Ibid., 2. See further *Everyone's United Nations,* 172.

278. See *The Arms Control Reporter,* Section 454.B, 3 *et seq.* (1990). The Soviet Union favored a South Asian NWFZ. It also had warned Pakistan about acquiring nuclear weapons. Similarly, the United States favors the nonproliferation of nuclear weapons in the region and has asked both Pakistan and India to discuss a common approach. Ibid.

279. Ibid., Section 503.A, 1.

280. Ibid.

281. Ibid.

282. Ibid., 2.

283. See also ibid., 4, 6.

284. Ibid.

285. Ibid.

286. Ibid.

287. Ibid., Section 458.A, 1–2.

288. Ibid. For a more detailed discussion of the obstacles and prospects for the demilitarization and denuclearization of the Korean Peninsula see generally: *The Korean Peninsula: Prospects for Arms Reduction under Global Détente,* eds. Taylor, W.J., Jr., C. Young-Koo, and J.Q. Blodgett (1990).

289. See *The Arms Control Reporter,* Section 457.A, 12 (1990).

290. Ibid.

291. Ibid.

292. See further *The Washington Post,* A1, A12 (March 22, 1994).

293. For a general discussion of the establishment of the South Pacific NWFZ see Fyfe, N. and Beeby, C., "The South Pacific Nuclear Free Zone Treaty," 17 *Victoria University of Wellington Law Review,* 34 *et seq.* (1987). For the full text of this treaty, including its annexes and protocols, see 24 *International Legal Materials,* 1442–1463 (1985).

294. See *The Arms Control Reporter,* Section 840, 323 *et seq.* (1996).

295. In contrast with the Treaty of Tlatelolco, the Rarotonga Treaty is not plagued by a complex system of acceptance. Article 12 provides a more flexible treaty acceptance mechanism. It calls simply for signature and ratification. Article 14 of the treaty states that

the treaty is not subject to reservation. See Macdonald, 64–65. Note further that Article 14 of the treaty states that the treaty is of permanent nature and shall remain in force indefinitely.

296. See Macdonald, 63. For a specific geographic description and delimitation of the South Pacific NFZ see Annex 1 of the Rarotonga Treaty.

297. See Macdonald, 62. Furthermore, the adoption and acceptance of the Rarotonga Treaty was certainly made easier because the South Pacific was already a de facto NFZ. See further Thakur, R., "The Treaty of Rarotonga: The South Pacific Nuclear-Free Zone" in Pitt and Thompson, 29.

298. See Article 5 of the Rarotonga Treaty. See also Macdonald, 62–63; and Lippman, M., "The South Pacific Nuclear-Free Zone Treaty: Regional Autonomy Versus International Law and Politics," 10 *Loyola of Los Angeles International and Comparative Law Journal,* 125 (1988).

299. See also Lippman, 125–126; and Gibbs, E.L., "In Furtherance of a Nuclear-Free Zone Precedent: The South Pacific Nuclear Free Zone Treaty," 4 *Boston University International Law Journal,* 402 *et seq.* (1986).

300. See Macdonald, 62–63.

301. See further Gibbs, 402–403.

302. See also Macdonald, 62; and Gibbs, 402.

303. See Macdonald, 63. The impetus for the conclusion of the Rarotonga Treaty did not only stem from long-standing concerns in the South Pacific over the testing of nuclear weapons and missiles, but also from the fear that Japan was about to dump radioactive waste and other radioactive matter at sea within the region. Ibid. Thus, Article 7 of the Rarotonga Treaty is designed to prevent and prohibit the pollution and contamination of the environment and the natural resources against the dumping of low-level radioactive materials by states inside and outside the South Pacific NFZ. See also Gibbs, 405–406.

304. See the view of Macdonald, 62.

305. See also Gibbs, 407.

306. Gibbs, 400 *et seq.*

307. See Macdonald, 64.

308. Macdonald, 64. See also Thakur, 29.

309. Thakur, 29.

310. Thakur, 29.

311. See also Macdonald, 64. For a more detailed comparative legal analysis of the Rarotonga Treaty and the Treaty of Tlatelolco, see Gibbs, 407–412.

312. Macdonald, 64; and Thakur, 30.

313. For the full text of Protocol I, II and III of the Rarotonga Treaty, see 24 *International Legal Materials,* 1459–1463 (1979).

314. See also the analysis of Macdonald, 64–65.

315. See *The Arms Control Reporter,* Section 840.B, 23 (1996).

316. See also Fyfe and Beeby, 48–49.

317. See *The Arms Control Reporter,* 4 (1996).

318. Quoted in Macdonald, 65.

319. Ibid.

320. See *The Arms Control Reporter,* Section 456.A, 4 (1996).

321. For a more detailed analysis of the militarization and nuclearization of the Pacific by the naval and aircraft nuclear-capable forces of the two superpowers see Lippman, 115–119.

322. See *The Arms Control Reporter,* Section 840.B, 23–24 (1996).

323. For the full text of the Moon Treaty see 18 *International Legal Materials,* 1434–1441 (1979).

324. See Christol, C.Q., "The Moon Treaty Enters Into Force," 79 *American Journal of International Law*, 163 (1985).

325. See further Singh and McWhinney, 237. For a more detailed analysis of the legal regulation of the exploration and uses of the Moon and other celestial bodies for the common benefit of humanity under the Moon Treaty see Christol, 164–165.

326. See also Singh and McWhinney, 237.

327. See also Singh and McWhinney, 237.

328. See also Dore, I.I., "International Law and the Preservation of the Ocean Space and Outer Space As Zones of Peace: Progress and Problems," 15 *Cornell International Law Journal*, 47–48 (1982).

329. See Moon Treaty, Article 15, 18 *International Legal Materials*, 1439–1440 (1979). See also Christol, 164.

330. See also Christol, 164.

331. See also ibid.

332. See further 18 *International Legal Materials*, 1419–1421 (1979).

333. Ibid. See the full text of the convention and its annexes in ibid., 1422–1433.

334. See *Treaties in Force* ed. US Department of State, 356 (1990).

335. For the full content of Article 1(a) and (b) see the convention, 18 *International Legal Materials*, 1422–1423 (1979). See also Annex II, 1433.

336. See the preamble and Article 1(c), ibid., 1423.

337. The convention serves the legal objective to avert the potential dangers posed by the unlawful taking and use of nuclear material while it encourages the transfer of such material for peaceful applications under the legal regime and controls of the NPT and under the safeguards of the IAEA. See also the preamble of the convention, ibid.

338. See Article 7, ibid., 1425–1426.

339. See Articles 7 and 8, ibid., 1425–1426.

340. Ibid.

341. See Articles 9–11, ibid., 1426–1427.

342. See *The Washington Times*, A15 (April 3, 1996).

343. See Articles 3 and 4, ibid., 1423–1424.

344. See Article 5, ibid., 1424–1425.

345. Ibid. See also Article 6, ibid., 1426.

346. Ibid. See also Article 17, ibid., 1429.

347. See *The Washington Times*, A4 (March 18, 1996).

Chapter 8

348. For a more detailed analysis of the US-Soviet NST negotiations in the 1980s with a specific concentration on the Gorbachev agenda on nuclear disarmament, see McCain, M., *Understanding Arms Control: The Options*, 176–198 (1989).

349. For a further discussion of the negative impact of the SDI program on the START and INF negotiations, see Risse-Kappen, 104.

350. See generally Gorbachev, M., *Perestroika: New Thinking for Our Country and the World* (1987), where Gorbachev himself provides the fundamental principles for a new all-embracing system of international security and for the global elimination of nuclear weapons. Also, for a further discussion of Gorbachev's leadership and new thinking about international security, global peace and nuclear disarmament, see Sagdeyev, R., "Soviet 'New Thinking' About International Security" in *Challenges for the 1990s for Arms Control and International Security*, ed. National Academy of Sciences, Committee on International Security and Arms Control, 28–35 (1989).

351. See Menos, *The Superpowers*, 30–31.

352. For an analysis of these Soviet proposals, see Risse-Kappen, 106.

353. For the Soviet concession to the SDI system see Bennett, P.R., *The Soviet Union and Arms Control: Negotiating Strategy and Tactics*, 81 (1989).

354. For a discussion of the Gorbachev-Reagan Geneva summit meeting and a specific description of what transpired between the two leaders see Adelman, K.L., *The Great Universal Embrace: Arms Summitry—A Skeptic's Account,* 121–160 (1989).

355. For some basic excerpts of the communiqué of the Geneva summit meeting see Menos, *The Superpowers*, 155–156. For a critical evaluation of the results of the Geneva summit see Risse-Kappen, 108.

356. See Menos, *The Superpowers*, 31.

357. See Risse-Kappen, 109.

358. Ibid.

359. See Menos, *The Superpowers*, 31.

360. See Risse-Kappen, 109–110. With respect to the Gorbachev proposal for a world nuclear disarmament by the year 2000, it must be noted that the NATO allies unanimously rejected this proposal. Risse-Kappen, 117.

361. For a more detailed discussion of the INF negotiations between February and September 1986 see Risse-Kappen, 110–115.

362. Risse-Kappen, 112.

363. For a general analysis of the preparation of the Reykjavik summit, including a specific account of what transpired between Gorbachev and Reagan in their NST negotiations, see Adelman, *The Great Universal Embrace*, 19–88.

364. See also the view of Risse-Kappen, 115.

365. See also Risse-Kappen, 114, *et seq.*

366. Ibid.

367. See Menos, *The Superpowers*, 156. For a further discussion of the Gorbachev proposals at Reykjavik for the beginning of a substantial legal process for superpower denuclearization and their impact on this question see Adeniran, T., "Nuclear Weapons: Toward Nuclear Arms Limitation and Global Disarmament after Reykjavik" in *Multilateral Aspects of the Disarmament Debate*, 32–47; Bessmertnykh, A., "Reykjavik and Prospects for a Nuclear-Free World" in ibid., 49–53; Carasales, J.C., "Possibilities After Reykjavik: Let Us Not Waste Them" in ibid., 54–59; and Payne, K.B., "The Dilemmas of Deterrence, Defense, and Disarmament," in *Strategic Arms Control After SALT*, ed. Cimbala, S.J., 115–133 (1989).

368. See Risse-Kappen, 114 *et seq.*

369. See Menos, *The Superpowers*, 156. Gorbachev in August 1986 stated that, although mountains of nuclear weapons were accumulated, yet the nuclear arms race continued, and that there existed a danger that it could extend into outer space. Ibid., 31.

370. See Risse-Kappen, 115.

371. For a more detailed discussion of the US-Soviet NST after the Reykjavik summit see Risse-Kappen, 143 *et seq.*; and Panofsky, W.K.H., "Reykjavik and Beyond: Implications of Deep Reductions in Strategic Nuclear Arsenals and the Future Direction of Arms Control" in *Reykjavik and Beyond*, 1–10 (1988). For a more detailed discussion of the progress and breakthroughs made in the INF negotiations after the Reykjavik summit, which led to the final conclusion of the INF Treaty in December 1987, see McCain, 194–196.

372. For a more specific analysis of the Shevardnadze-Shultz Agreement in Principle on the INF agreement, see Singh and McWhinney, 367.

373. For a general discussion of the Washington summit between Gorbachev and

Reagan, see Adelman, *The Great Universal Embrace*, 199–250. The author provides a detailed account on what transpired during this summit.

374. See Menos, *The Superpowers*, 157.

375. The full text of the INF Treaty, including its protocols and annex, can be found in 27 *International Legal Materials*, 90–254. For a brief description of the treaty's legal framework see Kokoski, R., and Koulik, S., *Verification of Conventional Arms Control in Europe: Technological Constraints and Opportunities*, 203 (1990).

376. For a description of the MOA of December 1989 see Kokoski and Koulik 203.

377. See Menos, *The Superpowers*, 158, and Risse-Kappen, 149. The ratification of the INF Treaty by the US Senate was simpler than initially expected. In fact, the Senate approved the INF Treaty by an overwhelming vote of 93–5. See Risse-Kappen, ibid.

378. See the preamble to the INF Treaty in 27 *International Legal Materials*, 90.

379. See the full text of Articles I and II of the treaty in 27 *International Legal Materials*, 90.

380. See the full text of Articles III and X (6) of the treaty in 27 *International Legal Materials*, 91 and 94–95.

381. See Menos, *The Superpowers*, 17.

382. See Article IV of the INF Treaty. For an analysis of this article see Risse-Kappen, 151.

383. See Article V of the treaty in 27 *International Legal Materials*, 91–92. See also Risse-Kappen, 153. According to Article V (2), both parties, within 90 days after the treaty's entry into force, had the legal duty to remove all of their nondeployed launchers of their shorter-range INF missiles to the elimination facilities.

384. See Article VI of the INF Treaty in 27 *International Legal Materials*, 92. Note, however, that Article VI (2) allows both parties to continue to use specific missile stages and boosters which would count as medium- or short-range missile systems. For a further analysis see Risse-Kappen, 154.

385. See Article X of the INF Treaty and it Protocol on Elimination in 27 *International Legal Materials*, 94–95 and 182–198.

386. See Risse-Kappen, 153–154. INF missiles can be eliminated by their launching pursuant to Article X (5) of the treaty and Article III of its Protocol on Elimination. But this process for the elimination of missiles was subject to inspection and observation by the parties.

387. Ibid. See also Menos, *The Superpowers*, 17, and Kokoski and Koulik, 203.

388. See Article X (4) of the treaty and Article IV of its Protocol on Elimination in 27 *International Legal Materials*, 94. See also Singh and McWhinney, 378.

389. See Kokoski and Koulik, 214 (note 1).

390. See *The Arms Control Reporter*, Section 403, A1–A2 (1996).

391. See also the views of Menos, *The Superpowers*, 17.

392. See Article XII of the treaty and its Protocol on Elimination in 27 *International Legal Materials*, 96–97.

393. For a more detailed and comprehensive description and analysis of the superpower NTM of verification see generally Kokoski, "National Technical Means" in Kokoski and Koulik, 17–55; Spitzer, H. "Aerial Observations and Overflights" in ibid., 89–122; Altmann, J. "Short-distance Sensors" in ibid., 123–138; and Fetter, S. and T. Garwin, "Tags" in ibid., 139–154.

394. See Article XII of the treaty in 27 *International Legal Materials*, 96–97. In accordance with this article, each party has the right to make six such requests per calendar year; only one deployment base must be subject to these cooperative measures at any one time. For a concise analysis of this article of the INF Treaty see Singh and McWhinney, 379.

395. See Kokoski and Koulik, 206–209. The US Arms Control and Disarmament Agency had submitted a classified report to the Senate stating that the United States by its NTM and intelligence capabilities could effectively verify Soviet compliance with the INF Treaty. Ibid.

396. See Article XI of the treaty and its Protocol on Inspections in 27 *International Legal Materials*, 95–96 and 183–255. See also Kokoski and Koulik, 205.

397. Risse-Kappen, 155–156, and Kokoski and Koulik, 205. The annex attached to the INF Treaty provides a specific legal regime in relation to the protection of the privileges and immunities of the inspectors and aircrew members.

398. See Risse-Kappen, 155.

399. See Kokoski and Koulik, 204. Based on the Memorandum of Understanding, there existed seven facilities in Eastern European countries and 12 in Western European countries associated with INF missile systems. See Risse-Kappen, 155.

400. See Article XIII of the INF Treaty in 27 *International Legal Materials*, 97. See further Kokoski and Koulik, 206. Additionally, the Nuclear Reduction Centers were established on September 15, 1987, by a relevant agreement between the Soviet Union and the United States. Their fundamental purpose is to reduce and ultimately eliminate the risk of outbreak of nuclear war between the two parties, particularly as a result of misinterpretation, miscalculation or accident.

401. See Kokoski and Koulik, 214 (note 1).

402. See *The Arms Control Reporter*, Section 403.A, 1–2 (1996).

403. The US allegations of Soviet violations of the Treaty, *inter alia*, included transferring of SS-23 missiles to some Eastern European countries, practices interfering with roof-opening cooperative measures and undeclared SS-4 and SS-5 treaty-limited items. For a further analysis see ibid., Section 403.B, 757–758. See also *The Washington Post*, A20 (July 24, 1991).

404. For a further discussion of the present status of the INF Treaty, see *The Arms Control Reporter*, Section 403.A, 1 *et seq.* (1996).

405. See also the view of Risse-Kappen, 157.

406. See further ibid., 157 *et seq.;* and Menos, *The Superpowers*, 17.

407. Menos, *The Superpowers*, 17.

408. After the signature of the INF Treaty the Soviet Union and the United States together maintained more than 10,000 tactical nuclear weapons in Europe consisting of short-range missiles, nuclear artillery, and nuclear capable aircraft. See Brauch, H.G., "Nuclear Weapons in Europe After the INF Agreement" in *Europe in Transition: Politics and Nuclear Security*, eds. Harle, V., and P. Sivonen, 155–178 (1989).

409. See *The Washington Times*, A17 (October 31, 1996).

410. See Menos, *The Superpowers*, 157. For a further analysis of the legal impact of the INF Treaty on the effective verification of nuclear disarmament treaties see generally: Orphanos, P.P., "INF Treaty On-Site Verification: An Emerging Standard for Policing Arms Control Treaty Obligations," 10 *New York Law School Journal of International and Comparative Law*, 421–450 (1989); and Trimble, P.R., "Beyond Verification: The Next Step in Arms Control," 102 *Harvard Law Review*, 885–912 (1989).

411. See Singh and McWhinney, 377–378.

412. For a concise analysis of the START negotiations during 1989 see *The Arms Control Reporter*, Section 611.A, 3 (1996).

413. For a more detailed discussion of the Gorbachev-Bush Malta summit see *The Arms Control Reporter*, Section 611.B, 595–597 (1996). During the Malta summit the leaders agreed to: (a) sign an agreement at their 1990 summit requiring the destruction of the US-Soviet chemical weapons down to 20 percent of the current US level; (b) provide joint US-Soviet support for a Conventional Forces Accord in Europe reducing their conventional

forces and to be signed into a treaty at the 1990 summit in Europe; and, (c) jointly undertake the efforts to constrain missile proliferation more effectively by observing the limits developed by the United States and its allies in the Missile Technology Control Regime. Ibid., 596.

414. For a general discussion of the negotiations on the START issues after the Malta summit and until the Washington summit see *The Arms Control Reporter,* Section 611.B, 630 *et seq* (1996). See also Lacayo, R., "A Hurry-Up Summit" in *Time*, April 16, 1990, 22–24; and Cox, D., "A Review of the Geneva Negotiations: 1989–1990" in Vol. 32 *Background Paper*, ed. Canadian Institute for International Peace and Security, 1–8 (1990).

415. See *The Arms Control Reporter*, Section 611.A, 1 (1996).

416. The full text of the treaty and its related documents can be found in Senate Treaty Document No. 20, 102d Congress, 1–1101 (1991). *Agreements*, ed. US Arms Control and Disarmament Agency (1991).

417. See the preamble to the START Treaty, ibid., 1.

418. See Article II of the treaty, ibid., 2. See also "A START Briefing Book" in *The Bulletin of the Atomic Scientists*, Nov. 1991, 24, which contains a detailed yet concise summary of the entire START Treaty provided by the US Arms Control and Disarmament Agency on July 29, 1991. For a legal definition and technical description of the various strategic nuclear weapon systems covered by the START Treaty, see the Definitions Annex to this treaty, 24–29, in *Arms Control and Disarmament Agreements* (1991). For a list of all categories of strategic nuclear arms covered by the treaty see the Memorandum of Understanding and its annexes, attached to this treaty, ibid., 120–144. For a discussion of the counting rules for the reduction of the strategic nuclear arms covered by the treaty see Article III of the treaty, ibid., 1–5.

419. See Article II of the treaty, ibid., 1. See also "A START Briefing Book," ibid., 24.

420. Ibid.

421. Ibid. For a specific analysis of the issue of downloading regulated by the treaty in relation to the reduction of the number of nuclear warheads of multiple-warhead ballistic missiles, see Marsh, G., "The Ups and Downs of Downloading" in *The Bulletin of the Atomic Scientists,* Nov. 1991, 21–23.

422. See "A START Briefing Book," 24.

423. Ibid.

424. Ibid.

425. Ibid., 24–25.

426. Ibid., 25.

427. See also Krass, A.S., "START" in *The Bulletin of the Atomic Scientists,* Nov. 1991, 13.

428. See *The Arms Control Reporter*, Section 611.B, 686 (1996).

429. See also ibid., Section 611.B, 686.

430. See Warnke, P., "Success Linked to ABM Treaty" in *The Bulletin of the Atomic Scientists*, Nov. 1991, 18. For a further discussion of the Soviet SS-18 ICBM and its destructive capabilities see Menos, *The Superpowers*, 9.

431. See also *The Arms Control Reporter*, Section 611.B, 689–690 (1996). The START Treaty does not require the destruction of nuclear warheads particularly because the American side wanted to reuse them on new weapons. In addition, the American side feared that observation of the destruction of nuclear warheads by the Soviets could compromise design secrets. Also, with respect to the elimination of launchers used for the delivery of strategic nuclear warheads, some of these launchers must be destroyed while the remaining can be used for other purposes. Indeed, the American side wanted to use such launchers for its SDI system. Ibid.

432. For a further analysis of the verification system of the START Treaty see also Drell, S.D., "Verification Triumphs" in *The Bulletin of the Atomic Scientists*, Nov. 1991, 28–29.

433. See also "A START Briefing Book," 25.

434. See also ibid.

435. See also ibid.

436. See also ibid.

437. See Article II of the Protocol on Inspections and Continuous Monitoring, 37–38. Almost immediately after the signature of the START Treaty both parties were preparing for the visits of each other's START inspection teams. See *The Arms Control Reporter*, Section 611.B, 691–692 (1996).

438. See also "A START Briefing Book," 25.

439. See Drell, "Verification Triumphs," 28–29.

440. See also *The Arms Control Reporter*, Section 611.B, 691 (1996).

441. See further ibid., 691–692.

442. I have heavily relied on Drell, "Verification Triumphs," 29. Both parties have recognized that the START Treaty has incorporated the most thorough and innovative verification provisions ever negotiated. Ibid. Additionally, for a general discussion of the reduction of US-Soviet strategic nuclear weapons through effective verification procedures see *Reversing the Arms Race: How to Achieve and Verify Deep Reductions in the Nuclear Arsenals,* eds. Von Hippel, F., and R. Sagdeyev (1990). See also *The Arms Control Reporter*, Section 614.A, 2 *et seq.* (1996).

443. See also the similar views of Krass, 13.

444. See further Warnke, 18; and Drell, 28.

445. See also Drell, "Verification Triumphs," 29.

446. See also *The Arms Control Reporter*, Section 611.B, 689; and Arbatov, A.G., "We Could Have Done Better" in *The Bulletin of the Atomic Scientists*, Nov. 1991, 36.

447. For a specific list of the superpower strategic nuclear forces by the end of 1999 see *The Arms Control Reporter,* Section 611.E–O, 3–4 (1996).

448. For a further analysis of this issue see Warnke, 18–19.

449. See *The Arms Control Reporter*, Section 611.B, 697–700 (1996). For a detailed analysis of the Soviet tactical nuclear weapons affected by the Gorbachev initiative see ibid., Section 408.E, 10–11; also see *The Washington Post,* A1 (October 6, 1991).

450. See *The Washington Post,* A14 (January 29, 1992).

451. Ibid.

452. See also ibid., A12.

453. See *The Washington Post,* A18 (January 30, 1992).

454. Ibid. Yeltsin announced that production of nuclear warheads for land-based tactical missiles had been stopped, and that Russia was eliminating one-third of sea-based tactical nuclear weapons and half the nuclear warheads for anti-aircraft missiles. Ibid.

455. Ibid.

456. Ibid.

457. Ibid.

458. See *The Washington Times*, A15 (September 24, 1996).

459. See *The Washington Post*, A18 (January 30, 1992).

460. The full text of the START II Treaty is in Senate, Treaty Document 101-1, 1–61 (1993) and in US Senate Executive Report 104-10, 2–40 (December 15, 1995).

461. For a discussion of Russia's failure to ratify the START II Treaty see *The Arms Control Reporter*, Section 614.B, 63 *et seq.* (1996). The United States ratified START II in January 1996. See Congressional Record, 104th Congress, Second Session, Vol. 142, No. 11, Daily Digest, D41 (January 26, 1996).

462. See *USA Today,* 2A (January 4, 1993).

463. Ibid.

464. See START II Treaty, Senate Treaty Doc. 103-1, 1–61.

465. Ibid.

466. See Friedman, T.L., "Reducing the Russian Arms Threat" in *The New York Times,* A11 (June 17, 1992).

467. See START II Treaty. Based on the terms of the START II Treaty, the parties have reached the legal understanding that by the end of the year 2003 they may reduce their respective strategic nuclear warheads to no more than 3,000 for each side. See also *The Washington Post,* A30 (June 17, 1992).

468. For a further analysis see *The Washington Post,* A1, A18 (January 4, 1993).

469. Ibid., A18.

470. For a more detailed analysis see *The Washington Post,* A30 (June 17, 1992). See also *The Arms Control Reporter,* Section 614.A, 1 *et seq.* (1996).

471. See *The New York Times,* A11 (June 17, 1992). See also *The Arms Control Reporter,* Section 614.B, 4 *et seq.* (1996).

472. See further *The New York Times,* A11 (June 17, 1992).

473. While it is not known whether the United States is engaged in the development and production of new types of nuclear weapon systems, American intelligence sources are presently reporting that Russia is developing a new version of the SS-25 mobile ICBM known as "Fatboy," and other types of sophisticated nuclear weapon systems. See *The Washington Times,* A19 (June 10, 1996).

474. Based on the partnership for peace plan, the NATO alliance would be expanded to include former Soviet republics and former Warsaw Pact member states. Presently, NATO and Russia are involved in negotiations because Russia is opposing the eastward NATO expansion. See *The Washington Times,* A13 (December 9, 1996).

475. See *The Arms Control Reporter,* Section 608.B, 291 (1994).

476. See *The Washington Post,* A1, A14 (March 16, 1994).

477. See *The Arms Control Reporter,* Section 611.B, 835 (1994).

478. See *The Arms Control Reporter,* Section 611.A, 2 (1996).

479. Ibid., Section 602.B, 296. See also *The Washington Times,* A12 (April 22, 1996).

480. See *The Washington Post,* A6 (February 5, 1992).

481. See *The Washington Post,* A7 (February 7, 1991). Furthermore, the United States has already made plans to keep a strategic reserve force of about 1,200 strategic nuclear warheads to ensure a post-nuclear war strategic advantage. See *The Washington Post,* A29 (July 21, 1991).

482. See *The Washington Post,* A18 (January 30, 1992).

483. For a more detailed analysis see *The Washington Post,* A1, A23 (May 24, 1992).

484. See *The Arms Control Reporter,* Section 611.E–2, 12. (1996). Moreover, President Yeltsin has stated that Russia needs nuclear arms to deal with any possible eventuality which might arise anywhere in the world and threaten Russia's security. See *The New York Times,* A11 (June 17, 1992). See also *The Washington Post,* A1, A14 (November 25, 1992). Also, for a discussion of President Clinton's nuclear strategy, see *The Washington Post,* A1, A26 (September 22, 1994).

485. For an analysis of this approach, see Rotblat, J., and V.I. Goldanskii, "The Elimination of Nuclear Arsenals: Is It Desirable? Is It Feasible?" in *Verification: Monitoring Disarmament,* eds. Calogero, F., M.L. Goldberger, and S.P. Kapitza, 210 (1991).

486. See also ibid., 205–208.

487. See also ibid., 211.

488. For a further analysis of the feasibility of such a proposal see generally: Davis,

Lynn E., *Assuring Peace In A Changing World: Critical Choices for the West's Strategic Arms Control Policies,* 55 *et seq.* (1990); Sagdeyev, R.J., and A.A. Kokoshin, "Stability of the Nuclear Balance After Deep Reductions" in Von Hippel, F., and R.Z. Sagdeyev, 19 *et seq.*; and Gaylor, N., "The Way Out: A General Nuclear Settlement," 5 *Yale Law and Policy Review,* 134–156 (1986). In addition, the Committee of Soviet Scientists for Peace and Against the Nuclear Threat has concluded on a scientific basis that a reduction of US-Russian nuclear weapons to a level of approximately 600–700 warheads for each side is feasible by the conclusion of a START III Treaty. See Von Hippel and Sagdeyev, 19.

489. In particular, the conclusion of a START III Treaty between Russia and the United States would increase the possibility of settling the question of global and comprehensive nuclear disarmament. See also *The Washington Post,* A19 (January 30, 1992).

490. See *The Arms Control Reporter,* Section 614.C, 10 (1996).

491. In his September 1997 interview, Russian Foreign Minister, Yevgeny Primakov stated that Russia was ready to start immediately START III negotiations. See *The Washington Post,* C2 (September 21, 1997).

492. See *The United Nations Disarmament Yearbook,* 87 (1990); and *The Arms Control Reporter,* Sections 801 *et seq.* (1991).

Chapter 9

493. See generally *The Arms Control Reporter* (1991), 85 *et seq.*

494. See further Rotblat and Goldanskii, 205.

495. For a detailed analysis of the Indian proposal, see Davydov, V. "The Indian Proposal at UNSSOD-III: Problems and Prospects" in *Nuclear Non-Proliferation and the Non-Proliferation Treaty,* eds. Fry, M.P., N.P. Keatinge, and J. Rotblat, 181–184 (1990).

496. See further Rotblat and Goldanskii 205 *et seq.* Russia, France and China are committed to a nuclear weapons-free world under certain conditions. China in 1988 sponsored resolution 44/116D entitled "Nuclear Disarmament," which was adopted by the UN General Assembly and which urged both nuclear superpowers to expedite their denuclearization and thus facilitate the multilateral legal process for global and comprehensive nuclear disarmament. See *The United Nations Disarmament Yearbook* (1990), 103–104.

497. See *The United Nations Disarmament Yearbook* (1990), 105–108.

498. Ibid., 27–28.

499. See generally ibid., 24–36, 386–387.

500. Ibid., 117–120. In 1989 the UN General Assembly adopted resolution 44/119E referring to the need for the cessation of the nuclear arms race and nuclear disarmament and prevention of nuclear war. Ibid., 120–121.

501. Ibid., 122–123.

502. Ibid., 109 *et seq.*

503. For the Gorbachev proposal for a pledge on a no first use of nuclear weapons by all nuclear weapon states, see *The Arms Control Reporter,* Section 806.A, 2, 699–700 (1996).

504. Ibid., Section 806.A, 2.

505. For a general discussion of the "Open Skies" Treaty, see ibid., Section 409.A, 1 *et seq.*

506. See ibid., Section 850, 423.

507. See ibid., 415 *et seq.*

508. For a more detailed analysis of India's nuclear weapon capabilities see generally: Hart, D., "India" in *A European Non-Proliferation Policy, Prospects and Problems,* ed. Muller,

H., 135–162 (1987); and Thomas, R.G.C., "Should India Sign the NPT?" in Pilat and Pendley, 133–150. Indian Foreign Secretary J.N. Dixit in 1992 denied reports that India possesses approximately 60 nuclear bombs. However, he acknowledged that India has the capacity to build and deliver one atomic bomb. See *The Washington Post,* C2 (January 5, 1997).

509. For a more specific analysis of Israel's nuclear weapon capabilities see: Fischer, D. "Drawing the Threshold States into a Regime of Restraint, by Joining the NPT or Otherwise" in Fry, 41–42; and Spector, L.S., "Nuclear Non-proliferation in the 1990s: The Storm After the Lull" in *New Threats,* 49–53. Although Israel has neither denied nor confirmed the reports on its nuclear weapon capabilities, it is widely believed to have constructed approximately 200 nuclear weapons. Israel has become the sixth nuclear power according to the number of its nuclear warheads. See generally, Hersh, S.M., *The Samson Option: Israel's Nuclear Arsenal and American Foreign Policy* (1991). See also *The Washington Times,* A10 (April 8, 1996).

510. For a detailed discussion of South Africa's nuclear weapon capabilities see Spector, 58–59. The South African government has announced that South Africa had developed six atomic bombs. See *The Washington Post,* A1, A31 (March 25, 1993).

511. See generally *New Threats,* 1.

512. For a general discussion of the emergence of the new nuclear age in the early 1970s and its evolution afterwards see Kapur, A., "World and Regional Power Relations Without the NPT" in Pilat and Pendley, 117–130. Iraq had launched a vigorous effort to acquire nuclear weapons before the Persian Gulf War. It is presently reported that the Iraqi nuclear weapons program has been dismantled by the United Nations carrying out the pertinent UN security resolutions to destroy the Iraqi nuclear weapons program. See *The Washington Post,* A33 (October 9, 1990). See also *The Washington Times,* A10 (April 8, 1996).

513. For a detailed discussion of Pakistan's nuclear weapon capabilities, including its ballistic missile delivery system, see Fischer, 37–39. See further *The Washington Post,* A21 (April 5, 1996).

514. For a more detailed discussion of the advanced nuclear programs of both Argentina and Brazil and their threshold nuclear weapons development capabilities see Spector, 40–44.

515. For a general discussion of the North Korean advanced nuclear program and its threshold nuclear weapon development status see ibid., 37–40. See also Oberdorfer, D., "N. Korea Seen Closer To A-Bomb" in *The Washington Post,* A1, A26 (February 23, 1992). See also *The Washington Times,* A10 (April 8, 1996).

516. See *The Washington Times,* A10 (April 8, 1996).

517. See *The Arms Control Reporter,* Section 455.A, 1 (1996).

518. See further *New Threats: An Aspen Strategy Group Report, 2 et seq.*

519. See also *The Washington Times,* A4 (March 13, 1996).

520. For a detailed discussion of the horizontal proliferation of ballistic missile systems capable of delivering nuclear weapons, see Nolan, J. and A. Wheelon, "Ballistic Missiles in the Third World" in *New Threats,* 89–103.

521. See *The Arms Control Reporter,* Section 602.A, 1–6–A1–A6, 309 (1996). See also *The Washington Post,* A12 (May 12, 1995).

522. *The Arms Control Reporter,* B310 (1996).

523. For a discussion of India's opposition to the NPT, see *The Arms Control Reporter,* Section 602.B, 295 (1996).

524. See also *The Washington Post,* A22 (March 24, 1994).

525. See generally *The Washington Times,* A19 (June 10, 1996), and *The Washington Times,* A15 (September 24, 1996).

526. For a discussion of China's efforts to expand its nuclear weapons arsenal and

its intercontinental ballistic capabilities, see *The Washington Times,* A16 (December 10, 1996).

527. See *The Arms Control Reporter*, Section 602.B, 213 (1992).

528. Britain, France and China expressed their willingness to participate in international treaties to reduce their nuclear weapons after both nuclear superpowers had made major reductions in their nuclear forces. See *The Washington Post,* A1, A19 (February 1, 1992).

529. See *The New York Times,* A3 (September 1, 1996).

530. For a discussion of the negotiations which led to the conclusion of the CTBT, see generally *The Arms Control Reporter,* Section 608.B, 427 *et seq.* (1996).

531. In particular, India has raised this problem of the CTBT. See further *The Washington Times,* A11 (September 11, 1996).

532. See *The Arms Control Reporter,* Section 608.B, 444 *et seq.* (1996).

533. For a general discussion of the CTBT verification measures, see ibid., Section 608.B, 448 *et seq.*

534. Ibid., 455.

535. Ibid., Section 457.A, 1.

536. Ibid., 5.

537. Ibid., 1.

538. Ibid., 2.

539. Ibid., 1. For a discussion of Japan's plutonium, see *Japan's Nuclear Future: The Plutonium Debate and East Asian Security,* ed. Harrison, S.S., 98 (1996).

540. *The Arms Control Reporter,* Section 458.A, 1 (1996).

541. An outline of the treaty establishing the Southeast Asian NWFZ can be found in ibid., Section 458.D, 1–4.

542. Ibid., 10.

543. China is dissatisfied with the treaty establishing this zone because China alleges that the treaty could include parts of the South China Sea claimed by China. The United States also disapproves of the treaty because it may bar the transit of nuclear powered or nuclear-armed ships. See ibid., Section 458.A, 2.

544. See ibid., Section 455.A, 1. South Africa had built six nuclear bombs. See *The Washington Post,* A31 (March 25, 1993).

545. *The Arms Control Reporter,* 455.B, 115 (1996).

546. Ibid., Section 455.A, 2.

547. For an outline of the treaty establishing the African NWFZ, see ibid., 3.

548. Ibid.

549. Ibid., 4–5.

550. For a discussion of these proposed NWFZs, see ibid., Section 850.A, 2, 6–8.

551. Ibid., Section 453.A, 1.

552. Ibid., 4. Israel has stated that it would agree to establish a Middle East NWFZ as the last step in a peace process. Ibid.

553. Ibid., 1–2.

554. Algeria, Egypt and Libya have research nuclear reactors. Syria has no such reactor. Iran has an advanced nuclear program, and it is reported that Iran will be capable of building a nuclear bomb within the next several years. Ibid., 3.

555. Ibid., 4.

556. See *The Arms Control Reporter,* Section 453.B, 129 (1992).

557. See *The Arms Control Reporter,* Section 454.A, 1 (1996).

558. Ibid.

559. Ibid., 2 *et seq.*

560. Ibid.

561. For an analysis of a future Indian-Pakistani Cold War and a catastrophic nuclear arms race, see generally *The Washington Post,* A21 (April 5, 1996). See also *The Washington Post,* C2 (January 5, 1997).

562. See also Adelman, K.L., "Just A Sideshow," *The Bulletin of the Atomic Scientists,* 19–21 (Nov. 1991). For a discussion of the withdrawal of tactical nuclear weapons by the United States and Russia from Europe and Asia, including other parts of the world see *The Arms Control Reporter,* Section 408.A, 1 *et seq.* (1992).

563. See also Shaw, M.N., "Nuclear Weapons and International Law," 1.

564. "First use" of nuclear weapons occurs when a nuclear weapon state is the first to use such weapons against an enemy state for aggressive purposes. See further Fujita, H., *International Regulation of the Use of Nuclear Weapons,* 43 *et seq.* (1988).

565. Ibid., 82–83. See also Shaw, 15–16.

566. *The Arms Control Reporter,* Section 850.A, 4–5 (1996).

567. See Falk, R., "Toward a Legal Regime for Nuclear Weapons," 28 *McGill Law Journal,* 520–541 (1983); Bleimaier, J.K., "Nuclear Weapons and Crimes Against Humanity Under International Law," 33 *The Catholic Lawyer,* 161–172 (1990); and Fujita, 82–83.

568. For a concise analysis of the UN General Assembly resolution 1653 (XVI) of 1961, see Grief, N., "The Legality of Nuclear Weapons" in Pogany, 38–39.

569. I have heavily relied on Corwin, D.M., "The Legality of Nuclear Arms Under International Law," 5 *Dickinson Journal of International Law,* 285 (1987).

570. For a detailed analysis of the use of strategic and tactical nuclear weapons in a self-defense scenario and the legal implications of such use, see Weston, B.H., "Nuclear Weapons and International Law: Illegality in Context," 13 *Denver Journal of International Law and Policy,* 1–15 (1983).

571. See Corwin, 284.

572. Ibid., 284–285.

573. Ibid.

574. Since a state cannot legally use bacteriological weapons in self-defense, it also cannot use nuclear weapons in self-defense. See Meyrowitz, E.L., "The Laws of War and Nuclear Weapons," 9 *Brooklyn Journal of International Law,* 243 (1983).

575. See Corwin, 285–286.

576. Ibid., 280–281.

577. Ibid.

578. Ibid., 282–283. The use of nuclear weapons for reprisals cannot be legally justified and permitted. Ibid.

579. I am indebted to the dissenting opinion of Judge Koroma to the advisory opinion of the ICJ of 8/7/1996.

580. The Declaration of St. Petersburg of 1868 was the result of a conference of European military officers who met to take action on a new type of bullet that expanded on entry into the body, causing painful wounds which were difficult to treat. The conferees reached an agreement forbidding the use of "any projectile of a weight below 400 grams which is either explosive or charged with fulminating or inflammable substance," and adopted more general principles which have had a lasting effect upon the development of the laws of war. See Meyrowitz, "The Laws of War," 233.

581. See Grief, 3–4.

582. I have heavily relied on Meyrowitz, "The Laws of War," 234–235.

583. See further Grief, 24.

584. See Corwin, 277. For a further discussion of the effects of the use of nuclear weapons, see generally Bates, D.G., "The Medical and Ecological Effects of Nuclear War," 28 *McGill Law Journal,* 716–731 (1983).

585. For a detailed discussion of the Shimoda case, see Falk, "The Shimoda Case," 759–793.

586. See Meyrowitz, "The Laws of War," 235.

587. See Corwin, 276. See also Meyrowitz, "The Laws of War," 235.

588. I have heavily relied on Meyrowitz, "The Laws of War." For a further analysis of the immediate and long-term poisonous effects of the detonation of nuclear weapons on human and other living organisms and the environment, see generally Bates.

589. See Meyrowitz, "The Laws of War," 235–236. See also Bleimaier, 164.

590. See Meyrowitz, "The Laws of War," 237. See also Corwin, 276–278.

591. See Corwin, 278.

592. See Meyrowitz, "The Laws of War," 238.

593. Ibid., 239.

594. For an analysis of Protocol I, see Singh and McWhinney, 319–320.

595. See Meyrowitz, "The Laws of War," 240–241. The use of atomic weapons against Hiroshima and Nagasaki in 1945 resulted in the indiscriminate killing of civilians. Ibid.

596. See Singh, N., *Nuclear Weapons and Contemporary International Law,* 106 (1959), cited in Meyrowitz, "The Laws of War," 242.

597. See Corwin, 279. It is suggested that the legal principle providing the protection of the territoriality of neutral states in an international armed conflict has become a customary rule of international law. Ibid. For an opposite view, see Macdonald, 71–72.

598. It has been further argued that if the German invasion of Belgium was condemned as a violation of international law in World War II and declared a war crime, then the use of nuclear weapons in circumstances in which the user knows that it is bound to injure neutral states must be considered a violation of international law and, if it involves the killing of innocent neutrals, a war crime. See Singh, 106.

599. See Meyrowitz, "The Laws of War," 227. For a more detailed analysis of the destructive capabilities and effects of nuclear weapons, see generally Bates, 717 *et seq.*

600. See Bleimaier, 167. For a further analysis of the Genocide Convention and its legal impact on the use of nuclear weapons, see Grief, 36 *et seq.*

601. See Bleimaier, 167.

602. Ibid., 168.

603. See Grief, 37.

604. See Bleimaier, 169–170.

605. See Grief, 37.

606. For detailed discussion of the use of nuclear weapons as a crime against peace, see Nanda, V.P., "Nuclear Weapons and the Right to Peace Under International Law," 9 *Brooklyn Journal of International Law,* 282–296 (1983).

607. For the full text of this convention, see *Arms Control and Disarmament Agreements,* 193–198 (1984).

608. See Bleimaier, 166.

609. See Shaw, 6.

610. See also Bleimaier, 166.

611. For a discussion of the prohibition of the deployment of nuclear weapons in these regions, see Paust, J.J., "Controlling Prohibited Weapons and the Illegal Use of Permitted Weapons," 28 *McGill Law Journal,* 611 (1983).

612. See Grief, 39–40. For the statement of the UN Human Rights Committee, see UN General Assembly Official Records, 37th Session, Suppl. No. 40 (Doc. A/37/40, *Report of the Human Rights Committee,* p. 93, Annex V, paragraph 2).

613. Grief, 40–41.

614. Grief, 40–41.

615. See further the similar views expressed in Grief, 40–42; and Bleimaier, 165–167.

616. See Shaw, 9–10.

617. See *The Arms Control Reporter,* Section 602.B, 310 (1996).

618. For a general analysis of the legality of the use of nuclear weapons under the pre-atomic rules of international law, see Fujita, 101 *et seq.* The Tokyo Court District in the Shimoda Case has concluded that the use of nuclear weapons against Hiroshima and Nagasaki in 1945 violated the pre-atomic rules of international law. See Corwin, 286–290. Particularly with relation to the justification for the use of atomic bombs on Hiroshima and Nagasaki in 1945, the Truman administration maintained that the use of atomic weapons spared the United States and the Allies from carrying out an invasion of the Japanese homeland, where the cost in lives would have been quite heavy. Revisionist assessments cast doubt upon whether the atomic attacks were ordered primarily to achieve the main war goals or whether there had been more geopolitical motivations, principally the intimidation of the Soviet Union. See generally, Alperovitz, 26 *et seq.*

619. See Grief, 42. The Nuclear Warfare Tribunal was organized by the British group of Lawyers for Nuclear Disarmament. Ibid., 52.

620. For a general discussion of the legality of nuclear weapons under international law, see Meyrowitz, E.L., *Prohibition of Nuclear Weapons: The Relevance of International Law* (1990).

Bibliography

Adelman, Kenneth L. *The Great Universal Embrace: Arms Summitry — A Skeptic's Account.* New York: Simon and Schuster, 1989.

_____. "Just A Sideshow." *The Bulletin of the Atomic Scientists* 47, No. 9 (November 1991), 19–21.

Adeniran, Tunde. "Nuclear Weapons: Toward Nuclear Arms Limitation and Global Disarmament After Reykjavik." In *Multilateral Aspects of the Disarmament Debate.* New York, Philadelphia, Washington, D.C., and London: Taylor & Francis, 1989.

Agreements for Arms Control: A Critical Survey. Ed. SIPRI. London and Cambridge, Massachusetts: Taylor & Francis, 1982.

Allison, G.T. "Conceptual Models and the Cuban Missile Crisis." In *International Relations: Contemporary Theory and Practice.* Eds. G.A. Lopez and M.S. Stohl. Washington, D.C.: CQ Press, 1989.

Almond, Harry H., Jr. "Demilitarization and Arms Control: Antarctica." *Case Western Reserve Journal of International Law* 17 (1985), 229–284.

Alperovitz, Gar. *Atomic Diplomacy: Hiroshima and Potsdam: The Use of the Atomic Bomb and the American Confrontation with Soviet Power.* New York: Simon and Schuster, 1965.

Altmann, Jurgen. "Short-distance Sensors." In *Verification of Conventional Arms Control in Europe: Technological Constraints and Opportunities.* Eds. Richard Kokoski and Sergey Koulik. Boulder, San Francisco and Oxford: Westview Press, 1990.

Arbatov, Alexei G. "We Could Have Done Better." In *The Bulletin of the Atomic Scientists* 47, No. 9 (November 1991), 36–40.

Arms Control: A Survey and Appraisal of Multilateral Agreements. Ed. Stockholm International Peace Research Institute. London: Taylor & Francis; New York: Crane, Russak, 1978.

Arms Control and Disarmament Agreements. Ed. United States Arms Control and Disarmament Agency. New Brunswick (USA) and London (UK): Transaction Books, 1980.

The Arms Control Reporter. Ed. Institute for Defense and Disarmament Studies. Arms Control and Disarmament Periodicals Since 1982. Brookline, Massachusetts.

Austin, Bonnie J., Thomas J. Irvin, Susan A. Kelly, and Gabriel P. Kralik. "The History of Nuclear Arms Negotiations Between the United States and the Soviet Union." *Journal of Legislation* 15 (1989), 199–228.

Bailey, K. "This Is Not Arms Control." *The Washington Post,* 17 December 1990, A11.

Bates, Don G. "The Medical and Ecological Effects of Nuclear War." *McGill Law Journal* 28 (1983), 716–731.

Bechoefer, Bernard G., and Eric Stein. "Atoms for Peace: The New International Atomic Energy Agency." *Michigan Law Review* 55 (1957), 747–798.

Bennett, Paul R. *The Soviet Union and Arms Control: Negotiating Strategy and Tactics.* New York: Praeger, 1989.

Bes, Daniel. "The Vertical Meaning of the Strategic Defense Initiative." In *Scientists, Peace and Disarmament*. Ed. Guillermo A. Lemarchand and Alberto R. Pedace. Singapore; River Edge, New Jersey; London and Hong Kong: World Scientific, 1988.

Bessmertnykh, Aleksandr. "Reykjavik and Prospects for a Nuclear-Free World." In *Multilateral Aspects of the Disarmament Debate*. New York, Philadelphia, Washington, D.C., London: Taylor & Francis, 1989.

Bhatia, Shyam. *Nuclear Rivals in the Middle East*. London and New York: Routledge, 1989.

Blacker, Coit D. *Reluctant Warriors: The United States, the Soviet Union, and Arms Control*. New York: W.H. Freeman and Company, 1987.

Blechman, Barry M., ed. *Preventing Nuclear War: A Realistic Approach*. Bloomington: Indiana University Press, 1985.

Bleimaier, John Kuhn. "Nuclear Weapons and Crimes Against Humanity Under International Law." *The Catholic Lawyer* 33 (1990), 161–172.

Boyle, Francis A. *The Future of International Law and American Foreign Policy*. Dobbs Ferry, New York: Transnational Publishers, Inc., 1989.

Brauch, H.G. "Nuclear Weapons in Europe After the INF Agreement." In *Europe in Transition: Politics and Nuclear Security*. Eds. Vilho Harle and Pekka Sivonen. London and New York: Printer Publishers, 1989.

Brodie, Bernard, ed. *The Absolute Weapon: Atomic Power and World Order*. New York: Harcourt, Brace and Company, 1946.

Calogero, Francesco, Marvin L. Goldberger, and Sergei P. Kapitza, eds. *Verification: Monitoring Disarmament*. Boulder: Westview Press, 1991.

Calvo-Goller, Notburga K., and Michel A. Calvo, *The SALT Agreements: Content-Application-Verification*. Dordrecht: Martinus Nijhoff, 1987.

Carasales, Julio C. "Possibilities After Reykjavik: Let Us Not Waste Them." In *Multilateral Aspects of the Disarmament Debate*. New York, Philadelphia, Washington, D.C., London: Taylor & Francis, 1989.

Carlton, David, and Carlo Schaerf, eds. *The Arms Race in the Era of STAR Wars*. New York: St. Martin's Press, 1988.

Cassese, Antonio. *Violence and Law in the Modern Age*. Princeton: Princeton University Press, 1988.

Cavers, David F. "International Cooperation in the Peaceful Uses of Atomic Energy." *Vanderbilt Law Review* 12 (1958-1959), 17–49.

Challenges for the 1990s for Arms Control and International Security. Washington, D.C.: National Academy Press, 1989.

Christol, Carl Q. "The Moon Treaty Enters Into Force." *American Journal of International Law* 79 (1985), 163–168.

Cimbala, Stephen J., ed. *Strategic Arms Control After SALT*. Wilmington, Delaware: Scholarly Resources, 1989.

Cioc, Mark. *Pax Atomica: The Nuclear Defense Debate in West Germany During the Adenauer Era*. New York: Columbia University Press, 1988.

Coates, Ken. "For A Nuclear-Free Europe." In *Nuclear-Free Zones*. Eds. David Pitt and Gordon Thompson. London, New York and Sydney: Croom Helm, 1987.

Corwin, David M. "The Legality of Nuclear Arms Under International Law." *Dickinson Journal of International Law* 5 (1987), 271–291.

Dahlitz, Julie. *Nuclear Arms Control with Effective International Agreements*. London and Boston: George Allen and Unwin, 1983.

Dallmeyer, Dorinda G. "Space Weapons: Arming Man's Last Frontier" in *Through the Straits of Armageddon: Arms Control Issues and Prospects*. Eds. Paul F. Diehl and Loch K. Johnson. Athens, Georgia, and London: University of Georgia Press, 1987.

Davies, T.H. "Soviet Atomic Espionage." In *The Atomic Age: Scientists in National and*

World Affairs. Eds. Morton Grodzins and Eugene Rabinowitz. New York: Basic Books, 1963.

Davis, Lynn E. *Assuring Peace in a Changing World: Critical Choices for the West's Strategic Arms Control Policies*. Lanham, Maryland: The Johns Hopkins University, 1990.

Davydov, Valeri. "The Indian Proposal at UNSSOD-III: Problems and Prospects." In *Nuclear Non-Proliferation and the Non-Proliferation Treaty*. Eds. M.P. Fry, N.P. Keatinge, and J. Rotblat. New York, London, Paris, Tokyo and Hong Kong: Springer-Verlag Berlin Heidelberg, 1990.

Dean, Arthur H. *Test Ban and Disarmament: The Path of Negotiation*. New York and London: Harper and Row, 1966.

De Tar, Richard A. "The Proposal for Reinterpreting the ABM Agreement: Death of a Treaty." *American University Journal of International Law and Policy*, 3 (1988), 419–450.

Diehl, Paul F., and Loch K. Johnson, eds. *Through the Straits of Armageddon: Arms Control Issues and Prospects*. Athens, Georgia, and London: The University of Georgia Press, 1987.

Disarmament: Negotiations and Treaties, 1946–1971. Ed. Keesing Publications. New York: Scribner, 1972.

Dockrill, Michael, and John W. Young, eds. *British Foreign Policy, 1945–1956*. New York: St. Martin's Press, 1989.

Dore, Isaak I. "International Law and the Preservation of the Ocean Space and Outer Space As Zones of Peace: Progress and Problems." *Cornell International Law Journal* 15 (1982), 1–61.

Drell, Sidney D. *Facing the Threat of Nuclear Weapons*. Seattle and London: University of Washington Press, 1989.

____. "Verification Triumphs." *The Bulletin of the Atomic Scientists* 47, No. 9 (November 1991), 28–29.

Dunn, Frederick S. "The Common Problem." In *The Absolute Weapon: Atomic Power and World Order*. Ed. Bernard Brodie. New York: Harcourt, Brace and Company, 1946.

Epstein, William. *The Last Chance: Nuclear Proliferation and Arms Control*. New York: The Free Press, 1976.

____. "A Nuclear-Weapon-Free Zone in Africa?" In *Nuclear-Free Zones*. Eds. David Pitt and Gordon Thompson. London, New York and Sydney: Croom Helm, 1987.

____. *The Prevention of Nuclear War: A United Nations Perspective*. Cambridge, Massachusetts: Oelgeschager, Gunn and Hain, 1984.

Everyone's United Nations. 10th ed. New York: United Nations, 1986.

Falk, Richard. "The Shimoda Case: A Legal Appraisal of the Atomic Attacks Upon Hiroshima and Nagasaki." *American Journal of International Law* 59 (1965), 759–793.

____. "Toward a Legal Regime for Nuclear Weapons." *McGill Law Journal* 28 (1983), 519–541.

Farmer, Fyke. "The Atomic Bomb Can Be Controlled." *Tennessee Law Review* 19 (1945), 40–43.

Feis, Herbert. *The Atomic Bomb and the End of World War II*. Princeton, New Jersey: Princeton University Press, 1966.

Fetter, Steve, and Thomas Garwin. "Tags." In *Verification of Conventional Arms Control in Europe: Technological Constraints and Opportunities*. Eds. Richard Kokoski and Sergey Koulik. Boulder, San Francisco and Oxford: Westview Press, 1990.

Fischer, D. "Drawing the Threshold States Into a Regime of Restraint, by Joining the NPT or Otherwise." In *Nuclear Non-Proliferation and the Non-Proliferation Treaty*.

Eds. M.P. Fry, N.P. Keatinge and J. Rotblat. New York, London, Paris, Tokyo and Hong Kong: Springer-Verlag Berlin Heidelberg, 1990.

Friedman, T.L. "Reducing the Russian Arms Threat." *The New York Times*, 17 June 1992.

Fry, M.P., N.P. Keatinge, and J. Rotblat, eds. *Nuclear Non-Proliferation and the Non-Proliferation Treaty*. New York, London, Paris, Tokyo and Hong Kong: Springer-Verlag Berlin Heidelberg, 1990.

Fujita, Hisakazu. *International Regulation of the Use of Nuclear Weapons*. Tokyo: Kansai University Press, 1988.

Fyfe, Niger, and Christopher Beeby. "The South Pacific Nuclear Free Zone Treaty." *Victoria University of Wellington Law Review* 17 (1987), 33–51.

Gall, Ruth. "Militarization of Space." In *Scientists, Peace and Disarmament*. Eds. Guillermo A. Lemarchand and Alberto R. Pedace. Singapore; River Edge, New Jersey; London and Hong Kong: World Scientific, 1988.

Gayler, Noel. "The Way Out: A General Nuclear Settlement." *Yale Law and Policy Review* 5 (1986), 134–156.

George, James L. *The New Nuclear Rules: Strategy and Arms Control after INF and START*. New York: St. Martin's Press, 1990.

Gibbs, Elizabeth L. "In Furtherance of a Nuclear-Free Zone Precedent: The South Pacific Nuclear-Free Zone Treaty." *Boston University International Law Journal* 4 (1986), 387–421.

Goldman, Nathan C. *American Space Law, International and Domestic*. 1st ed. Ames: Iowa State University Press, 1988.

Gorbachev, Mikhail. *Perestroika: New Thinking for Our Country and the World*. 1st ed. Cambridge and New York: Harper and Row, 1987.

Gowing, M. "Britain, America and the Bomb." In *British Foreign Policy, 1945– 1956*. Eds. Michael Dockrill and John W. Young. New York: St. Martin's Press, 1989.

____. *Britain and Atomic Energy: 1939–1945*. New York: St. Martin's Press, 1964.

Grief, N. "The Legality of Nuclear Weapons." In *Nuclear Weapons and International Law*. Ed. Istvan Pogany. New York: St. Martin's Press, 1987.

Grodzins, Morton, and Eugene Rabinowitz, eds. *The Atomic Age: Scientists in National and World Affairs*. New York: Basic Books, 1963.

Gross, Donald G. "Negotiated Treaty Amendment: The Solution to the SDI-ABM Treaty Conflict." *Harvard International Law Journal*, 28 (1987), 31–68.

Grossman, Jerome. "The Politics of 'Star Wars'." *Journal of Legislation*, 15 (1989), 93–101.

Halsted, T.A. "Nuclear Testing — No End in Sight?" In *The Arms Race in the Era of Star Wars*. Eds. D. Carlton, and C. Schaerf. New York: St. Martin's Press, 1988.

Harle, Vilho, and Pekka Sivonen. *Europe in Transition: Politics and Nuclear Security*. London and New York: Printer Publishers, 1989.

Harrison, Selig S., ed. *Japan's Nuclear Future: The Plutonium Debate and East Asian Security*. Washington, D.C.: Carnegie Endowment for International Peace, 1996.

Hart, D. "India." In *A European Non-Proliferation Policy: Prospects and Problems*. Ed. H. Muller. Oxford: Clarendon Press; New York: Oxford University Press, 1987.

Heere, Wybo P., ed. *International Law and Its Sources*. Denver, Antwerp, London, Frankfurt, Boston and New York: Kluwer Law and Taxation Publishers, 1988.

Herken, Gregg. *The Winning Weapon: The Atomic Bond in the Cold War, 1945–1950*. New York: Knopf, 1980.

Hersh, Seymour M. *The Samson Option: Israel's Nuclear Arsenal and American Foreign Policy*. New York: Random House, 1991.

Holden, Gerard. *The Warsaw Pact, Soviet Security and Block Politics*. Oxford, UK; New York, New York, USA: B. Blackwell; Tokyo, Japan: United Nations Press, 1989.

International Negotiations of the Seabed Arms Control Treaty. Washington, D.C.: United States Arms Control and Disarmament Agency, 1973.

Johnson, Loch K. "Three Windows on Armageddon." In *Through the Straits of Armageddon: Arms Control Issues and Prospects.* Eds. Paul F. Diehl, and Loch K. Johnson. Athens, Georgia, and London: The University of Georgia Press, 1987.

Johnson, T.H. "Technologies of Ballistic Missile Defense." In *The ABM Treaty: To Defend or Not to Defend?* Eds. Walther Stützle, Jasani Bhupendra, and Regina Cowen. SIPRI. Oxford and New York: Oxford University Press, 1987.

Kapur, A. "World and Regional Power Relations Without the NPT." In *Beyond 1995: The Future of the NPT Regime.* Eds. Joseph F. Pilat and Robert E. Pendley. New York and London: Plenum Press, 1990.

Kelsen, H. "The Old and the New League: The Covenant and the Dumbarton Oaks Proposals." *American Journal of International Law* 39 (1945), 45–83.

Kintner, William R., and Robert L. Pfaltzgraff. *SALT: Implications for Arms Control in the 1970s.* Pittsburgh: University of Pittsburgh Press, 1973.

Kokoski, Richard. "National Technical Means." In *Verification of Conventional Arms Control in Europe: Technological Constraints and Opportunities.* Eds. Richard Kokoski, and Sergey Koulik. Boulder, San Francisco and Oxford: Westview Press, 1990.

Kokoski, Richard, and Sergey Koulik. *Verification of Conventional Arms Control in Europe: Technological Constraints and Opportunities.* Boulder, San Francisco and Oxford: Westview Press, 1990.

Krass, Allan S. "START." *The Bulletin of the Atomic Scientists,* 47 No. 9 (November 1991), 13–17.

Krepon, Michael. *Arms Control in the Reagan Administration.* Lanham, Maryland: University Press of America, 1989.

Lacayo, R. "A Hurry-Up Summit." *Time,* 16 April 1990, 22–24.

Lemarchand, Guillermo A. and Alberto R. Pedace, eds. *Scientists, Peace and Disarmament.* Singapore; River Edge, New Jersey; London and Hong Kong: World Scientific, 1988.

Lenefsky, David. "The United Nations Security Council Resolution on Security Assurances for Non-Nuclear Weapon States." *New York University Journal of International Law and Politics* 3 (1970), 56–71.

Lin, Herbert. *New Weapon Technologies and the ABM Treaty.* Washington, D.C., New York and Oxford: Pergamon-Brassey's International Defense Publishers, Inc., 1988.

Lippman, Matthew. "The South Pacific Nuclear-Free Zone Treaty: Regional Autonomy Versus International Law and Politics." *Loyola of Los Angeles International and Comparative Law Journal* 10 (1988), 109–133.

Lopez, George A. "Forward: The Reagan Legacy and the Strategic Defense Initiative." *Journal of Legislation* 15 (1989), 77–87.

Lopez, George A., and Michael S. Stohl. *International Relations: Contemporary Theory and Practice.* Washington, D.C.: CQ Press, 1989.

Lundestad, Geir. *East, West, North, South: Major Developments in International Politics, 1945–1986.* Oslo: Norwegian University Press, 1986.

McBride, James H. *The Test Ban Treaty: Military, Technological, and Political Implications.* Chicago: Henry Regnery Co., 1967.

McCain, Morris. *Understanding Arms Control: The Options.* New York and London: W.W. Norton, 1989.

Macdonald, R. St. J. "Nuclear Weapon-Free Zones and Principles of International Law." In *International Law and Its Sources.* Ed. Wybo P. Heere. Denver, Antwerp, London, Frankfurt, Boston and New York: Kluwer Law and Taxation Publishers, 1988.

McNamara, Robert S. *Out of the Cold: New Thinking for American Foreign and Defense Policy in the 21st Century.* New York: Simon and Schuster, 1989.

McNight, Allan D. *Atomic Safeguards: A Study In International Verification*. New York: United Nations Institute for Training and Research, 1971.

McWhinney, Edward. *The International Law of Détente*. Alphen aan den Rijn, The Netherlands: Sijthoff and Noordhoff International Publishers, 1978.

Mandelbaum, Michael. *The Nuclear Revolution: International Politics Before and After Hiroshima*. Cambridge; New York: Cambridge University Press, 1981.

Marks, Anne W., ed. *NPT: Paradoxes and Problems*. Washington, D.C.: Carnegie Endowment for International Peace, 1975.

Marsh, Gerald. "The Ups and Downs of Downloading." *The Bulletin of the Atomic Scientists* 47, No. 9 (November 1991), 21–23.

Menos, Dennis. *The Superpowers and Nuclear Arms Control: Rhetoric and Reality*. New York: Praeger, 1990.

____. *World at Risk: The Debate Over Arms Control*. Jefferson, North Carolina, and London: McFarland and Co., 1986.

Meredith, Pamela M. "The Legality of a High-Technology Missile Defense System: The ABM and Outer Space Treaties." *American Journal of International Law*, 78 (1984), 418–423.

Meyrowitz, Elliot L. "The Laws of War and Nuclear Weapons." *Brooklyn Journal of International Law* 9 (1983), 227–258.

____. *Prohibition of Nuclear Weapons: The Relevance of International Law*. Dobbs Ferry, New York: Transnational Publishers, 1990.

Moulton, Harland B. *From Superiority to Parity: The United States and the Strategic Arms Race, 1961–1971*. Westport, Connecticut: Greenwood Press, 1973.

Muller, Harald, ed. *A European Non-Proliferation Policy: Prospects and Problems*. Oxford: Clarendon Press; New York: Oxford University Press, 1987.

Multilateral Aspects of the Disarmament Debate. New York, Philadelphia, Washington, D.C. and London: Taylor & Francis, 1989.

Myhre, Jeffrey D. *The Antarctic Treaty System: Politics, Law and Diplomacy*. Boulder: Westview Press, 1986.

Nanda, Ved P. "Nuclear Weapons and the Right to Peace Under International Law." *Brooklyn Journal of International Law* 9 (1983), 282–296.

New Threats: Responding to the Proliferation of Nuclear, Chemical, and Delivery Capabilities in the Third World. Lanham, Maryland: The Aspen Strategy Group and University Press of America, 1990.

Newhouse, John. *Cold Dawn: The Story of SALT*. 1st ed. Oxford and New York: Pergamon-Brassey's International Defense Publishers, Inc., 1989.

Noel-Baker, Philip. *The Arms Race; A Programme for World Disarmament*. London: Atlantic Books, 1958.

Nogee, Joseph L., and Robert H. Donaldson. *Soviet Foreign Policy Since World War II*. 3d ed. New York: Pergamon Press, 1988.

Nuclear Weapons: Report of the Secretary-General of the United Nations. Brookline, Massachusetts: Autumn Press, Inc., 1980.

Oberdorfer, D. "N. Korea Seen Closer to A-Bomb." *The Washington Post*, 23 February 1992.

Orphanos, Peter P. "INF Treaty On-Site Verification: An Emerging Standard for Policing Arms Control Treaty Obligations." *New York Law School Journal of International and Comparative Law* 10 (1989), 421–450.

Ozinga, James R. *The Rapacki Plan: The 1957 Proposal to Decnuclearize Central Europe, and an Analysis of Its Rejection*. Jefferson, North Carolina, and London: McFarland and Company, 1989.

Pamir, Peri. "The Quest for a Balkan Nuclear-Weapons-Free Zone." In *Nuclear-Free Zones*.

Eds. David Pitt and Gordon Thompson. London, New York and Sydney: Croom Helm, 1987.

Panofsky, W.K.H. "Reykjavik and Beyond: Implications of Deep Reductions in Strategic Nuclear Arsenals and the Future Direction of Arms Control." In *Reykjavik and Beyond: Deep Reductions in Strategic Nuclear Arsenals and the Future Direction of Arms Control.* Washington, D.C.: National Academy Press, 1988.

Paterson, Thomas G. *Meeting the Communist Threat: Truman to Reagan.* New York: Oxford University Press, 1988.

Paust, Jordan J. "Controlling Prohibited Weapons and the Illegal Use of Permitted Weapons." *McGill Law Journal* 28 (1983), 608–627.

Payne, Keith B. "The Dilemmas of Deterrence, Defense, and Disarmament." In *Strategic Arms Control After SALT.* Ed. Stephen J. Cimbala. Wilmington, Delaware: Scholarly Resources, Inc., 1989.

Payne, Samuel B., Jr. *The Soviet Union and SALT.* Cambridge, Massachusetts, and London: MIT Press, 1980.

Pilat, Joseph F., and Robert E. Pendley. *Beyond 1995: The Future of the NPT Regime.* New York and London: Plenum Press, 1990.

Pitt, David. "Nuclear-Free Zones: An Idea Whose Time Has Come." In *Nuclear-Free Zones.* Eds. David Pitt and Gordon Thompson. London, New York, Sydney: Croom Helm, 1987.

Pitt, David, and Gordon Thompson, eds. *Nuclear-Free Zones.* London, New York and Sydney: Croom Helm, 1987.

Pogany, Istvan, ed. *Nuclear Weapons and International Law.* New York: St. Martin's Press, 1987.

Pope, Ronald R. *Soviet Views on the Cuban Missile Crisis: Myth and Reality In Foreign Policy Analysis.* Washington, D.C.: University Press of America, 1982.

Potter, William C. *Verification and SALT: The Challenge of Strategic Deception.* Boulder: Westview Press, 1980.

Powaski, Ronald E. *March to Armageddon: The United States and the Nuclear Arms Race, 1939 to the Present.* New York: Oxford University Press, 1987.

Reitzel, William, Morton A. Kaplan, and Constance G. Coblenz. *United States Foreign Policy, 1945–1955.* Washington: Brookings Institution, 1956.

Reykjavik and Beyond: Deep Reductions in Strategic Nuclear Arsenals and the Future Direction of Arms Control. Washington, D.C.: National Academy Press, 1988.

Risse-Kappen, Thomas. *The Zero Option: INF, West Germany, and Arms Control.* Boulder and London, Westview Press, 1988.

Robles, Alfonso Garcia. *The Denuclearization of Latin America.* Carnegie Endowment for International Peace, 1967.

____. "The Treaty for the Prohibition of Nuclear Weapons in Latin America." In *Nuclear-Free Zones.* Eds. David Pitt and Gordon Thompson. London, New York and Sydney: Croom Helm, 1987.

Rostow, W.W. *Open Skies: Eisenhower's Proposal of July 21, 1955.* Austin: University of Texas Press, 1982.

Rotblat, J., and V.I. Goldanskii. "The Elimination of Nuclear Arsenals: Is It Desirable? Is It Feasible?" In *Verification: Monitoring Disarmament.* Eds. F. Calogero, M.L. Goldberger and S.P. Kapitza. Boulder: Westview Press, 1991.

Rourke, John T. *Making Foreign Policy: United States, Soviet Union, China.* Pacific Grove, California: Brooks/Cole, 1990.

Sagdeyev, R.Z. "Soviet 'New Thinking' About International Security." In *Challenges for the 1990s for Arms Control and International Security.* Washington, D.C.: National Academy Press, 1989.

Sagdeyev, R.Z., and A.A. Kokoshin. "Stability of the Nuclear Balance After Deep Reductions." In *Reversing the Arms Race: How to Achieve and Verify Deep Reductions in the Nuclear Arsenals*. Eds. F. Von Hippel and R.Z. Sagdeyev. New York: Gordon and Breach Science Publishers, 1990.

Sagdeyev, R.Z., Yevgeni Velikhov, and A.A. Kokoshin. "Strategic and Political Aspects of the Strategic Defense Initiative: A Soviet Viewpoint." *Journal of Legislation* 15 (1989), 179–198.

Schoenbaum, T.J. "A Historical Perspective on Arms Control Agreements." In *Through the Straits of Armaggedon: Arms Control Issues and Prospects*. Eds. Paul F. Diehl and Loch K. Johnson. Athens, Georgia, and London: The University of Georgia Press, 1987.

Seaborg, Glenn T. *Kennedy, Khrushchev and the Test Ban*. Berkeley: University of California Press, 1981.

Shaker, M.I. "The Non-Proliferation Treaty Regime, a Reading Before 1995." In *Beyond 1995: The Future of the NPT Regime*. Eds. J.F. Pilat and R.E. Pendley. New York and London: Plenum Press, 1990.

Shaw, M.N. "Nuclear Weapons and International Law." In *Nuclear Weapons and International Law*. Ed. Istvan Pogany. New York: St. Martin's Press, 1987.

Sheehan, Michael. *Arms Control: Theory and Practice*. Oxford: Blackwell, 1988.

Shills, Edward. "The Failure of the United Nations Atomic Energy Commission: An Interpretation." *University of Chicago Law Review* 15 (1948), 855–876.

Simma, Bruno, ed. *The Charter of the United Nations: A Commentary*. New York: Oxford University Press, 1995.

Simpson, John, and Anthony G. McGrew, eds. *The International Nuclear Non-Proliferation System: Challenge and Choices*. New York: St. Martin's Press, 1984.

Singh, Nagendra, and Edward McWhinney. *Nuclear Weapons and Contemporary International Law*. 2d ed. Dordrecht, Boston and London: Martinus Nijhoff , 1989.

Smyth, Henry D. *Atomic Energy for Military Purposes: The Official Report on the Development of the Atomic Bomb Under the Auspices of the United States Government, 1940–1945*. Princeton, New Jersey: Princeton University Press, 1948.

Snyder, Jed C., and Samuel F. Wells, Jr., eds. *Limiting Nuclear Proliferation*. Cambridge, Massachusetts: Ballinger Publishing Co., 1985.

Sofaer, Abraham D. "The ABM Treaty and the Strategic Defense Initiative." *Harvard Law Review* 99 (1986), 1972–1985.

Sohn, Louis B. "Verification Dilemmas." In *Through the Straits of Armageddon: Arms Control Issues and Prospects*. Eds. Paul F. Diehl and Loch K. Johnson. Athens, Georgia, and London: The University of Georgia Press, 1987.

The Soviet Stand on Disarmament. New York: Crosscurrents Press, 1962.

Spector, L.S. "Nuclear Nonproliferation in the 1990s: The Storm After the Lull." In *New Threats: Responding to the Proliferation of Nuclear, Chemical, and Delivery Capabilities in the Third World*. Lanham, Maryland: The Aspen Strategy Group and University Press of America, 1990.

Spitzer, Hartwig. "Aerial Observation and Overflights." In *Verification of Conventional Arms Control in Europe Technological Constraints and Opportunities*. Eds. Richard Kokoski and Sergey Koulik. Boulder, San Francisco and Oxford: Westview Press, 1990.

"A START Briefing Book." *The Bulletin of the Atomic Scientists* 47, No. 9 (November 1991), 24–25.

Stützle, Walther, Jasani Bhupendra, and Regina Cowen. *The ABM Treaty: To Defend or Not to Defend?* Oxford and New York: Oxford University Press, 1987.

Taylor, William J., Jr., Cha Young-Koo, and John Q. Blodgett, eds. *The Korean Penin-*

sula: Prospects for Arms Reduction Under Global Détente. Boulder, San Francisco and Oxford: Westview Press, 1990.

Thakur, Ramesh. "The Treaty of Rarotonga: The South Pacific Nuclear-Free Zone." In *Nuclear-Free Zones*. Eds. David Pitt, and Gordon Thompson. London, New York and Sydney: Croom Helm, 1987.

Thomas, R.G.C. "Should India Sign the NPT?" In *Beyond 1995: The Future of the NPT Regime*. Eds. J.F. Pilat, and R.E. Pendley. New York and London: Plenum Press, 1990.

Treaties in Force. Washington, D.C.: United States Department of State, 1990.

Trimble, Philip R. "Beyond Verification: The Next Step in Arms Control." *Harvard Law Review* 102 (1989), 885–912.

The United Nations and Disarmament: 1945–1985. New York: United Nations, 1985.

The United Nations and Disarmament: 1945–1970. New York: United Nations, 1970.

The United Nations and Disarmament: 1945–1965. New York: United Nations, 1965.

The United Nations and Disarmament: 1970–1975. New York: United Nations, 1976.

The United Nations Disarmament Yearbook. New York: United Nations, 1979–1982, 1990.

United States Treaties and Other International Agreements. Washington, D.C.: United States Department of State, 1963.

Ury, William L. *Beyond the Hotline: How Crisis Control Can Prevent Nuclear War*. Boston: Houghton Mifflin Co., 1985.

Von Hippel, Frank, and Roald Z. Sagdeyev, eds. *Reversing the Arms Race: How to Achieve and Verify Deep Reductions in the Nuclear Arsenals*. New York: Gordon and Breach Science Publishers, 1990.

Warburg, James P. *Disarmament: The Challenge of the Nineteen Sixties*. Garden City, New York: Doubleday, 1961.

Warnke, Paul C. "Success Linked to ABM Treaty." *The Bulletin of the Atomic Scientists* 47, No. 9 (November 1991), 18–19.

Westerkamp, J.F. "On the Strategic Defense Initiative and the Anti-Ballistic Missile Treaty." In *Scientists, Peace and Disarmament*. Eds. Guillermo A. Lemarchand and Alberto R. Pedace. Singapore; River Edge, New Jersey; London and Hong Kong: World Scientific, 1988.

Weston, Burns H. "Nuclear Weapons and International Law: Illegality in Context." *Denver Journal of International Law and Policy* 13 (1983), 1–15.

Wilmhurst, M.J. "The Development of Current Non-Proliferation Policies." In *The International Nuclear Non-Proliferation System: Challenge and Choices*. Eds. John Simpson and Anthony G. McGrew. New York: St. Martin's Press, 1984.

Wolfe, Thomas W. *The SALT Experience*. Cambridge, Massachusetts: Ballinger Publishing Company, 1979.

York, H.F. "'Star Wars': Origins and Overview." In *The Arms Race in the Era of STAR Wars*. Eds. David Carlton and Carlo Schaerf. New York: St. Martin's Press, 1988.

Index